A crucially important historicity of the cultural narrative and framing of the death penalty in Britain from the nineteenth century to abolition. Lizzie Seal's study is a fascinating enquiry into media reporting and popular reception of the circumstances surrounding murders and the imposition of executions. This book is a cogent reminder of the real potential of miscarriages of justice in capital cases, and will help to keep political attention on human rights rather than retribution through an archaic punishment.

Jon Yorke, *Reader in Law and Director, Centre for American Legal Studies, Birmingham City University, UK*

Lizzie Seal's Capital Punishment in Twentieth-Century Britain offers a fresh look at the press and public imagination of the state's ultimate penalty in a period when its reality was hidden behind prison walls. Combining extensive primary research with a broad engagement with secondary literature, Seal generates new perspectives on well-known cases and sheds light on the experiences of many of the now-forgotten British condemned. Her book is a pioneering and intellectually exciting contribution to the rapidly developing historiography of crime and criminal justice in twentieth-century Britain.

John Carter Wood, *Leibniz Institute of European History, Germany*

With multiple points of insight, Seal offers a meaning-centered analysis of the demise of capital punishment in Britain. By contrast with accounts of this as an elite-driven activity that defied entrenched public beliefs, Seal shows widespread unease and ambivalence in popular attitudes and circulating media representations. The upshot is a thickened understanding of a surprisingly complex field.

Philip Smith, *Professor of Sociology, Yale University, USA*

This important book is a valuable addition to the literature on capital punishment in twentieth-century Britain. By examining the cultural history of capital cases and endeavouring to ascertain opinions of the general public (albeit often refracted through a range of popular representations), Lizzie Seal has opened up exciting new perspectives on the popular politics of the death penalty.

Dr Anne Logan, *University of Kent, UK*

Capital Punishment in Twentieth-Century Britain

Capital punishment for murder was abolished in Britain in 1965. At this time, the way people in Britain perceived and understood the death penalty had changed – it was an issue that had become increasingly controversial, high-profile and fraught with emotion. In order to understand why this was, it is necessary to examine how ordinary people learned about and experienced capital punishment.

Drawing on primary research, this book explores the cultural life of the death penalty in Britain in the twentieth century, including an exploration of the role of the popular press and a discussion of portrayals of the death penalty in plays, novels and films. Popular protest against capital punishment and public responses to and understandings of capital cases are also discussed, particularly in relation to conceptualisations of justice. Miscarriages of justice were significant to capital punishment's increasingly fraught nature in the mid-twentieth century and the book analyses the unsettling power of two such high-profile miscarriages of justice. The final chapters consider the continuing relevance of capital punishment in Britain after abolition, including its symbolism and how people negotiate memories of the death penalty.

Capital Punishment in Twentieth-Century Britain is groundbreaking in its attention to the death penalty and the effect it had on everyday life. It is the only text on this era to place public and popular discourses about, and reactions to, capital punishment at the centre of the analysis. Interdisciplinary in focus and methodology, it will appeal to historians, criminologists, sociologists and socio-legal scholars.

Lizzie Seal is Senior Lecturer in Criminology at the University of Sussex. Her research interests include gender representations of women who kill, cultural criminology, historical criminology and capital punishment. Her previous publications include *Women, Murder and Femininity: Gender Representations of Women Who Kill* (Palgrave, 2010) and, with Maggie O'Neill, *Transgressive Imaginations: Crime, Deviance and Culture* (Palgrave, 2012).

Routledge SOLON Explorations in Crime and Criminal Justice Histories

Edited by Kim Stevenson, University of Plymouth
Judith Rowbotham, Nottingham Trent University and
David Nash, Oxford Brookes University

This series is a collaboration between Routledge and the SOLON consortium (promoting studies in law, crime and history), to present cutting-edge inter-disciplinary research in crime and criminal justice history, through monographs and thematic collected editions which reflect on key issues and dilemmas in criminology and socio-legal studies by locating them within a historical dimension. The emphasis here is on inspiring use of historical and historio-graphical methodological approaches to the contextualising and understanding of current priorities and problems. This series aims to highlight the best, most innovative interdisciplinary work from both new and established scholars in the field, through focusing on the enduring historical resonances to current core criminological and socio-legal issues.

Capital Punishment in Twentieth-Century Britain

Audience, justice, memory

Lizzie Seal

Routledge
Taylor & Francis Group

LONDON AND NEW YORK

First published 2014
by Routledge

Published 2014 by Routledge
2 Park Square, Milton Park, Abingdon, Oxfordshire, OX14 4RN

and by Routledge
711 Third Avenue, New York, NY 10017

Routledge is an imprint of the Taylor and Francis Group, an informa business

First issued in paperback 2015

British Library Cataloguing in Publication Data
A catalogue record for this book is available from the British Library

Library of Congress Cataloging-in-Publication Data
Seal, Lizzie, 1977-
Capital punishment in twentieth-century Britain : audience, justice,
memory / Lizzie Seal.
  pages cm
1. Capital punishment--Great Britain--History--20th century. I. Title.
  HV8699.G8S43 2014
  364.660941'0904--dc23
        2013037317

ISBN 978-0-415-62244-8 (hbk)
ISBN 978-1-138-96129-6 (pbk)
ISBN 978-0-203-10470-5 (ebk)

Typeset in Times New Roman
by Taylor & Francis Books

For my Mom and Dad

Contents

Acknowledgements

Two grants funded much of the primary research on which this book is based: Socio-Legal Studies Association Small Grant awarded 2009 and British Academy Small Grant awarded 2010. Financial support was also provided by the School of Applied Social Sciences, Durham University.

I would like to thank the Mass Observation Archive for granting me permission to quote from their collections.

I would also like to thank the series editors for their guidance and feedback during the conception and writing of this book.

Reproduced with permission of Curtis Brown Group Ltd., London, on behalf of the Trustees of the Mass Observation Archive.

Series Editors Introduction

The volumes in this series contribute to the unashamedly interdisciplinary exercise in which SOLON has engaged since its inception in 2000: something now enhanced by the collaboration with Routledge to present cutting edge interdisciplinary research in crime and criminal justice history. The focus is on issues which, while rooted in the past, have also a crucial current resonance and so the volumes reflect on key issues and dilemmas which persist in terms of contemporary priorities.

*****

This volume, on capital punishment and its abolition in the twentieth century, highlights just such an issue. Any particularly heinous crime (particularly a child killing, for instance) leads to demands for the culprit to be executed, reminding us of the fact that there is still, in the early twenty-first century when the 'extreme sanction' has been fully removed from the statute book, a high level of public support for a return of capital punishment. But what Lizzie Seal admirably illustrates here is the complexity that lies behind that apparently popular demand for capital punishment to be on the statute book. It rightly deals with the everyday or mass dimension to the issue of executions for murder (by the twentieth century this was, in practice, the only crime in peacetime for which capital punishment was the penalty). The important point here is that just as what constitutes a crime needs public support for that to become a reality within the criminal justice system, so punishments for crimes need to be supported by public opinion if the criminal justice process is going to be identified as working by society. Behind its humour, W.S. Gilbert's Mikado was making a serious point when he claimed that his 'object all sublime' was to 'make the punishment fit the crime'. Death sentences have been supported by those who have felt that there is a need for a punishment of sufficient seriousness to match the seriousness of an individual crime. But – as this volume reveals so effectively – popular reactions could be very mixed when the full details of a murder were laid out in court, and in the press. There tends to be a difference between an abstract belief in the appropriate- ness of a punishment and actual support for an individual punishment in an individual case. Certainly during the last half of the nineteenth century, even before the timeframe for this volume, every conviction for murder was accompanied by at least one petition for the death sentence to be commuted to imprisonment – often featuring members of the jury that had convicted. The importance of this volume is that it underlines for us, through its examination of what used to be the extreme legal punishment and the campaign for its removal, just how complex public reactions to criminal punishments are. Trying to make the 'punishment fit the crime' is no easy task and this book provides a useful reminder of this reality.

Judith Rowbotham, Kim Stevenson, David Nash

Introduction

This book began with a cache of letters. Carrying out research in the National Archives some years ago, I called up the files that relate to Ruth Ellis, the last woman to be hanged in Britain. At the time, I was researching gender representations of women who kill, not capital punishment. The files of a woman as famous as Ruth Ellis have a special allure, promising a look behind the scenes of a landmark case and extra chapters to a fascinating story. They contained the usual documents that the state produced in a case of capital murder, such as witness statements, medical reports and trial transcripts and, at the time, this was the stuff that I sought out. However, the files also contained documents the state had not produced – hundreds of letters, nearly all handwritten and expressing heartfelt views on the execution of Ruth Ellis. Whether they urged a reprieve (which most of them did) or saw her as an immoral woman who deserved to die, one thing was for sure. The hanging of Ruth Ellis really mattered to the people who wrote those letters. They sparked my interest in how the twentieth-century public responded to capital punishment – not in the abstract of idle speculation about it but in the actuality of reactions to real cases. When I grew this initial interest into a research project, a further seed was planted, which was to know more about capital punishment in twentieth-century Britain. Not more about what was said in the House of Commons necessarily but more about how the death penalty would have figured in the day-to-day lives of ordinary people – my grandparents, my parents, my own life. Most people's lives. What did it mean to us and how did we experience it?

The cultural meanings of capital punishment in Britain changed over the course of the twentieth century. Although an already ambivalent practice capable of provoking anxiety, the contestation of execution by hanging deepened and intensified in the mid-twentieth century. In the 1950s, representations of and reflections on the death penalty and the individuals subject to it were frequent in popular and 'highbrow' culture. By this time, actual executions had become increasingly rare but capital punishment had assumed a more prominent and more anxious place in the everyday. This prominence declined after abolition of the death penalty for murder in 1965 but the imaginary power of execution did not disappear. Today, the issue of capital punishment emerges periodically in representations of its place in Britain's past and debates over whether it has a role to play in its future. It retains multiple symbolic meanings about which there is no consensus and which signal wider concerns about and perceptions of the state of British society.

This book is about the everyday meanings and cultural life of capital punishment in twentieth-century Britain. There is no other sustained examination of everyday culture and the death penalty in Britain at this time, and there is relatively little scholarship on capital punishment in twentieth-century Britain more generally. Understandably, much research has tended to focus on the processes leading to abolition. This has led to a concentration on 'high' politics, rather than the death penalty's wider, symbolic meanings. The public, if they figure in the story at all, are mentioned for their occasional emotional outbursts in response to controversial cases like Ruth Ellis and Derek Bentley, or to make the point that abolition was driven by elites as the majority of the public was retentionist up until and after abolition. An exception to this is Langhamer's recent article on capital punishment and the 'politics of emotion' in the 1940s and 50s. She notes that '[n]o historian to date has placed public, rather than political or campaigning opinion, center stage' and draws on the Mass Observation Archive to analyse how death penalty feeling was 'framed by time and culture'.[1]

The overall lack of attention to the cultural life of capital punishment in twentieth-century Britain is puzzling given the rich historiography that exists in relation to the seventeenth to nineteenth centuries, which draws on concepts such as sacredness, spectacle and the aesthetic. Attention is paid to the behaviour and perception of the execution crowd as well as the portrayal of the death penalty in visual art, novels, broadsides and songs. There is no equivalent to this historical literature for the twentieth-century, despite the fact that executions were carried out until 1964. As Grant argues, there is also a need to understand the cultural effects of abolition and the echoes of the death penalty in late twentieth and early twenty-first century penal cultures.[2] Capital punishment continues to have cultural uses even after abolition.[3]

We have valuable but partial knowledge about capital punishment in twentieth-century Britain. Rowbotham rightly argues that, although there are certainly exceptions, the historiography for this era has exhibited 'conceptual timidity'.[4] Indispensable studies explore the Parliamentary and interest group move towards abolition, the changing position of the Church of England and the execution of

1 C. Langhamer, '"The Live Dynamic Whole of Feeling and Behaviour": Capital Punishment and the Politics of Emotion, 1945–57', *Journal of British Studies*, 2012, 51(2): 416–41, pp. 419–20.
2 C. Grant, *Crime and Punishment in Contemporary Culture*, Abingdon: Routledge, 2004, p. 128.
3 E. Girling, 'European Identity and the Mission Against the Death Penalty in the United States', A. Sarat and C. Boulanger (eds), *The Cultural Lives of Capital Punishment*, Stanford, CA: Stanford University Press, 2005, p. 113.
4 J. Rowbotham, 'Execution as Punishment in England: 1750–2000', A. Kilday and D. Nash (eds), *Histories of Crime: Britain 1600–2000*, Basingstoke: Palgrave Macmillan, 2010, p. 188.

women.[5] In recent work, elite cultures have received analysis. Hammel discusses debates on capital punishment amongst European elites, including in Britain, arguing that twentieth-century abolitionism came to stand for humane enlightenment government[6] and Kaufman-Osborn examines the emphasis the Royal Commission on Capital Punishment, 1949–53 placed on 'humanity, certainty and decency' in its consideration of execution methods.[7] However, the wider symbolic meanings associated with and generated by the death penalty in Britain, especially its popular meanings, remain largely unexplored, as do the ways in which ordinary people would have experienced it.

There are two probable root causes of this conceptual timidity. Hanging was removed from public view in 1868 and became a private, bureaucratic affair. The lack of attention to its cultural life after privatisation can perhaps be explained in part by this transition of capital punishment into something that excluded the community and was 'petty, tedious and mean'.[8] Ostensibly, gone was the sacred, the spectacle and the aesthetic. The other is the abolition of capital punishment in Britain in the 1960s. Unlike the United States, where use of the death penalty intensified in certain states in the 1990s raising questions about the culture in which it flourished, capital punishment slipped down the political agenda in Britain. There were periodic calls for reintroduction but none that was likely to be successful. The spur to a more ambitious conceptual reckoning with twentieth-century capital punishment was missing.

Capital punishment – shifting the centre

The end of public hanging did not mean that the public ceased to experience it, rather their experiences were transformed.[9] Execution came to be largely experienced through representation and imagination. This book moves beyond the political centre and turns its attention to this imaginary, twentieth-century death penalty. In doing so, it seeks to shed light not only on the cultural place of

---

5 On abolition, see V. Bailey, 'The Shadow of the Gallows: The Death Penalty and the British Labour Government, 1945–51', *Law and History Review*, 2000, 18(2): 305–50 and N. Twitchell, *The Politics of the Rope*, Bury St. Edmunds: Athena, 2012. On the Church of England, see H. Potter, *Hanging in Judgment: Religion and the Death Penalty in England*, London: SCM Press Ltd, 1993 and on the cases of the 15 women executed in twentieth-century England and Wales, see A. Ballinger, *Dead Woman Walking: Executed Women in England and Wales, 1900–55*, Aldershot: Ashgate, 2000.
6 A. Hammel, 'Civilized Rebels', A. Sarat and J. Martschukat (eds), *Is the Death Penalty Dying? European and American Perspectives*, Cambridge: Cambridge University Press, 2011, p. 196.
7 T. V. Kaufman-Osborn, 'The Death of Dignity', A. Sarat and J. Martschukat (eds), *Is the Death Penalty Dying?*, p. 213.
8 R. McGowen, 'Civilizing Punishment: The End of the Public Execution in England', *Journal of British Studies*, 1994, 33(3): 257–82, p. 281.
9 A. Linders, 'The Execution Spectacle and State Legitimacy: The Changing Nature of the Execution Audience, 1833–1937', *Law and Society Review*, 2002, 36(3): 607–56. Linders' analysis is of the American death penalty.

capital punishment, but also penal culture as an aspect of everyday life in Britain. Such a study inevitably intersects and overlaps with major policy shifts such as abolition but this is not the story of how abolition was brought about, detailed accounts of which exist elsewhere.

Capital punishment's everyday meanings were constructed and expressed through newspaper articles, television programmes, films, novels, songs and plays, as well as 'crime talk'.[10] If we are to find its presence in day-to-day life, we must turn to sources such as these, as this is how people unconnected to the criminal justice system learned about capital cases and the practice of execution. These are also the sources that expressed the range of cultural meanings carried by the death penalty.[11] They do not tell us which were the precise bureaucratic steps taken to change death penalty policy or the exact mechanisms that enabled abolition. However, they do let us know the ways in which the vast majority of people would have experienced and imagined capital punishment in twentieth-century Britain. The sources that constituted popular culture are of particular interest due to their comparatively large audiences.[12] These spaces helped to construct folk knowledge about the death penalty. However, the discussion and representation of capital punishment in more 'highbrow' cultural forms is also important as they too were part of everyday experience (albeit for a smaller number of people), and the highbrow and the popular influence one another. Similarly, the specific form of state mandated capital punishment operating within a society and its wider political context is also inevitably relevant to everyday meanings and experiences.[13]

The popular press, both at the national and local level, forms an important source for understanding everyday experiences of capital punishment. Coverage and debates in the 'quality' press enable analysis of anxieties about the death penalty in 'highbrow' culture, which were not restricted to the parliamentary process. Attention to the reporting of particular cases and executions – often cultural events or flashpoints – well illustrates how the variety of narratives surrounding the death penalty were not abstract concerns but were expressed in relation to particular people at particular times. Execution most frequently appeared in newspapers as a penal practice in relation to a specific criminal for a specific crime. As such, discussion of these cases was tied to questions of

10 T. Sasson, *Crime Talk: How Citizens Construct a Social Problem*, New York: Aldine De Gruyter, 1995.

11 On cultural representations of the death penalty, see C. Boulanger and A. Sarat, 'Putting Culture into the Picture', A. Sarat and C. Boulanger (eds), *The Cultural Lives of Capital Punishment*, Stanford, CA: Stanford University Press, 2005.

12 As Sarat and Boulanger argue, popular culture has a life of its own, ibid., p. 18.

13 E. Carrabine, 'The Iconography of Punishment', *The Howard Journal*, 2011, 50(5): 452–64. In relation to image analysis, Carrabine contends that 'images and texts are embedded in the social worlds that produced them', which includes the need to pay attention to institutions and social structures, pp. 454–5.

identity, understandings of justice and the construction of communities of sentiment.[14]

The visibility of capital punishment to the public in twentieth-century Britain was maintained by press reports, but also in fictional portrayals on stage, screen and in print. Such portrayals exemplified an important cultural use of capital punishment – as entertainment. The continued cultural life of the death penalty in post-abolition Britain has been sustained through news reporting, films, books and television documentaries and, as such, these are important sources.

In addition to cultural narratives, newspaper stories are useful for what they can reveal about ordinary people's responses to capital punishment that might not have been preserved in any other source. This includes the reactions of relatives of the condemned and the behaviour of execution crowds. Newspaper reports do not provide unproblematic access to the 'truth' of what happened and were of course written according to the conventions and requirements of their form. However, they do enable interpretation of reactions that would otherwise be unrecorded. Another valuable source of public reaction that can be found in the official archive is letters sent to Home Secretaries in relation to particular cases, like those mentioned at the outset in relation to Ruth Ellis. Unlike letters sent directly to the condemned or their relatives,[15] these have survived as they are part of the state's record. Mass Observation has a topic collection on capital punishment, most of which relates to its surveys on the same from the 1940s and 50s, which contained some open-ended questions. Oral history interviews are a means of gaining access to how cultural memories of capital punishment and its post-abolition meanings in twentieth-century Britain were negotiated.

Chapter One outlines the conceptual approach that is employed in the book and also provides an overview of capital punishment in Britain since it moved behind prison walls in 1868. Chapter Two examines how the execution audience in the twentieth century was largely sustained through reading newspapers. It highlights a significant shift in the mid-twentieth century when an emotional public sphere developed around the issue of the death penalty, deepening its cultural ambivalence. Chapter Three addresses the continuing role in the twentieth century of capital punishment as a form of entertainment, and the cultural anxieties that this provoked, particularly in terms of 'taste'. Chapter Four turns its attention to popular protest against the death penalty,

14 Girling employs Appadurai's notion of 'community of sentiment' in relation to the death penalty to refer to 'people who imagine and feel things together', E. Girling, '"Looking Death in the Face": The Benetton Death Penalty Campaign', *Punishment and Society*, 2004, 6(3): 271–87, p. 284. See also A. Appadurai, *Modernity at Large: Cultural Dimensions of Modernity*, Minneapolis: University of Minnesota Press, 1996.

15 See J. C. Wood, *The Most Remarkable Women in England: Poison, Celebrity and the Trials of Beatrice Pace*, Manchester: Manchester University Press, 2012, Ch. 9 for a discussion of letters sent to Pace, who was acquitted of her husband's murder in 1928. These were saved by her solicitor.

exploring spontaneous protests that erupted in relation to certain cases, as well as Violet van der Elst's long-running campaign against capital punishment. Chapter Five analyses public responses to the death penalty as they were expressed in letters to the Home Office about specific cases. In particular, it examines how justice was a crucial symbol in reactions to these cases. Chapter Six further probes the ambivalence of twentieth-century execution by focusing on two high-profile miscarriages of justice – Edith Thompson and Timothy Evans. It employs the concept of 'haunting' to explore these cases' lingering power to unsettle. Chapter Seven discusses significant currents in penal culture in the post-abolition era and how they did not all flow in the same direction. Drawing on oral history interviews from the Millennium Memory Bank, Chapter Eight explores the negotiation of cultural memories of the death penalty, and the ways in which these are multiple and contested in nature and relate to wider cultural themes.

Bibliography

Appadurai, A., *Modernity at Large: Cultural Dimensions of Modernity*, Minneapolis: University of Minnesota Press, 1996.

Bailey, V., 'The Shadow of the Gallows: The Death Penalty and the British Labour Government, 1945–51', *Law and History Review*, 2000, 18(2): 305–50.

Ballinger, A., *Dead Woman Walking: Executed Women in England and Wales, 1900–55*, Aldershot: Ashgate, 2000.

Boulanger, C. and Sarat, A., 'Putting Culture into the Picture', A. Sarat and C. Boulanger (eds), *The Cultural Lives of Capital Punishment*, Stanford, CA: Stanford University Press, 2005, 1–47.

Carrabine, E., 'The Iconography of Punishment', *The Howard Journal*, 2011, 50(5): 452–64.

Girling, E., '"Looking Death in the Face": The Benetton Death Penalty Campaign', *Punishment and Society*, 2004, 6(3): 271–87.

——'European Identity and the Mission Against the Death Penalty in the United States', A. Sarat and C. Boulanger (eds), *The Cultural Lives of Capital Punishment*, Stanford, CA: Stanford University Press, 2005, 112–28.

Grant, C., *Crime and Punishment in Contemporary Culture*, Abingdon: Routledge, 2004.

Hammel, A., 'Civilized Rebels', A. Sarat and J. Martschukat (eds), *Is the Death Penalty Dying? European and American Perspectives*, Cambridge: Cambridge University Press, 2011, 173–203.

Kaufman-Osborn, T. V., 'The Death of Dignity', A. Sarat and J. Martschukat (eds), *Is the Death Penalty Dying? European and American Perspectives*, Cambridge: Cambridge University Press, 2011, 204–35.

Langhamer, C., '"The Live Dynamic Whole of Feeling and Behaviour": Capital Punishment and the Politics of Emotion, 1945–57', *Journal of British Studies*, 2012, 51(2): 416–41.

Linders, A., 'The Execution Spectacle and State Legitimacy: The Changing Nature of the Execution Audience, 1833–1937', *Law and Society Review*, 2002, 36(3): 607–56.

McGowen, R., 'Civilizing Punishment: The End of the Public Execution in England', *Journal of British Studies*, 1994, 33(3): 257–82.

Potter, H., *Hanging in Judgment: Religion and the Death Penalty in England*, London: SCM Press Ltd, 1993.

Rowbotham, J., 'Execution as Punishment in England: 1750–2000', A. Kilday and D. Nash (eds), *Histories of Crime: Britain 1600–2000*, Basingstoke: Palgrave Macmillan, 2010, 180–202.

Sasson, T., *Crime Talk: How Citizens Construct a Social Problem*, New York: Aldine De Gruyter, 1995.

Twitchell, N., *The Politics of the Rope*, Bury St. Edmunds: Athena, 2012.

Wood, J. C., *The Most Remarkable Women in England: Poison, Celebrity and the Trials of Beatrice Pace*, Manchester: Manchester University Press, 2012.

1 Capital punishment in Britain since 1868

Concepts and context

First, this chapter outlines the conceptual approach that will be taken to understand capital punishment in twentieth-century Britain. This draws from the 'cultural turn' in the sociology of punishment and analyses of the 'cultural life' of the death penalty, which highlight its symbolic resonance. The significance is explored of capital punishment as an ambivalent practice that generates anxiety and conflicted feelings. The chapter then undertakes a discussion of the changing policies and practices of capital punishment in Britain since 1868, as well as considering some of its wider cultural representations. It argues that continuing attempts to civilise and modernise execution, and to resolve its contradictions, showed its ongoing, deepening ambivalence. As a bodily punishment starkly enacting the state's violence, hanging became increasingly out of place in twentieth-century Britain, with its developing Welfare State and expanded notions of citizenship. However, the death penalty also retained its profound retributive appeal. The social categories of gender and age are particularly significant to understanding restrictions placed on the death penalty in the earlier part of the twentieth century, and also highlight important ambivalences that deepened in the 1950s. These uncertainties related back to understandings of civilisation and modernity.

The cultural life of capital punishment

The cultural turn in the sociology of punishment has encouraged scholars to explore how punishment 'is practiced and played with in daily life'.[1] Penal cultures are not only generated by ruling elites and the personnel of the criminal justice system, but also in everyday talk and representations. Punishment lives in 'the quotidian as well as the majestic'.[2] This needs to be understood if we are to appreciate not just how the wider culture shapes penal practice, but also

---

1 M. Brown, *The Culture of Punishment: Prison, Society and Spectacle*, New York: New York University Press, 2009, p. 94.
2 B. D. Steiner, W. J. Bowers and A. Sarat, 'Folk Knowledge as Legal Action: Death Penalty Judgments and the Tenet of Early Release in a Culture of Mistrust and Punitiveness', *Law & Society Review*, 1999, 33(2): 461–505, p. 461.

how forms of punishment have a role in shaping the wider culture.[3] In order to gain a fuller picture of the place of capital punishment in twentieth-century Britain, it is necessary to analyse how it figured in people's day-to-day lives.[4] We can interpret this both in relation to how people reacted to the death penalty while it was in use and in terms of how it lives on in cultural memory. Perceptions of capital punishment created and create 'folk knowledge' – 'everyday, taken-for-granted understandings'[5] about this practice – which is as much a part of its historical and cultural legacy as its construction in political and legal processes.

This attention to the everyday is not intended to replace political and legal understandings, which are also part of the culture of capital punishment (and are primarily responsible for the specific form in which it is practised and, of course, whether it is practised).[6] However, the story of the death penalty in everyday life in twentieth-century Britain remains largely untold by historians and sociologists, meaning that this crucial aspect of the culture of capital punishment needs sustained examination.

The death penalty is particularly well suited to a cultures of punishment approach. It necessarily exists as the most severe punishment in societies that employ it and is the state's ultimate sanction. More than any other punishment, execution demonstrates the state's authority and monopoly on violence, which extends to power over life and death of its own citizens.[7] It carries echoes of the absolute power historically exercised by monarchs and as such symbolises and defines the sovereignty of the state.[8] Capital punishment is highly expressive as it communicates moralities and demarcates behaviour that is to be totally reviled. This can be understood as its pedagogical function.[9] For example, Jarvis describes the execution of Julius and Ethel Rosenberg as Communist spies in Cold War America in 1954 as a 'political education' for the wider American populace.[10]

Capital punishment is also highly ritualistic and performatively constitutes aspects of the character of the society in which it is exercised.[11] The

3 M. Smith, R. Sparks and E. Girling, 'Educating Sensibilities: The Image of the "Lesson" in Children's Talk about Punishment', *Punishment & Society*, 2000, 2(4): 395–415, p. 397.

4 Ibid., p. 396.

5 Steiner *et al.* 'Folk Knowledge', p. 462.

6 See J. Q. Whitman, 'Response to Garland', *Punishment & Society*, 2005, 7(4): 389–96, p. 390.

7 D. Garland, *Peculiar Institution: America's Death Penalty in an Age of Abolition*, Oxford: Oxford University Press, 2010, p. 91.

8 A. Sarat, 'Capital Punishment as Legal, Political, and Cultural Fact: An Introduction', A. Sarat (ed.), *The Killing State: Capital Punishment in Law, Politics and Culture*, Oxford: Oxford University Press, 1999.

9 Ibid., p. 9 and S. A. Bandes, 'The Heart has its Reasons: Examining the Strange Persistence of the American Death Penalty', *Law, Politics and Society*, 2008, 42: 21–52, p. 23.

10 B. Jarvis, *Cruel and Unusual: Punishment and U.S. Culture*, London: Pluto Press, 2004, p. 67.

11 J. Martschukat, 'Nineteenth-Century Executions as Performances of Law, Death and Civilization', A. Sarat and C. Boulanger (eds), *The Cultural Lives of Capital Punishment*, Stanford, CA: Stanford University Press, 2005, p. 52.

proclamation of the death sentence has an 'incantatory power' that illustrates the ceremonial function of the death penalty.[12] Changes in the method of execution indicate shifts in how the governing elite of a society sees itself and wishes to be seen.[13] In the United States, the replacement of hanging with the electric chair, and the electric chair with lethal injection, demonstrated an ongoing project to perform a civilised, modern type of execution that was efficient and free of pain and gore.[14] The communicative, ritualistic nature of the death penalty gives it the potential to be laden with overflowing meaning.[15] Some of these meanings are communicated by the state as part of its stage management of the execution scene but such an elemental event expresses and can be assigned with a multiplicity of meanings that can subvert and resist the dominant message.[16] Smith examines how the condemned can subvert and re-appropriate the execution scene. Through a performance of penitence and piety, Ruth Ellis, the last woman to be hanged in Britain, rewrote her state mandated role of murderess and bad woman.[17]

The symbolic potency of the death penalty means that it generates discourses and narratives that communicate meanings beyond the punishment of wrongdoing, and the life and death of the condemned, to wider social and cultural issues.[18] These can relate to perceptions of respectability, the construction of social identities and inequalities in terms of class, race and gender,[19] understandings of national identity and the contemporary state of society.[20] As such, the discourses and narratives surrounding capital punishment reflect and reproduce hopes and anxieties about the past, present

12 F. E. Zimring and G. Hawkins, *Capital Punishment and the American Agenda*, Cambridge: Cambridge University Press, 1986, p. 11.

13 T. V. Kaufman-Osborn, *From Noose to Needle*, Ann Arbor: University of Michigan Press, 2002.

14 T. V. Kaufman-Osborn, 'The Death of Dignity', A. Sarat and J. Martschukat (eds), *Is the Death Penalty Dying? European and American Perspectives*, Cambridge: Cambridge University Press, 2011, p. 213 and D. Garland, 'The Problem of the Body in Modern Punishment', *Social Research*, 2011, 78(3): 767–98, pp. 779–80.

15 P. Smith, *Punishment and Culture*, Chicago, IL: University of Chicago Press, 2008, pp. 38–43.

16 M. Madow, 'Forbidden Spectacle: Executions, the Public and the Press in Nineteenth-Century New York', *Buffalo Law Review*, 1995, 43(2): 461–562, p. 485.

17 P. Smith, 'Executing Executions: Aesthetics, Identity and the Problematic Narratives of Capital Punishment Ritual', *Theory and Society*, 1996, 25(2): 235–61.

18 C. Boulanger and A. Sarat, 'Putting Culture into the Picture', A. Sarat and C. Boulanger (eds), *The Cultural Lives of Capital Punishment*, Stanford, CA: Stanford University Press, 2005, pp. 1–9.

19 See, inter alia, A. Ballinger, *Dead Woman Walking,* Aldershot: Ashgate, 2000; C. Strange, 'Masculinities, Intimate Femicide and the Death Penalty in Australia, 1890–1920', *British Journal of Criminology*, 2003, 43(2): 310–39 and B. Fleury-Steiner, 'Death in "Whiteface"', C. J. Ogletree Jr. and A. Sarat (eds), *From Lynch Mobs to the Killing State*, New York: New York University Press, 2006.

20 R. McGowen, 'Introduction', D. Garland, R. McGowen and M. Meranze (eds), *America's Death Penalty Between Past and Present*, New York: New York University Press, 2011, pp. 17–18 and A. Sarat and J. Martschukat, 'Introduction: Transatlantic Perspectives on Capital Punishment', A. Sarat and J. Martschukat (eds), *Is the Death Penalty Dying?*

and future.[21] The significance of gender in particular to cultural analysis of the death penalty has frequently been ignored or underplayed.[22] In relation to twentieth-century Britain, gender – especially constructions of femininity – cannot be sawn off from a cultural analysis of capital punishment because gendered understandings were absolutely integral to it.

The significance of emotions has been recognised as increasingly important in analyses of crime and punishment.[23] As a matter of life and death, the death penalty has the potential to generate particularly strong emotional reactions and it has been argued that people's views on capital punishment are primarily shaped by how they feel about it.[24] The heavily symbolic nature of capital punishment is tied to its strong emotional resonance. Belief in the need for the death penalty as a deterrent can be allied to fear of crime and wider feelings of insecurity.[25] Arguments that execution is uncivilised are associated with feelings of disgust at bodily punishment.[26] Disgust can also be significant to gaining capital convictions for especially 'heinous' murders.[27] Reactions to particular cases often involve personal identification and empathy, either on behalf of the condemned or with the relatives of the victim.[28]

Capital punishment and ambivalence

Franklin Zimring has highlighted the significance of ambivalence to American policies and practices of capital punishment. He identifies conflicted feelings

21 For a similar approach in relation to policing, see I. Loader and A. Mulcahy, *Policing and the Condition of England: Memory, Politics and Culture*, Oxford: Oxford University Press, 2003. Loader and Mulcahy explore the place of policing in 'the English social imaginary', p. 36.

22 Ballinger critiques Garland's gender blindness, arguing that this misses key 'contradictions, contestations and complexities', A. Ballinger, '"Clear Eyed Description and Objective Analysis": A Peculiar History of the Death Penalty', A Symposium of Reviews of *Peculiar Institution*, *British Journal of Criminology*, 2012, 52(1): 202–6, p. 205.

23 See, inter alia, S. Karstedt, 'Emotions and Criminal Justice', *Theoretical Criminology*, 2002, 6(3): 299–317; L. W. Sherman, 'Reason for Emotion: Reinventing Justice with Theories, Innovations and Research', *Criminology*, 2003, 41(1): 1–38 and S. Karstedt, I. Loader and H. Strang (eds), *Emotions, Crime and Justice*, Oxford: Hart Publishing, 2011.

24 S. P. Garvey, 'The Emotional Economy of Capital Sentencing', *New York University Law Review*, 2000, 75(1): 26–73 and S. A. Bandes, 'Repellent Crimes and Rational Deliberation: Emotion and the Death Penalty', *Vermont Law Review*, 2009, 33(3): 489–518.

25 See S. A. Bandes, 'Fear Factor: The Role of Media in Covering and Shaping the Death Penalty', *Ohio State Journal of Criminal Law*, 2003, 1(2): 585–98 and J. Simon, 'Capital Punishment as Homeowner's Insurance', A. Sarat and J. Martschukat (eds), *Is the Death Penalty Dying?*

26 H. Haines, 'Flawed Executions, The Anti-Death Penalty Movement, and the Politics of Capital Punishment', *Social Problems*, 1992, 39(2): 125–38.

27 M. C. Nussbaum, *Hiding from Humanity: Disgust, Shame and the Law*, Princeton, NJ: Princeton University Press, 2006, pp. 163–6.

28 L. Seal, 'Ruth Ellis and Public Contestation of the Death Penalty', *The Howard Journal*, 2011, 50(5): 492–504 and S. A. Bandes, 'Empathy, Narrative and Victim Impact Statements', *University of Chicago Law Review*, 1996, 63(2): 361–412.

about the death penalty at the legal, political and public levels within states.[29] Following the Supreme Court's decision in *Gregg v Georgia* in 1976,[30] which ended the national moratorium on execution in the United States established by *Furman v Georgia* in 1972,[31] many states passed death penalty statutes in the 1980s. However, not all of these actually executed death sentenced prisoners, creating the new phenomenon in certain states, such as California, of large death row populations but few or no actual executions.

Zimring argues that this 'reflected conflict and uncertainty about capital punishment in the states themselves'.[32] He examines New York as a prime example of this 'internal ambivalence' towards the death penalty, where the re-election of anti-capital punishment governors meant the vetoing of death penalty legislation. When the capital punishment statute finally passed in 1995, it was for a death penalty with a very narrow application, meaning that actual executions were unlikely.[33] This reflected the climate of moral uncertainty regarding capital punishment in New York. The campaign for the successful statute focused on passing the legislation, rather than the execution of prisoners, creating a measure that reflected the ambivalent feelings amongst politicians and the public within the state. Similarly, the capital punishment legislation that was passed in Kansas in 1994 was narrow in scope, signalling the state's 'normative ambivalence' about the death penalty.[34] Galliher and Galliher describe this legislation as symbolic because it could only be applied to a small number of cases. It can be understood as an attempt to fill 'an ever-shifting, ambivalent "cultural space" for Kansans',[35] as a seldom used death penalty is able to fulfil competing demands.

Since the nineteenth century, American capital punishment can be best comprehended as an ambivalent, uneasy practice 'with a shaky consensus often contingent on a complex variety of racial, cultural, and criminological considerations'.[36] Although American public opinion is frequently described as supportive of the death penalty, it is 'both complicated and ambivalent', shifting according to the specific wording of survey questions,[37] and in relation to certain triggering events.[38] It is often noted in death penalty scholarship

29 F. E. Zimring, 'Ambivalence in State Capital Punishment Policy: An Empirical Sounding', *New York Review of Law and Social Change*, 1990–91, 18(3): 729–42.
30 *Gregg v Georgia* 428 US 153 (1976).
31 *Furman v Georgia* 408 US 238 (1972).
32 Zimring, 'Ambivalence', p. 729.
33 F. E. Zimring, 'The Wages of Ambivalence: On the Context and Prospects of New York's Death Penalty', *Buffalo Law Review*, 1996, 44(2): 303–24, p. 322.
34 J. M. Galliher and J. F. Galliher, '"Déjà vu All Over Again": The Recurring Life and Death of Capital Punishment Legislation in Kansas', *Social Problems*, 1997, 44(3): 369–85, p. 372.
35 Ibid., p. 389.
36 R. J. Cottrol, 'Finality with Ambivalence: The American Death Penalty's Uneasy History', *Stanford Law Review*, 56(6): 1641–73, p. 1643.
37 F. E. Zimring, *The Contradictions of American Capital Punishment*, Oxford: Oxford University Press, 2003, p. 10.
38 Galliher and Galliher, 'Déjà vu', p. 377.

that abolition in Western European countries usually took place without a broad base of public support.[39] Anxiety and unease in relation to aspects of capital punishment or to certain cases 'may also help to explain public tolerance for the abolition of capital punishment even when substantial majorities say they want a death penalty to continue'.[40]

These insights into capital punishment as a culturally ambivalent practice are relevant to its symbolic status and operation in twentieth-century Britain. Its continuing de-ritualisation and the restriction of its use indicated unease with the practice at the political level. The reinvigoration of the abolitionist movement in the mid-twentieth century reflected growing uncertainty. Intensifying press and public contestation of particular high-profile capital cases, as well as heightened attention to capital punishment as an issue, also demonstrated a deepening ambivalence in the wider culture. At stake were understandings of Britain as a modern, civilised society and notions of what it meant to be a citizen in that society. In 1957, legal scholar, HLA Hart, compared capital punishment in the United States and England, arguing 'English people have probably been more disturbed and more divided by the use of the death penalty for murder than any people who still retain it as a form of punishment for that offense'.[41] The rest of the chapter provides contextual background in relation to the operation of capital punishment in Britain since the late nineteenth century.

The late nineteenth century

Following the publication of the report of the Royal Commission on Capital Punishment in 1866, hanging ceased to be a fully public event in 1868 and was from then on to take place within prison grounds. The exclusion of the crowd from the execution scene on the one hand 'appeased [the] squeamishness',[42] that was part of the developing Victorian middle-class culture of sensibility, and on the other meant that hanging could be carried out as a more orderly, bureaucratic affair, over which the state had firmer control.[43] By the mid-nineteenth century, spectating an execution had become 'uncivilised', with the sight of bodily punishment increasingly regarded as repugnant.[44] This did not necessarily signal greater sympathy with the condemned but rather the

---

39 See, for example, D. Garland, *Peculiar*, p. 130 and P. Spierenburg, 'The Green, Green Grass of Home', A. Sarat and J. Martschukat (eds), *Is the Death Penalty Dying?*, p. 40.

40 Zimring, *Contradictions*, p. 24.

41 H. L. A. Hart, 'Murder and the Principles of Punishment: England and the United States', *Northwestern University Law Review*, 1957, 52(4): 433–61, p. 433.

42 V. A. C. Gatrell, *The Hanging Tree: Execution and the English People, 1770–1868*, Oxford: Oxford University Press, 1996, p. 596.

43 Ibid., p. 611 and R. McGowen, 'Civilizing Punishment: The End of the Public Execution in England', *Journal of British Studies*, 1994, 33(3): 257–82, pp. 280–82.

44 P. Spierenburg, *The Spectacle of Suffering*, Cambridge: Cambridge University Press, 1984, pp. 185–201. Spierenburg's study is of punishment in the Netherlands.

need to establish new, respectable standards of conduct.[45] Alongside the sensibility of squeamishness were middle-class and elite fears of the 'dangerous classes' of the sort that were likely to congregate at a hanging. Public order was easier to secure by reducing opportunities for festive, raucous behaviour, and by attempting to remove the danger that the crowd would identify with the condemned rather than his or her punishers.[46] Belief in the need to control the misbehaviour of the urban working class was demonstrated by a hardening of penal measures in the 1860s.[47] At the same time, 'murderers came to be seen as less than human', brutes from whom the respectable classes needed protection.[48]

The mid-nineteenth century witnessed the emergence of a thriving abolitionist movement.[49] However, the privatisation of execution dampened abolitionist fervour, seeming to have solved the problems of the savagery of hanging as entertainment and the incipient rebelliousness of the crowd. Nevertheless, the abolitionist movement did not disappear and bills for abolition were read in Parliament in the 1870s and 1880s. In the late nineteenth century, the supporters of abolitionism were drawn from Liberals, radicals, spiritualists and theosophists. Although the cause itself had limited appeal, abolitionists were able to mobilise campaigns for reprieve in relation to certain contentious cases, such as Florence Maybrick and Mary Ann Ansell.[50] After retiring, long-serving hangman, James Berry, gave public lectures against hanging and a new abolitionist society was established at the turn of the twentieth century.[51]

Anxiety about the gallows peaked in the 1860s but was not completely assuaged by their concealment behind prison walls. Death, pain and violence were increasingly unacceptable in public spaces in the nineteenth century. Death was becoming more private and deritualised, its occurrence a potential source of embarrassment and shame.[52] The nineteenth-century 'civilising offensive' meant that the infliction of physical suffering was increasingly

---

45 McGowen, 'Civilizing Punishment', pp. 265–7.

46 Ibid., pp. 268–72; Gatrell, *The Hanging Tree*, p. 591.

47 J. Gregory, *Victorians Against the Gallows*, London: I. B. Tauris, 2012, p. 223. On these measures, which emphasised the need for discipline, morality and character development, see M. J. Wiener, *Reconstructing the Criminal: Culture, Law, and Policy in England, 1830–1914*, Cambridge: Cambridge University Press, 1990, pp. 141–58.

48 R. McGowen, 'History, Culture and the Death Penalty: The British Debates', *Historical Reflections*, 2003, 29(2): 229–50, p. 242.

49 See Gregory, *Victorians* for a study of Victorian abolitionism.

50 Florence Maybrick was reprieved in 1889, following conviction for the murder of her husband. She became a cause *cèlébre* as the evidence for the supposed poisoning was circumstantial and to her supporters it seemed that her infidelity had influenced the verdict. See G. Robb, 'Circe in Crinoline: Domestic Poisonings in Victorian England', *Journal of Family History*, 1997, 22(2): 176–90, p. 184. Mary Ann Ansell was hanged in 1899 after being found guilty of her sister's murder (also a poisoning). A press campaign on her behalf highlighted doubts about her mental soundness. See M. J. Wiener, 'Convicted Murderers and the Victorian Press: Condemnation vs. Sympathy', *Crimes and Misdemeanours*, 2007, 1/2: 110–25, p. 117.

51 Gregory, *Victorians*, pp. 231–38.

52 R. Evans, *Rituals of Retribution*, Oxford: Oxford University Press, 1995, p. 20.

stigmatised and the social legitimacy of violence had narrowed.[53] A 'culture of refinement' amongst the middle classes demarcated itself from the 'savagery' of the working classes. This culture abjured public displays of violence.[54] Increasingly, too, values of 'respectability' amongst the Victorian working classes made violence in public more unacceptable.[55] Humanitarians emphasised the corrupting influence of witnessing pain, which could reduce empathy and inspire violence. Pain was redefined as shocking and obscene – but this redefinition enhanced its moral dangerousness as it was also illicit, exciting and a source of voyeurism.[56] The 'civilised classes' sought to put distance between themselves and the visibility of pain, which at the same time enhanced the pornographic appeal of bodily suffering. This remained a problem for the civilised exercise of bodily punishments as, even once they were removed from public view, they remained a source of fascination and became the subject of erotic fantasy.[57]

Holding humanitarian, progressive views such as abolitionism could be a 'mark of distinction', which separated the educated and sensitive from the brute masses.[58] The capacity to empathise with the condemned, who was usually from lower down the social class structure than the humanitarian, demonstrated refined feelings. For the aspirant middle class and new, respectable social elite, such refinement could also distinguish them from the callousness and moral bankruptcy of the aristocracy. However, empathy sometimes sat uneasily alongside another imperative of nineteenth-century civilisation – rationality.[59]

The civilised person's capacity for cool rationality required detachment from emotional situations in order to make calm judgments.[60] It was important that empathy with the condemned did not become sentimentality or, worse, hysteria. In 1868, *The Times* congratulated John Stuart Mill for his disregard of sentimentality in stating that the abolition of capital punishment would bring 'an enervation and effeminacy in the general mind of the country'.[61] The interlinking of the exercise of the death penalty with national sovereignty meant that it was closely associated with issues of warfare and defence, and support for the retention of capital punishment was a norm of

---

53 M. J. Wiener, *Men of Blood: Violence, Manliness and Criminal Justice in Victorian England*, Cambridge: Cambridge University Press, 2004, p. 11 and J. C. Wood, *Violence and Crime in Nineteenth-Century England: The Shadow of Our Refinement*, London: Routledge, 2004, p. 5.
54 Wood, p. 6.
55 Wiener, *Men of Blood*, p. 13.
56 K. Halttunen, 'Humanitarianism and the Pornography of Pain in Anglo-American Culture', *American History Review*, 1995, 100(2): 303–34, pp. 318–25.
57 Ibid.
58 A. Hammel, 'Civilized Rebels', A. Sarat and J. Martschukat, *Is the Death Penalty Dying?*, p. 175.
59 Ibid., p. 196.
60 Wood examines how the 'civilised mentality' of the nineteenth-century emphasised rationality and restraint, *Violence and Crime*, p. 14.
61 L. Radzinowicz and R. Hood, *A History of English Criminal Law and its Administration Vol. 5: The Emergence of Penal Policy*, London: Stevens and Sons, 1986, p. 686.

mid-nineteenth-century British masculinity.[62] The ongoing tension between empathy and rationality can be identified in twentieth-century humanitarian campaigns for the abolition of capital punishment. Too much empathic identification risked the sin of sentimentality.

The need to be civilised and to become modern can be understood as concerns underlying the practice of the death penalty and as guiding the reforms made to it in the late nineteenth and early twentieth centuries.[63] The execution audience had been significantly modified by the Capital Punishment (Amendment) Act 1868 and most ordinary people no longer witnessed the hanging of the condemned. However, executions were still performed and still conveyed meaning to the distanced audience. As Martschukat argues, civilisation is something that must be performatively constituted and the privatisation of execution was a performance of what it meant to be rational and humane.[64] The reproduction of civilisation and modernity necessitated avoiding the 'maimed, disfigured body',[65] meaning that execution had to become painless and invisible. The ceremonial aspects of capital punishment were gradually removed, but this did not mean that it ceased to be a ritualistic practice. Rather, the nature of the ritual changed into one that was private, bureaucratic and within the authorities' control.[66] This transformation of the death penalty deepened its ambivalence as it tacitly acknowledged capital punishment's damaging and derogatory effects, whilst it was retained as a necessary measure in the state's arsenal of punishment.[67]

In the light of these imperatives botched executions were problematic, especially as they could become public knowledge through newspaper reporting, which often provided graphic accounts.[68] This compromised the privacy of the execution but also its civilised nature – a widely reported botched hanging was neither painless nor invisible.[69] In the 1880s, the lack of circumspection of James Berry, the hangman, was cause for official concern. He presided over several flawed executions and also gave talks at which he would demonstrate his equipment, publicising his trade.[70] In 1886, the

---

62 Gregory, *Victorians*, p. 186.
63 McGowen, 'History': McGowen explores how the imperatives of civilisation and modernity were important to both abolitionists and retentionists in the mid-nineteenth century.
64 Martschukat's arguments are made in relation to Germany but are highly applicable to Britain, 'Nineteenth-Century Executions', pp. 52–5. See also Madow, 'Forbidden Spectacle', p. 476.
65 Martschukat, p. 62.
66 Haines, 'Flawed Executions', p. 126.
67 Martschukat, 'Nineteenth-Century Executions', p. 57.
68 H. Potter, *Hanging in Judgment: Religion and the Death Penalty in England*, London: SCM Press, 1993, pp. 102–4.
69 Smith explores how the first execution by electric chair, in New York in 1890, was 'horribly botched', failing to kill the condemned, William Kemmler, quickly. The *New York Times* described it as a 'disgrace to civilization', Smith, *Punishment*, p. 151.
70 On botched hangings in the 1880s, see Execution of Sentence of Death, Notes as to Practice, 1920, TNA/HO45/25843, pp. 20–1. This document records that there were no significant gallows mishaps after 1891.

Aberdare Committee was established in order to suggest improvements to execution practice. Its 1888 report recommended the adoption of standardised gallows apparatus and produced an official table of drops to help ensure the prisoner would die through their neck breaking rather than by asphyxiation. It also established the practice of prison governors filing reports on each execution.[71] These late nineteenth-century moves towards standardisation and record keeping further entrenched the performance of capital punishment as a civilised, bureaucratic ritual and brought it more firmly under Home Office control. Further vestiges of the ceremonial were removed from the execution event at the turn of the twentieth century, when the tolling of the bell ceased to happen during the execution but instead could only ring out afterwards. In 1902, the raising of the black flag after a hanging was stopped.[72]

The twentieth century

An abolitionist movement continued to exist in the early twentieth century but its profile was low.[73] Certain contentious executions attracted public attention, debate and dispute but capital punishment was not a prominent issue.[74] However, anxiety and unease with the application of the death penalty was stoked in certain quarters by the 361 military executions for desertion and cowardice of British soldiers during the First World War,[75] especially as they had limited legal representation and inadequate rights of appeal. Although there was not a strong public reaction against such executions, a small number of Labour and Liberal MPs pursued a parliamentary campaign to restrict the use of capital punishment against soldiers, resulting in the Army Act 1930, which confined the military death penalty to treachery.[76] This campaign was boosted by the formation of the Labour minority government in 1923,[77] and the consolidation of the Labour Party as a parliamentary force would be crucial to putting abolitionism on the political agenda.[78]

---

71 Potter, *Hanging in Judgment*, pp. 102–4.
72 Ibid., p. 105 and Execution of Sentence of Death, HO45/25843, p. 21.
73 See E. O. Tuttle, *The Crusade Against Capital Punishment in Britain*, London: Stevens and Sons, 1961, p. 27 on the founding of the Penal Reform League in 1907.
74 B. P. Block and J. Hostettler, *Hanging in the Balance: A History of the Abolition of Capital Punishment in Britain*, Winchester: Waterside Press, 1997, pp. 79–83.
75 D. Hay, 'Hanging and the English Judges: The Judicial Politics of Retention and Abolition', Garland, McGowen and Meranze (eds), *America's Death Penalty*, p. 153.
76 J. McHugh, 'The Labour Party and the Parliamentary Campaign to Abolish the Military Death Penalty 1919–30', *The Historical Journal*, 1999, 42(1): 233–49 and C. Corns and J. Hughes-Wilson, *Blindfold and Alone: British Military Executions in the Great War*, London: Cassell, 2001, pp. 403–63.
77 McHugh, p. 249.
78 V. Bailey, 'The Shadow of the Gallows: The Death Penalty and the British Labour Government, 1945–51', *Law and History Review*, 2000, 18(2): 305–50.

In 1927, the party took an abolitionist stance in its *Manifesto on Capital Punishment*.[79]

As in many other places and times, execution was least contentious in twentieth-century Britain when applied to the healthy, adult male body. Discomfort and disagreement were provoked when the condemned did not fit this type – when they were drawn from the too young, the too old and the female. No-one aged below 18 had been executed in Britain since 1887,[80] although hanging was not officially ended for under 16s until 1908 and under 18s in 1933.[81] The execution of young men between the ages of 18 and 23 had the power to provoke controversy, especially when it appeared that there were strong mitigating circumstances or when the murder was clearly unpremeditated. Straddling the boundary between adolescence and adulthood, the hanging of teenagers in particular could cause press and public unease. Examples included Henry Jacoby in 1922 (see Chapter Two) and Derek Bentley in 1953. Youth alone was frequently not considered adequate grounds for reprieve, meaning that there were mismatches between public and official views on the legitimacy of executing very young men. In their 1961 book, *Hanged by the Neck*, Koestler and Rolph pointed out that 50 of the 123 people executed 1949–60 were under 25, and described this as 'a repudiation of modern penology and of common sense'.[82] In 1960, the impending execution of 18-year-old Francis Forsyth inspired a letter to *The Times* signed by leading abolitionists as well as cultural figures such as Kingsley Amis, J. B. Priestly and Michael Redgrave. This argued '[t]here could be no greater affront to either the Christian or the humanist conscience than to kill, in cold blood, a youth of 18'.[83]

Old age, on the other hand, was treated as grounds for reprieve,[84] with the Home Office exhibiting unwillingness to highlight the brutal – and potentially uncivilised – nature of hanging by breaking an already frail body. It was believed that public opinion would be offended by execution of the elderly and the modern, democratic governments of the twentieth century needed to avoid wielding power too cruelly against their citizens.[85]

79 J. Rowbotham, 'Execution as Punishment in England: 1750–2000', A. Kilday and D. Nash (eds), *Histories of Crime: Britain 1600–2000*, Basingstoke: Palgrave MacMillan, 2010, p. 186.

80 Potter, *Hanging in Judgment*, p. 109.

81 Tuttle, *The Crusade*, p. 27.

82 A. Koestler and C. H. Rolph, *Hanged by the Neck*, London: Penguin, 1961, p. 139.

83 'Sentenced to Death', Letter to the Editor, *The Times*, 1 November 1960. Forsyth and 23-year-old Norman Harris were hanged for the 'footpath murder' of Allen Jee, whom they beat to death and robbed on Hounslow footpath.

84 See L. Seal, 'Public Reactions to the Case of Mary Wilson, the Last Woman to be Sentenced to Death in England and Wales', *Papers from the British Criminology Conference*, 2008, 8: 65–84. Mary Wilson, 66, was reprieved in 1958; Rab Butler judged her execution would be 'a shock to public opinion', p. 65. Only one person over the age of 70 was hanged in the twentieth century.

85 D. Reicher, 'Bureaucracy, "Domesticated" Elites, and the Abolition of Capital Punishment. Processes of State Formation and the Number of Executions in England and Habsburg Austria between 1700 and 1914', *Crime, Law and Social Change*, 2010, 54(3/4): 279–97. Reicher

From the late eighteenth century, executing women was a significant cause of ambivalence in relation to capital punishment in Britain.[86] As subsequent chapters discuss, the hangings of Edith Thompson in 1923 and Ruth Ellis in 1955 were important moments in terms of stirring anxiety about capital punishment and for the reinvigoration of abolitionism. Women's increased social and political status in the early twentieth century was reflected in the campaign to establish the Infanticide Act 1922, which made the murder of a newborn child by its mother a separate, lesser offence that was not subject to the death penalty (this was extended to cases of children under one in 1938). Although this Act has sometimes been interpreted as a paternalistic gesture, which encoded the reproductive female body as pathological,[87] it was achieved after feminist and women's groups pursued a sustained campaign on this issue.[88] Hanging for pregnant women was legislatively abolished in 1931,[89] although as with the Infanticide Act, this codified well-established existing practice.

Women's executions had the potential to be especially symbolic, as the behaviour and treatment of (white) women were key signifiers of national civilisation and modernity.[90] At the same time, hanging women demonstrated how these two imperatives were open to multiple interpretations and could pull in different directions. Women's bodies, especially since the nineteenth century, were perceived to be more delicate than the male body.[91] The

examines how democratization in England ameliorated the harshness of physical punishment. Through a comparison with Austria, he argues that democratization was not a prerequisite for this process, as Austria was more lenient than nineteenth-century England.

86 See R. McGowen, 'The Body and Punishment in Eighteenth Century England', *The Journal of Modern History*, 1987, 59(4): 651–79 and M. J. Wiener, 'Alice Arden to Bill Sikes: Changing Nightmares of Intimate Violence in England, 1559–1869', *Journal of British Studies*, 2001, 40(2): 184–212, pp. 194–9.

87 For debates on the Infanticide Act, see T. Ward, 'The Sad Subject of Infanticide: Law, Medicine and Child Murder, 1860–1938', *Social and Legal Studies*, 1999, 8(2): 163–80 and K. J. Kramar and W. D. Watson, 'The Insanities of Reproduction: Medico-Legal Knowledge and the Development of Infanticide Law', *Social and Legal Studies*, 2006, 15(2): 237–55.

88 A. Logan, *Feminism and Criminal Justice*, Basingstoke: Palgrave MacMillan, 2008, pp. 131–3 and D. J. R. Grey, 'Women's Policy Networks and the Infanticide Act 1922', *Twentieth Century British History*, 2010, 21(4): 441–63.

89 Block and Hostettler, *Hanging in the Balance*, p. 89.

90 Particularly in the mid-twentieth century, British women's citizenship was tied to their reproductive role, as they 'could bear healthy white citizens', J. Garrity, *Step-Daughters of England: British Women Modernists and the National Imaginary*, Manchester: Manchester University Press, 2003, p. 1. On mid-twentieth-century associations between femininity and modernity, see C. Geraghty, *British Cinema in the Fifties: Gender, Genre and the 'New Look'*, London: Routledge, 2000 and J. Giles, 'Narratives of Gender, Class and Modernity in Women's Memories of Mid Twentieth-Century Britain', *Signs*, 2002, 28(1): 21–41.

91 See C. Gallagher and T. Laqueur (eds), *The Making of the Modern Body: Sexuality and Society in the Nineteenth Century*, London: University of California Press, 1987. As Strange argues, there are important distinctions between the cultural meanings of men's and women's bodies, which are highly relevant to the exercise of bodily punishment, C. Strange, 'The Undercurrents of Penal Culture: Punishment of the Body in Mid Twentieth-Century Canada', *Law & Society Review*, 2001, 19(2): 343–85, p. 367.

execution of a woman was a reminder of the visceral aspects of capital punishment, something exemplified by concerns that the hanging of Edith Thompson was botched, causing her womb to 'fall out'.[92] As Chapter Six discusses, this contradicted the supposed modernity and civilisation – and cleanness – of the twentieth-century death penalty. The execution of a woman entailed the breaking of the maternal body, which highlighted the 'powers of horror' of bodily punishment and violated the sacred meanings of motherhood.[93]

Debates over what it meant to be civilised were brought into stark relief by the hanging of women. As Grant argues, 'the severe punishment of a woman not only legitimates, but also uncomfortably reveals, the violence which underpins the state's authority'.[94] Proposals to exempt women from capital punishment were made on the basis that it was uncivilised to hang women – but the urge to be modern meant that women and men needed to be subject to the same penalties on the grounds of equality. A leader in the *Manchester Guardian* on Edith Thompson's impending execution commented, '[i]t is difficult these days to plead for the exemption of women from the death penalty'.[95] Suggestions to restrict capital punishment to men only were rejected by the Royal Commission on Capital Punishment 1949–53, the Report found 'no rational grounds on which discrimination between men and women on this matter could be justified'.[96]

Whilst hanging women may have been necessary for the appearance of equality, it very rarely happened. Over 90 per cent of women sentenced to death in the twentieth century were reprieved and only 16 women were hanged between 1900 and 1965, the last of these being Ruth Ellis in 1955.[97] Both for the reasons discussed above and because of this rarity, women's capital cases were often cultural flashpoints. Concerns that particular women were being treated unfairly, either because mitigating circumstance had not been recognised or because it seemed that a man in the same situation would be reprieved, raised questions of the unequal treatment of women under the law. Feminist campaigners for Edith Thompson argued that she faced hanging for her immorality, as the evidence against her was shaky.[98] Ruth Ellis was another prime example – the 'double standard' that forgave sexual experience in men but deplored it in women was perceived to be in operation.[99] The

---

92 R. Kennedy, 'The Media and the Death Penalty: The Limits of Sentimentality, the Power of Abjection', *Humanities Research*, 2007, 14(2): 29–48.

93 Ibid., p. 34 and C. Grant, *Crime and Punishment in Contemporary Culture*, Abingdon: Routledge, 2004, p. 129.

94 Grant, p. 126.

95 'The Death Penalty', *Manchester Guardian*, 6 January 1923.

96 *Report of the Royal Commission on Capital Punishment, 1949–1953*, Cmd. 8932, London: HMSO, p. 65.

97 Ballinger, *Dead*, p. 328. This figure does not include women executed in Ireland before independence.

98 Logan, *Feminism*, pp. 133–4.

99 Seal, 'Ruth Ellis', pp. 499–500.

equal treatment argument was not always made in favour of reprieve. In 1945, Elizabeth Jones was reprieved for her part in the 'Cleft Chin' murder of a taxi driver, while her partner in crime, Karl Hulten, was hanged. Many argued that Jones and Hulten should have received the same penalty, and in parts of the country factory girls threatened strike action over this perceived inequality.[100] Therefore, the execution of women raised a number of issues that had the potential to intensify anxieties about the use of capital punishment. These derived not only from old fashioned, 'chivalric' views, but also from concerns about women's equal treatment.

Issues of race and ethnicity did not fire cultural reaction in the way that youth and femininity did. Possible inequities in the application of the death penalty to people born outside of Britain and/or who were minority ethnic requires further research and analysis. Somalian sailor, Mahmood Mattan, was hanged in Cardiff in 1952 for the murder of a shopkeeper, Lily Volpert. Koestler and Rolph noted that Mattan's defence counsel described him as 'a half child of nature, a semi-civilized savage'.[101] It now seems highly unlikely that the murder was committed by Mattan and his case was the first to be referred to the Court of Appeal by the Criminal Cases Review Commission. His conviction was quashed in 1998.[102] Mattan was not a cause cèlébre and the execution of those outside of British citizenship and the community of sentiment had low cultural salience, even as the death penalty's cultural ambivalence deepened in the 1950s.

Moving towards abolition

Abolitionism started to gather strength in the 1920s, one of the spurs being Edith Thompson's execution in 1923.[103] The Howard League took a referendum of its members in this year and adopted abolition as one of its campaigning priorities.[104] The National Council for the Abolition of the Death Penalty was founded in 1925, with Roy Calvert as its secretary.[105] Calvert emphasised the need for abolitionist arguments to be based on logic, rationalism and science and that research was needed in order to provide statistics in support of the abolitionist position. His approach exemplified the 'civilised rebellion' explored by Hammel, whereby the principles of civilisation and modernity were central to campaigns against capital punishment.[106] The first

---

100 C. Dyhouse, *Girl Trouble: Panic and Progress in the History of Young Women*, London: Zed Books, 2013, p. 111.
101 Koestler and Rolph, *Hanged by the Neck*, p. 119.
102 See J. Minkes and M. Vanstone, 'Gender, Race and the Death Penalty: Lessons from Three 1950s Murder Trials', *Howard Journal*, 2006, 45(4): 403–20, pp. 411–13 on racialised language in the trial of Mattan.
103 Logan, *Feminism*, pp. 130–1.
104 G. Rose, *The Struggle for Penal Reform*, London: Stevens and Sons, 1961, p. 203.
105 Ibid., p. 204.
106 Hammel, 'Civilised Rebels'.

full Parliamentary debate on capital punishment in the twentieth century was held in 1929 and resulted in the establishment of a Select Committee on the issue.[107]

The Select Committee's report was published in 1930. Despite the fact that the majority of British witnesses had advocated retention of the death penalty, the report recommended an experimental five-year period of abolition.[108] It argued that examination of other countries 'has increasingly convinced us in the assurance that capital punishment may be abolished in this country without endangering life or property, or impairing the security of society'.[109] However, the report was neither debated nor discussed in the Commons,[110] demonstrating the low political saliency of this issue at the time. Two heavily contrasting active campaigns for abolition were waged in the 1930s. The Howard League and National Campaign for the Abolition of the Death Penalty launched an abolitionist journal, the *Penal Reformer*, in 1934 and conducted a sober campaign which pointedly eschewed emotionalism, as this compromised rationality.[111] As part of this, they refrained from intervening in individual cases but rather opposed all capital punishment. Wealthy businesswoman, Violet van der Elst, funded her own direct action campaign against the death penalty, which is discussed in Chapter Four. This involved a mixture of techniques, including flying planes trailing banners over the prison on execution morning, employing 'sandwich men' to display anti-capital punishment slogans and addressing the crowd outside the prison through a loud hailer, often leading them in song.[112]

Anti-death penalty feeling was expressed by some authors in the hugely popular 'golden age' detective fiction of the 1930s.[113] Dorothy L Sayers' Lord Peter Wimsey was keenly aware that solving the puzzle of the crime would send the murderer to the gallows and had a 'Gothic intimacy with wrongdoers' rather than being separate from them.[114] Ngaio Marsh held abolitionist views and conferred her own 'repugnance for that terrible practice' upon her detective, Roderick Alleyn, and the woman he marries, Agatha Troy.[115] Also in the 1930s, F Tennyson Jesse's *A Pin to See the Peepshow* (based on Edith

---

107 Block and Hostettler, *Hanging in the Balance*, pp. 90–3.
108 Potter, *Hanging in Judgment*, pp. 130–4.
109 *Report from the Select Committee on Capital Punishment*, London: HMSO, 1930, p. 94.
110 Potter, p. 135.
111 Tuttle, *The Crusade*, pp. 45–50.
112 Ibid., p. 48.
113 'Golden age' detective fiction refers to the development in the interwar period of mysteries as a distinct genre. Such stories and novels were based on murder as an intellectual puzzle that needed to be solved. Female authors writing about male sleuths predominated, the most widely read being Agatha Christie, Dorothy L. Sayers, Josephine Tey, Ngaio Marsh and Margery Allingham. K. G. Klein, *The Woman Detective: Gender and Genre*, Urbana: University of Illinois Press, 2nd edition, 1995, pp. 95–121.
114 S. Rowland, 'House not Ho(l)mes', L. Hockley and L. Gardner (eds), *House: The Wounded Healer on Television*, Hove: Routledge, 2011, p. 138.
115 N. Marsh, 'Portrait of Troy', *Death in Ecstasy-Vintage Murder-Artists in Crime Omnibus*, London: Harper, 2009, p. x.

Thompson) and Graham Greene's *It's a Battlefield* highlighted flaws in capital punishment.[116]

After the Second World War, the prospect of abolition appeared to be within reach and chances were improved by the large Labour victory in 1945.[117] Abolitionist Labour MP, Sydney Silverman, added a clause to the Criminal Justice Bill 1948, which passed in the Commons by 247 votes to 224. Capital punishment was suspended between February and November of that year, although the Criminal Justice Act passed without the abolition clause.[118] A Royal Commission was established in 1949 with a narrow remit to examine whether eligibility for the death penalty should be limited or modified.[119] Before it reported in September 1953, two cases had shaken the legitimacy of capital punishment and raised anxiety about its application. Nineteen-year-old Derek Bentley was executed in January for the murder of a policeman, despite the fact that his friend, Christopher Craig, had actually shot the officer while Bentley was under arrest. In July, John Christie was hanged for the murder of his wife and confessed to killing six other women whose remains were found in and outside his Notting Hill flat. One of these victims was Beryl Evans, the wife of Timothy Evans, who had been hanged in 1950. Evans had named Christie as the murderer of his wife and baby, and it appeared highly likely that an innocent man had been executed.[120]

In February 1955, the Conservative Government announced that it could not accept any of the Royal Commission's recommendations.[121] Silverman retaliated with a motion for abolition, which was supported by James Chuter Ede, Home Secretary when Evans was executed.[122] Although this motion was defeated, the breakdown of votes demonstrated that the composition of Conservative MPs was changing to include more abolitionists.[123] In July 1955, Ruth Ellis was hanged amidst public consternation that a woman who had been so mistreated by the man she killed had failed to win a

---

116 F. T. Jesse, *A Pin to See the Peepshow*, London: Heinemann, 1934 (discussed further in Chapter Six). G. Greene, *It's a Battlefield*, London: Heinemann, 1934. Greene's main theme is the arbitrariness of justice; M. R. Maamri, 'Cosmic Chaos in *The Secret Agent* and Graham Greene's *It's a Battlefield*', *Conradiana*, 2008, 40(2): 179–91, p. 179.

117 Potter, *Hanging in Judgment*, p. 308.

118 Detailed accounts can be found in J. B. Christoph, *Capital Punishment and British Politics*, London: George Allen & Unwin, 1962 pp. 38–75 and Bailey, 'Shadow', pp. 320–46.

119 For a discussion of the Royal Commission from one of its Commissioners, see L. Radzinowicz, *Adventures in Criminology*, London: Routledge, 1999, pp. 245–69. The Report suggested that it should be left to the jury to decide whether a murderer received the death sentence or imprisonment. It cautioned against the adoption of degrees of murder, which would be too rigid to be workable, *Report of the Royal Commission on Capital Punishment*, pp. 212–15.

120 These well-known cases have been recounted many times and are widely recognised to have deepened anxiety regarding capital punishment. Radzinowicz states that 'their cumulative weight produced a deep and disturbing effect on public opinion', 1999, p. 272.

121 Christoph, *Capital Punishment*, p. 127.

122 T. Morris, *Crime and Criminal Justice since 1945*, Oxford: Wiley-Blackwell, 1989, p. 83.

123 Tuttle, *The Crusade*, p. 105 and Christoph, *Capital Punishment*, p. 128.

reprieve.[124] In the wake of her execution, the National Campaign for the Abolition of Capital Punishment was set up by Victor Gollancz with the support of Arthur Koestler and gained 20,000 members within a short space of time.[125] Unlike the Howard League, this campaign sought to engage public emotion and outrage.[126] According to Twitchell, the NCACP was the most influential abolitionist group and was 'a very high powered organisation supported by a roll call of eminent individuals from all walks of life'.[127] Although successful in the Commons, Silverman's 1956 Death Penalty Abolition Bill was voted down in the Lords (and the Conservative Government did not invoke the Parliament Act to pass it). Significantly, though, a majority of MPs was now in favour of abolishing capital punishment.[128]

In the mid-1950s, sections of the popular press enthusiastically supported abolition. The *Daily Mirror* polled its readers after the Ellis execution, attracting double the amount of responses in favour of abolition as for retention.[129] The *Picture Post* named hanging its 'moral issue of the year' in 1955 and commenced 1956 with a 'complete investigation on the subject'.[130] It also published several letters received from figures such as Victor Gollancz and Hugh Klare of the Howard League.[131] In the late 1950s, novels and films promoted abolitionist sentiment. The novel, *My Mother was Hanged*, portrays a young man who is driven to murder his friend after discovering that his mother was executed when he was a small child. He becomes obsessed with her case and with sharing her experience.[132] The publicity for the film, *Yield to the Night*, about a woman facing the death penalty, directly asked the public 'Would you hang Mary Hilton?'.[133] The film was intended by its scriptwriter, Joan Henry, and director, Lee Thompson, as 'a propaganda drama in the campaign against hanging'.[134]

The Homicide Act 1957 was a compromise in relation to capital punishment, as it limited the death penalty's application to certain types of murder,

---

124 Seal, 'Ruth Ellis', pp. 497–9.
125 Potter, *Hanging in Judgment*, p. 170.
126 For an account of the National Campaign for the Abolition of Capital Punishment by someone who was personally involved with it, see P. Duff, *Left, Left, Left*, London: Allison and Busby, 1971, pp. 104–11. Duff describes the NCACP as 'a very different sort of campaign', p. 106.
127 N. Twitchell, *The Politics of the Rope*, Bury St Edmunds: Arena, 2012, p. 45. The NCACP's Committee of Honour included Benjamin Britten, Cecil Day-Lewis, Henry Moore and J. B. Priestley, p. 34.
128 See Christoph, *Capital Punishment*, pp. 135–50.
129 'Verdict in Great "Mirror" Poll is – ABOLISH HANGING!', *Daily Mirror*, 18 July 1955. The *Mirror* did not conduct its poll 'scientifically' and simply asked readers to return a coupon.
130 'The Moral Issue of the Year', *Picture Post*, 31 December 1955.
131 V. Gollancz, 'The Campaign Grows' and H. Klare, 'A Moral Issue', Letters to the Editor, *Picture Post*, 7 January 1956.
132 E. S. Willards, *My Mother was Hanged*, London: Heinemann, 1958.
133 S. Chibnall, 'The Anti Heroines of Holloway', P. Mason (ed.), *Captured by the Media: Prison Discourse in Popular Culture*, Willan: Cullompton, 2006, p. 183.
134 Ibid., p. 179.

as well as introducing the defence of diminished responsibility and widening the provocation defence.[135] This Act was a crucial turning point in the history of capital punishment in Britain, as death was no longer the automatic penalty for murder. If intended to salve the growing contentiousness of the death penalty, the Homicide Act was a failure as the justification for its categories of capital murder was open to debate,[136] and it did not resolve the issue of the apparently arbitrary nature of the reprieve system. Between the passing of the Act in March 1957 and the last executions in December 1964, three or four people were hanged per year.[137] Execution itself had become rare but was the subject of much impassioned debate. Fears of miscarriage of justice had become firmly attached to the issue of hanging and were further stoked by the execution of James Hanratty in 1962 as uncertainty surrounded his guilt.[138] Abolition seemed increasingly likely and possible. Silverman's Private Member's Bill of 1964 was passed as the Death Penalty (Abolition) Act in 1965. This was to be based on an initial suspension period of five years, although final abolition of capital punishment for murder took place in 1969, when the Commons voted 343 to 185 for permanent abolition.[139]

The last executions to take place in Britain were in 1964. In themselves, they were not a major event[140] but they occurred at a point at which capital punishment had become ambivalent and anxious, with questions frequently raised about its legitimacy and the dangers of executing the innocent. This did not mean that abolition was a popular measure. It would be most accurate to state that widespread public approval for capital punishment remained, but that application of the death sentence for all murders became culturally untenable in the 1950s. In this sense, the Homicide Act 1957 should be interpreted as the key legislative turning point as this meant that murder

135 For contemporary discussions of the Act, see S. Prevezer, 'The English Homicide Act: A New Attempt to Revise the Law of Murder', *Columbia Law Review*, 1957, 57(5): 624–42 and J. Edwards, 'The Homicide Act, 1957: A Critique', *British Journal of Delinquency*, 1957, 8: 49–61. Capital murder was now restricted to those carried out with a gun or by explosion, those made in the course or furtherance of theft, murder whilst resisting arrest, murder of a police or prison officer, and where murder had been committed on two separate occasions.

136 The first execution after the Homicide Act, of John Vickers in July 1957, exposed the Act's inconsistencies. Vickers killed an old woman in the course of theft, making his a capital crime but the killing was not intentional and so not one of the 'worst' murders, Twitchell, *Politics*, p. 104.

137 Potter, *Hanging in Judgment*, p. 192. Around 40 per cent of the condemned were still being reprieved, demonstrating that the Act had not been successful in restricting the death sentence to the 'death worthy'.

138 See L. Blom-Cooper, *The A6 Murder: Regina vs James Hanratty, the Semblance of Truth*, Harmondsworth: Penguin, 1963. Hanratty was hanged for the murder of Michael Gregston, who was shot dead at the side of the road. Doubt surrounded the witness identification used to convict him. His case remains controversial.

139 See Block and Hostettler, *Hanging in the Balance*, pp. 235–66.

140 *The Times* reported as 'News in Brief' that Peter Allen and Gwynne Evans would not be reprieved for murdering John West 'in the course or furtherance of theft' – 'No Reprieve for Two', 12 August 1964. They were executed on 13 August at Liverpool and Manchester.

was no longer automatically a capital crime. However, this limitation of capital punishment did not stop the questioning of reprieve decisions or ameliorate the death penalty's cultural ambivalence.

Abolition can be understood to largely have been driven by elites, although the popular abolitionism of Violet van der Elst, and of news media such as the *Daily Mirror, Daily Herald* and *Picture Post* should not be ignored. This underlines the fact that debates about the death penalty, and associated discussions of what it meant to be civilised and modern, were not restricted to official and highbrow culture.[141] The complete removal of the death penalty for murder was achieved by parliamentary interest group activity, led by MPs such as Sydney Silverman, and was made within the context of the liberalising reforms of the mid to late 1960s.[142] However, a wider loss of faith in the adequate use of the reprieve system and in the criminal justice system to convict the right person was not confined to elites and characterised much popular discourse in Britain by the mid-twentieth century. The automatic death sentence for murder needed to be removed. Understanding this difference is crucial because it modifies the rather too straightforward view that elites effected abolition in opposition to public opinion. In fact, whilst abolition of the death penalty for the 'worst' murderers was not popular, capital punishment had become sufficiently ambivalent in Britain by the 1950s that its restriction became a necessary *response* to public opinion, even if that opinion was sporadic, volatile and contradictory.

Shifts in the meaning and constitution of British citizenship in the twentieth century can help to explain the deepening ambivalence and anxiousness of the death penalty. The increased inclusion of ordinary, working-class British people within the definition of 'citizen', and of women of any class, expanded its boundaries. This expansion did not incorporate everyone – it was primarily for the respectable, white working class.[143] However, the secrecy that shrouded the post-conviction execution process became increasingly jarring in a country that was more democratic and developing a more inclusive version of citizenship. This did not necessarily dispose the wider population to be abolitionist – but as the death penalty became a high-profile issue that was debated and discussed frequently in print and other media, the perceived inequities in certain cases were magnified. This called the effectiveness of the

---

141 'Official' is used here to describe the state's bureaucratic culture, rather than carrying a broader meaning of a 'high' culture that can be distinguished from 'popular' culture. For a similar usage, see A. W. B. Simpson, 'Shooting Felons: Law, Practice, Official Culture, and Perceptions of Morality', *Journal of Law and Society*, 2005, 32(2): 241–66.

142 These reforms include the legalisation of homosexuality and abortion, and the relaxing of the divorce laws and theatre censorship. The House of Lords had greater Labour representation by the 1960s and the 1955 and 1959 intakes of Conservative MPs added to the liberal element within the Conservative Party, Twitchell, *Politics*, pp. 320–30.

143 See S. O. Rose, *Which People's War? National Identity and Citizenship in Britain 1939–1945*, Oxford: Oxford University Press, 2003. Rose highlights the Second World War as the turning point in creating this version of British citizenship.

operation of capital punishment into question, as well as its morality. Even those satisfied with the latter were not necessarily sanguine about the former.

Abolition created its own contentions, and calls for the reintroduction of the death penalty were made soon after its final suspension. Free votes on the issue were held in every parliamentary session until 1998,[144] and the issue of restoration continues to receive media attention.[145] However, the terms of the debate have fundamentally shifted. Chapter Seven explores how certain crimes have been especial focal points for cultural anxiety and for punitive reactions, such as the Moors murders, tried in 1966 shortly after abolition, and the terrorist bombings perpetrated by IRA members on mainland Britain in the 1970s. The perceived injustice of hanging the innocent, the mentally ill, the developmentally disadvantaged, the mistreated and the desperate can no longer inflame feelings against the death penalty. Post-abolition miscarriages of justice, not least the release of the Guildford Four in 1989 and the Birmingham Six in 1991, underlined the ongoing fallibility of criminal convictions for the worst crimes.[146] The final chapters in Britain's legislative death penalty were closed when in 1998 the Labour Government abolished capital punishment for treason and piracy with violence, and in 1999 when it ratified the abolitionist protocols of the European Court of Human Rights and the International Covenant on Civil and Political Rights.[147]

Archival collections

The National Archives, Home Office (HO)

Newspapers and Magazines

Daily Mirror
Manchester Guardian

---

144 Rowbotham, 'Execution', p. 187.
145 For example, *The Sun* newspaper carried out a poll of its readers in 2008, finding 99 per cent approval for reintroducing capital punishment, J. Clench and A. West, 'Death Penalty: Your Verdict', *The Sun*, 25 February 2008: www.thesun.co.uk/sol/homepage/news/justice/841077/Death-penalty-Your-verdict-99-of-Sun-readers-from-our-poll-vote-in-favour-of-reintroducing-capital-punishment.html. In 2011, it ran a feature on whether capital punishment should be brought back, which related to online petitions that aimed to get the issue considered for a Commons debate, 'Should Britain Bring Back the Death Penalty?', *The Sun*, 5 August 2011: www.thesun.co.uk/sol/homepage/news/3734341/Should-Britain-bring-back-the-death-penalty.html. Both stories reported the views of relatives of murder victims in order to present the for and against sides of the argument. Channel Four screened a documentary style drama in 2009, which envisioned a near future in which the death penalty had been reintroduced, not only for murder but also for sex offences against children, R. Coldstream, *The Execution of Gary Glitter* [Television Movie], Juniper Communications, UK, 2009.
146 R. Hood and C. Hoyle, *The Death Penalty: A Worldwide Perspective*, Oxford: Oxford University Press, 2008, p. 147.
147 Ibid.

Picture Post
The Sun
The Times

Bibliography

Bailey, V., 'The Shadow of the Gallows: The Death Penalty; British Labour Government, 1945–51', *Law and History Review*, 2000, 18(2): 305–50.

Ballinger, A., *Dead Woman Walking: Executed Women in England and Wales, 1900–55*, Aldershot: Ashgate, 2000.

——'"Clear Eyed Description and Objective Analysis": A Peculiar History of the Death Penalty', A Symposium of Reviews of *Peculiar Institution*, *British Journal of Criminology*, 2012, 52(1): 202–6.

Bandes, S. A., 'Empathy, Narrative and Victim Impact Statements', *University of Chicago Law Review*, 1996, 63(2): 361–412.

——'Fear Factor: The Role of Media in Covering and Shaping the Death Penalty', *Ohio State Journal of Criminal Law*, 2003, 1(2): 585–98.

——'The Heart has its Reasons: Examining the Strange Persistence of the American Death Penalty', *Law, Politics and Society*, 2008, 42: 21–52.

——'Repellent Crimes and Rational Deliberation: Emotion and the Death Penalty', *Vermont Law Review*, 2009, 33(3): 489–518.

Block, B. P. and Hostettler, J., *Hanging in the Balance: A History of the Abolition of Capital Punishment in Britain*, Winchester: Waterside Press, 1997.

Blom-Cooper, L., *The A6 Murder: Regina vs James Hanratty, the Semblance of Truth*, Harmondsworth: Penguin, 1963.

Boulanger, C. and Sarat, A., 'Putting Culture into the Picture', A. Sarat and C. Boulanger (eds), *The Cultural Lives of Capital Punishment*, Stanford, CA: Stanford University Press, 2005, 1–47.

Brown, M., *The Culture of Punishment: Prison, Society and Spectacle*, New York: New York University Press, 2009.

Chibnall, S., 'The Anti Heroines of Holloway', P. Mason (ed.), *Captured by the Media: Prison Discourse in Popular Culture*, Willan: Cullompton, 2006, 172–90.

Christoph, J. B., *Capital Punishment and British Politics*, London: George Allen & Unwin, 1962.

Coldstream, R., *The Execution of Gary Glitter* [Television Movie], Juniper Communications, UK, 2009.

Corns, C. and Hughes-Wilson, J., *Blindfold and Alone: British Military Executions in the Great War*, London: Cassell, 2001.

Cottrol, R. J., 'Finality with Ambivalence: The American Death Penalty's Uneasy History', *Stanford Law Review*, 2004, 56(6): 1641–73.

Duff, P., *Left, Left, Left*, London: Allison and Busby, 1971.

Dyhouse, C., *Girl Trouble: Panic and Progress in the History of Young Women*, London: Zed Books, 2013.

Edwards, J., 'The Homicide Act, 1957: A Critique', *British Journal of Delinquency*, 1957, 8: 49–61.

Evans, R., *Rituals of Retribution*, Oxford: Oxford University Press, 1995.

Fleury-Steiner, B., 'Death in "Whiteface"', C. J. Ogletree Jr. and A. Sarat (eds), *From Lynch Mobs to the Killing State*, New York: New York University Press, 2006, 150–81.

Furman v Georgia 408 US 238 (1972).

Gallagher, C. and Laqueur, T. (eds), *The Making of the Modern Body: Sexuality and Society in the Nineteenth Century*, London: University of California Press, 1987.

Galliher, J. M. and Galliher, J. F., '"Déjà vu All Over Again": The Recurring Life and Death of Capital Punishment Legislation in Kansas', *Social Problems*, 1997, 44(3): 369–85.

Garland, D., *Peculiar Institution: America's Death Penalty in an Age of Abolition*, Oxford: Oxford University Press, 2010.

——'The Problem of the Body in Modern Punishment', *Social Research*, 2011, 78(3): 767–98.

Garrity, J., *Step-Daughters of England: British Women Modernists and the National Imaginary*, Manchester: Manchester University Press, 2003.

Garvey, S. P., 'The Emotional Economy of Capital Sentencing', *New York University Law Review*, 2000, 75(1): 26–73.

Gatrell, V. A. C., *The Hanging Tree: Execution and the English People, 1770–1868*, Oxford: Oxford University Press, 1996.

Geraghty, C., *British Cinema in the Fifties: Gender, Genre and the 'New Look'*, London: Routledge, 2000.

Giles, J., 'Narratives of Gender, Class and Modernity in Women's Memories of Mid Twentieth-Century Britain', *Signs*, 2002, 28(1): 21–41.

Grant, C., *Crime and Punishment in Contemporary Culture*, Abingdon: Routledge, 2004.

Greene, G., *It's a Battlefield*, London: Heinemann, 1934.

Gregg v Georgia 428 US 153 (1976).

Gregory, J., *Victorians Against the Gallows*, London: I.B. Tauris, 2012.

Grey, D. J. R., 'Women's Policy Networks and the Infanticide Act 1922', *Twentieth Century British History*, 2010, 21(4): 441–63.

Haines, H., 'Flawed Executions, The Anti-Death Penalty Movement, and the Politics of Capital Punishment', *Social Problems*, 1992, 39(2): 125–38.

Halttunen, K., 'Humanitarianism and the Pornography of Pain in Anglo-American Culture', *American History Review*, 1995, 100(2): 303–34.

Hammel, A., 'Civilized Rebels', A. Sarat and J. Martschukat (eds), *Is the Death Penalty Dying? European and American Perspectives*, Cambridge: Cambridge University Press, 2011, 173–203.

Hart, H. L. A., 'Murder and the Principles of Punishment: England and the United States', *Northwestern University Law Review*, 1957, 52(4): 433–61.

Hay, D., 'Hanging and the English Judges: The Judicial Politics of Retention and Abolition', D. Garland, R. McGowen and M. Meranze (eds), *America's Death Penalty Between Past and Present*, New York: New York University Press, 2011, 129–65.

Hood, R. and Hoyle, C., *The Death Penalty: A Worldwide Perspective*, Oxford: Oxford University Press, 2008.

Jarvis, B., *Cruel and Unusual: Punishment and U.S. Culture*, London: Pluto Press, 2004.

Jesse, F. T., *A Pin to See the Peepshow*, London: Heinemann, 1934.

Karstedt, S., 'Emotions and Criminal Justice', *Theoretical Criminology*, 2002, 6(3): 299–317.

Karstedt, S., Loader, I. and Strang, H. (eds), *Emotions, Crime and Justice*, Oxford: Hart Publishing, 2011.

Kaufman-Osborn, T. V., *From Noose to Needle*, Ann Arbor: University of Michigan Press, 2002.

——'The Death of Dignity' A. Sarat and J. Martschukat (eds), *Is the Death Penalty Dying? European and American Perspectives*, Cambridge: Cambridge University Press, 2011, 204–35.

Kennedy, R., 'The Media and the Death Penalty: The Limits of Sentimentality, the Power of Abjection', *Humanities Research*, 2007, 14(2): 29–48.

Klein, K. G., *The Woman Detective: Gender and Genre*, Urbana: University of Illinois Press, 2nd edition, 1995.

Koestler, K. and Rolph, C. H., *Hanged by the Neck*, London: Penguin, 1961.

Kramar, K. J., and Watson, W. D., 'The Insanities of Reproduction: Medico-Legal Knowledge and the Development of Infanticide Law', *Social and Legal Studies*, 2006, 15(2): 237–55.

Loader, I. and Mulcahy, A., *Policing and the Condition of England: Memory, Politics and Culture*, Oxford: Oxford University Press, 2003.

Logan, A., *Feminism and Criminal Justice*, Basingstoke: Palgrave MacMillan, 2008.

Maamri, M. R., 'Cosmic Chaos in *The Secret Agent* and Graham Greene's *It's a Battlefield*', *Conradiana*, 2008, 40(2): 179–91.

Madow, M., 'Forbidden Spectacle: Executions, the Public and the Press in Nineteenth-Century New York', *Buffalo Law Review*, 1995, 43(2): 461–562.

Marsh, N., 'Portrait of Troy', *Death in Ecstasy-Vintage Murder-Artists in Crime Omnibus*, London: Harper, 2009.

Martschukat, J., 'Nineteenth-Century Executions as Performances of Law, Death and Civilization', A. Sarat and C. Boulanger (eds), *The Cultural Lives of Capital Punishment*, Stanford, CA: Stanford University Press, 2005, 49–68.

McGowen, R., 'The Body and Punishment in Eighteenth Century England', *The Journal of Modern History*, 1987, 59(4): 651–79.

——'Civilizing Punishment: The End of the Public Execution in England', *Journal of British Studies*, 1994, 33(3): 257–82.

——'History, Culture and the Death Penalty: The British Debates', *Historical Reflections*, 2003, 29(2): 229–50.

——'Introduction', D. Garland, R. McGowen and M. Meranze (eds), *America's Death Penalty Between Past and Present*, New York: New York University Press, 2011, 1–29.

McHugh, J., 'The Labour Party and the Parliamentary Campaign to Abolish the Military Death Penalty 1919–30', *The Historical Journal*, 1999, 42(1): 233–49.

Minkes, J. and Vanstone, M., 'Gender, Race and the Death Penalty: Lessons from Three 1950s Murder Trials', *Howard Journal*, 2006, 45(4): 403–20.

Morris, T., *Crime and Criminal Justice since 1945*, Oxford: Wiley-Blackwell, 1989.

Nussbaum, M. C., *Hiding from Humanity: Disgust, Shame and the Law*, Princeton, NJ: Princeton University Press, 2006.

Potter, H., *Hanging in Judgment: Religion and the Death Penalty in England*, London: SCM Press Ltd, 1993.

Prevezer, S., 'The English Homicide Act: A New Attempt to Revise the Law of Murder', *Columbia Law Review*, 1957, 57(5): 624–42.

Radzinowicz, L., *Adventures in Criminology*, London: Routledge, 1999.

——and Hood, R., *A History of English Criminal Law and its Administration Vol. 5: The Emergence of Penal Policy*, London: Stevens and Sons, 1986.

Reicher, D., 'Bureaucracy, "Domesticated" Elites, and the Abolition of Capital Punishment. Processes of State Formation and the Number of Executions in England

and Habsburg Austria between 1700 and 1914', *Crime, Law and Social Change*, 2010, 54(3/4): 279–97.

Report from the Select Committee on Capital Punishment, London: HMSO, 1930.

Report of the Royal Commission on Capital Punishment, 1949–1953, Cmd. 8932, London: HMSO, 1953.

Robb, G., 'Circe in Crinoline: Domestic Poisonings in Victorian England', *Journal of Family History*, 1997, 22(2): 176–90.

Rose, G., *The Struggle for Penal Reform*, London: Stevens and Sons, 1961.

Rose, S. O., *Which People's War? National Identity and Citizenship in Britain 1939–1945*, Oxford: Oxford University Press, 2003.

Rowbotham, J., 'Execution as Punishment in England: 1750–2000', A Kilday and D Nash (eds), *Histories of Crime: Britain 1600–2000*, Basingstoke: Palgrave Macmillan, 2010, 180–202.

Rowland, S., 'House not Ho(l)mes', L. Hockley and L. Gardner (eds), *House: The Wounded Healer on Television*, Hove: Routledge, 2011, 133–51.

Sarat, A., 'Capital Punishment as Legal, Political, and Cultural Fact: An Introduction', A. Sarat (ed.), *The Killing State: Capital Punishment in Law, Politics and Culture*, Oxford: Oxford University Press, 1999, 3–25.

Sarat, A. and Martschukat, J., 'Introduction: Transatlantic Perspectives on Capital Punishment', A. Sarat and J. Martschukat (eds), *Is the Death Penalty Dying?* Cambridge: Cambridge University Press, 2011, 1–15.

Seal, L., 'Public Reactions to the Case of Mary Wilson, the Last Woman to be Sentenced to Death in England and Wales', *Papers from the British Criminology Conference*, 2008, 8: 65–84.

——'Ruth Ellis and Public Contestation of the Death Penalty', *The Howard Journal*, 2011, 50(5): 492–504.

Sherman, L. W., 'Reason for Emotion: Reinventing Justice with Theories, Innovations and Research', *Criminology*, 2003, 41(1): 1–38.

Simon, J., 'Capital Punishment as Homeowner's Insurance', A. Sarat and J. Martschukat (eds), *Is the Death Penalty Dying?* Cambridge: Cambridge University Press, 2011, 78–107.

Simpson, A. W. B., 'Shooting Felons: Law, Practice, Official Culture, and Perceptions of Morality', *Journal of Law and Society*, 2005, 32(2): 241–66.

Smith, M., Sparks, R. and Girling, E., 'Educating Sensibilities: The Image of the "Lesson" in Children's Talk about Punishment', *Punishment & Society*, 2000, 2(4): 395–415.

Smith, P., 'Executing Executions: Aesthetics, Identity and the Problematic Narratives of Capital Punishment Ritual', *Theory and Society*, 1996, 25(2): 235–61.

——*Punishment and Culture*, Chicago, IL: University of Chicago Press, 2008.

Spierenburg, P., *The Spectacle of Suffering*, Cambridge: Cambridge University Press, 1984.

——'The Green, Green Grass of Home', A. Sarat and J. Martschukat (eds), *Is the Death Penalty Dying?* Cambridge: Cambridge University Press, 2011, 17–46.

Steiner, B. D., Bowers, W. J. and Sarat, A., 'Folk Knowledge as Legal Action: Death Penalty Judgments and the Tenet of Early Release in a Culture of Mistrust and Punitiveness', *Law & Society Review*, 1999, 33(2): 461–505.

Strange, C., 'The Undercurrents of Penal Culture: Punishment of the Body in Mid Twentieth-Century Canada', *Law & Society Review*, 2001, 19(2): 343–85.

——'Masculinities, Intimate Femicide and the Death Penalty in Australia, 1890–1920', *British Journal of Criminology*, 2003, 43(2): 310–39.

Tuttle, E. O., *The Crusade Against Capital Punishment in Britain*, London: Stevens and Sons, 1961.

Twitchell, N., *The Politics of the Rope*, Bury St. Edmunds: Athena, 2012.

Ward, T., 'The Sad Subject of Infanticide: Law, Medicine and Child Murder, 1860–1938', *Social and Legal Studies*, 1999, 8(2): 163–80.

Whitman, J. Q., 'Response to Garland', *Punishment & Society*, 2005, 7(4): 389–96.

Wiener, M. J., *Reconstructing the Criminal: Culture, Law, and Policy in England, 1830–1914*, Cambridge: Cambridge University Press, 1990.

——'Alice Arden to Bill Sikes: Changing Nightmares of Intimate Violence in England, 1559–1869', *Journal of British Studies*, 2001, 40(2): 184–212.

——*Men of Blood: Violence, Manliness and Criminal Justice in Victorian England*, Cambridge: Cambridge University Press, 2004.

——'Convicted Murderers and the Victorian Press: Condemnation vs. Sympathy', *Crimes and Misdemeanours*, 2007, 1/2: 110–25.

Willards, E. S., *My Mother was Hanged*, London: Heinemann, 1958.

Wood, J. C., *Violence and Crime in Nineteenth-Century England: The Shadow of Our Refinement*, London: Routledge, 2004.

Zimring, F. E., 'Ambivalence in State Capital Punishment Policy: An Empirical Sounding', *New York Review of Law and Social Change*, 1990–91, 18(3): 729–42.

——'The Wages of Ambivalence: On the Context and Prospects of New York's Death Penalty', *Buffalo Law Review*, 1996, 44(2): 303–24.

——*The Contradictions of American Capital Punishment*, Oxford: Oxford University Press, 2003.

Zimring, F. E. and Hawkins, G., *Capital Punishment and the American Agenda*, Cambridge: Cambridge University Press, 1986.

2 Audience, publicity and emotion

The pedagogical role of capital punishment means that it is carried out for an audience, which is the 'key element in the perception, organisation and delivery of the death penalty'.[1] The audience is an essential aspect for capital punishment to exist as a public institution.[2] After the privatisation of execution in the mid-nineteenth century, the audience was no longer physically present but this did not mean it had disappeared. Rather, it had transformed. Around the same time that execution was privatised in Britain and many other jurisdictions, the penny press was developing, offering an increasingly literate population an entertaining means of reading about crime and punishment, as well as the assurance that the punishment had been carried out.[3] As newspapers and newspaper reading expanded, a potentially much larger and wider population could learn about particular executions than could have attended them in person.[4] Sarat *et al.* rightly argue in relation to America that 'in an era when executions were moved behind prison walls, newspapers played a critical mediating role between the execution and the … public'.[5] The press now enjoyed a monopoly on eyewitness accounts, either as related by their own journalists or as told to journalists.[6]

1 A. Linders, 'The Execution Spectacle and State Legitimacy: The Changing Nature of the American Execution Audience, 1833–1937', *Law and Society Review*, 2002, 36(3): 607–56, p. 645.
2 Ibid.
3 On England, see J. Rowbotham and K. Stevenson, 'Introduction', J. Rowbotham and K. Stevenson (eds), *Criminal Conversations: Victorian Crimes, Social Panic and Moral Outrage*, Columbus: Ohio State University Press, 2005, p. xxiv and J. Tulloch, 'The Privatising of Pain: Lincoln Newspapers, "Mediated Publicness" and the End of Public Execution', *Journalism Studies*, 2006, 7(3): 437–51. On the United States and Germany, see L. Masur, *Rites of Execution: Capital Punishment and the Transformation of American Culture, 1776–1865*, Oxford: Oxford University Press, 1991, pp. 114–16 and R. Evans, *Rituals of Retribution: Capital Punishment in Germany, 1600–1987*, Oxford: Oxford University Press, 1995, p. 403.
4 L. Friedman, *Crime and Punishment in American History*, New York: Basic Books, 1993, p. 170.
5 A. Sarat *et al.* 'Gruesome Spectacles: The Cultural Reception of Botched Executions in America, 1890–1920', *British Journal of American and Legal Studies*, 2012, 1(1): 1–30, p. 1.
6 M. Madow, 'Forbidden Spectacle: Executions, the Public and the Press in Nineteenth-Century New York', *Buffalo Law Review*, 1995, 43(2): 461–562, p. 555.

The growth of affordable, accessible print media both signalled and helped to create a new kind of mass public that was able to participate in a shared popular culture.[7] The burgeoning popular cultures of the nineteenth and early twentieth centuries had an 'accelerating interest in lurid stories of crime and bloodshed',[8] which acted as the 'brazen counterpoint' to the creation of an 'orderly and civil society'.[9] The emergence of a mass public, served by a print-based popular culture, was an important aspect of modernity, 'in which publicness no longer depends on sharing a particular location, was cut off from face-to-face interaction and involved the transformation of the link between publicness and sense perception'.[10] The sensationalist nature of popular culture's approach to representing crime and punishment was frequently regarded as at best suspect and at worst damaging and debasing from the perspective of 'high' and 'official' culture.[11] Popular culture's portrayals of crime and punishment were perceived by its detractors to be in 'bad taste'.[12] This suspicion and disdain related to ongoing class-based assumptions about the harmfulness of popular culture, which was understood to be consumed by working-class and uneducated people.[13] It was also tied to gendered understandings of the sensationalist elements of popular culture as being harmful to women in particular – and women's participation in sensationalism was seen as indicative of cultural decline.[14] Therefore, the transformed continuation of the spectacle and spectatorship of execution developed with modernity but, seen from the perspective of high and official culture, was opposed to civilisation.[15]

This chapter is the first of two which explore the ways in which twentieth-century British people were able to experience and imagine execution in an era when public hanging had receded firmly into the past. It discusses newspaper reports of capital punishment as these were the primary means through which people would have learned of executions. For the earlier part of the century, concentration is mainly on provincial newspapers, shifting to the popular national press for the mid-twentieth century. Coverage of execution in 'quality' papers is also discussed. Tulloch notes that execution became rarer in the Victorian era but more central to the cultural imagination because of its mass

---

7 Evans, *Rituals*, p. 413.
8 M. Trotti, *The Body in the Reservoir: Murder and Sensationalism in the South*, Chapel Hill: University of North Carolina Press, 2008, p. 6.
9 Ibid., p. 8.
10 Tulloch, 'The Privatising', p. 440.
11 See H. Gans, *Popular Culture and High Culture: An Analysis and Evaluation of Taste*, New York: Basic Books, 1999, 2nd edition, p. 29. Gans' study was in relation to the United States, but his insights into the relationship between class, culture and 'taste' have wider relevance.
12 For Bourdieu, taste is a marker of class: P. Bourdieu, *Distinction: A Social Critique of Judgment and Taste*, London: Routledge and Kegan Paul, 1984, p. 2.
13 Gans, *Popular Culture*, p. 29.
14 For a brief overview of this paternalistic, gendered view of popular culture, see J. Fiske, *Understanding Popular Culture*, Abingdon: Routledge, 1989, pp. 58–68.
15 Gans highlights the reduction of civilisation as one of the main critiques levelled at popular culture, *Popular Culture*, p. 29.

audience, mediated via the press.[16] Execution continued to be rare in the twentieth century and was increasingly so by the middle of the century. However, as abolition loomed capital punishment's cultural potency strengthened. In relation to the death penalty, the mediated public sphere became an increasingly emotional one, in which the tragic impact of hanging on the relatives of the condemned was brought to the fore.

Newspapers and the execution scene

Nineteenth-century news weeklies such as the *News of the World* and *Lloyd's Weekly News* 'played a major role in propelling the newspaper to the heart of British popular culture'[17] and local evening newspapers of the era increased the readership of daily news.[18] Beginning with the launch of the *Daily Mail* in 1896, the early twentieth century saw the development of a new, popular national daily press that by the mid-twentieth century also included the *Daily Mirror, Daily Herald, Daily Express* and *News Chronicle*.[19] Bingham argues that the national dailies in particular came to symbolise mass society, bringing news values that 'elevated the popular and commercial'.[20] This meant giving space to human interest and features articles of the kind that would engage female, as well as male, readers.[21] After the First World War, newspaper reading expanded rapidly. By the mid-twentieth century, the majority of British adults read a national daily newspaper and over 90 per cent read a Sunday.[22] The British were enthusiastic consumers of newspapers, reading double the amount in comparison with Americans and treble that of the French.[23] The centrality of newspapers to everyday life in twentieth-century Britain highlights their importance as a means of communicating stories of capital punishment and the necessity of paying attention to them in order to understand the death penalty's contested place within the culture. Bingham states that '[p]opular curiosity and elite disgust have been long entwined in the history of newspapers'[24] and the same can be said of the gallows.

The Capital Punishment Amendment Act 1868, which privatised executions, restricted attendance to the sheriff, executioners, prison chaplain, prison doctor and other prison personnel as required, plus the option for the sheriff

16 Tulloch, 'The Privatising', p. 440.
17 A. Bingham, 'Reading Newspapers: Cultural Histories of the Popular Press in Modern Britain', *History Compass*, 2012, 10(2): 140–50, p. 141.
18 A. Bingham, *Gender, Modernity, and the Popular Press in Inter-War Britain*, Oxford: Clarendon Press, 2004, p. 25.
19 Ibid., pp. 12–22.
20 Ibid., p. 10.
21 Ibid., p. 35. This imperative also meant that popular news was viewed, from the position of high culture, as lowbrow.
22 A. Bingham, *Family Newspapers? Sex, Private Life, and the British Popular Press, 1918–1978*, Oxford: Oxford University Press, 2009, pp. 16–18.
23 Bingham, 'Reading Newspapers', p. 141.
24 Ibid.

to admit other people as he saw fit, such as relatives of the condemned. This last proviso meant that journalists could be permitted to attend and report on hangings. The last journalist to be admitted to an execution was in 1934, although it had become rare by the early twentieth century. Explicit press reports 'endanger[ed] the very purpose of private executions' and,[25] in line with the imperatives of civilisation and modernity in execution practice discussed in Chapter One, sheriffs and then prison governors were increasingly disinclined to allow reporters in. Despite this, journalists could sometimes glean the important details from other eye witnesses, such as whether the prisoner had confessed at the last moment or whether their legs twitched after the drop. This level of publicity for the execution scene itself did not persist beyond the early twentieth century. Home Office rules prevented the prison governor from stating anything about the execution, beyond the fact it had happened 'expeditiously and without a hitch' and governors were not to discuss whether a confession had been made.[26] The Memorandum of Conditions for the executioner was modified in 1952 specifically to prohibit revealing 'to any person, whether for publication or not, any information about his work as an Executioner'.[27]

Blood and gore

By 1900, the more sanguinary details of the British execution process did not necessarily reach the public.[28] This accords with the analysis of modern attempts to remove the body from capital punishment, which are interpreted as in keeping with the removal of bodily functions from public space more generally. In particular, the body in pain became increasingly intolerable and profane.[29] However, whilst the body of the condemned was a problem for official culture, which needed to erase elements of cruelty from the death penalty, it remained a source of fascination in popular culture. This is part of the ambivalence of modern punishment.[30] As Lynch argues, it is important to take account of 'subcultural

---

25 H. Potter, *Hanging in Judgment: Religion and the Death Penalty in England*, London: SCM Press, 1993, p. 104.

26 In 1936, a Home Office memorandum modified this to state that hitches or 'unusual events' must 'of course be stated, and a full explanation given'. This later became contentious when first in the *Picture Post*, and then in *The Observer*, Arthur Koestler reported the earlier version as an illustration of the secrecy surrounding the death penalty. See report dated 31 December 1955 in TNA/PCOM9/1776. This is discussed further in Chapter Six.

27 PCOM9/2025.

28 Mid-nineteenth-century execution stories emphasised the shocking and sensational, V. A. C. Gatrell, *The Hanging Tree: Execution and the English People, 1770–1868*, Oxford: Oxford University Press, 1994, p. 599. Tulloch examines the reporting of Priscilla Biggadike's execution in 1868 in the *Lincoln Gazette*, which described her hanging as 'horribly revolting' and Priscilla as a 'poor half dead woman', 'The Privatising', p. 448.

29 D. Garland, 'The Problem of the Body in Modern Punishment', *Social Research*, 2011, 78(3): 767–98.

30 M. Lynch, 'On-Line Executions: The Symbolic Use of the Electric Chair in Cyberspace', *POLAR*, 1999, 23(2): 1–20.

norms, populist sensibilities and social artifacts, which all may play a powerful role in shaping or influencing state punishment'.[31] In the context of the modern American death penalty, she identifies an ongoing public attraction to death machinery and the suffering body of the condemned.

Early twentieth-century British newspapers sought to sate what they clearly understood to be readers' fascination with the body as it was put to death by reporting on executions in other countries. These were either places where execution still took place in public, such as France, or where the gory details of botched executions became publicly known, such as the United States. Therefore, the bodies of the condemned did not disappear from the pages of the newspaper, even if they were not British bodies.

Various mistakes and mishaps could make a foreign execution scene newsworthy. One was slow, suffering death due to the incompetence of the executioner. The *Gloucester Citizen* reported how the unfortunate Johan Woboril of Vienna, 'began to show signs of life' after being hanged. The executioner's assistant 'held him fast by the legs, and a dreadful struggle continued'.[32] Bungled executions could produce scenes of horror – and gore. The guillotining of an Algerian convict in a public square in Paris in 1906 ended badly due to the executioner being 'so clumsy and nervous that the knife of the guillotine fell before the condemned man's head was in posi-tion, the result being that the top of the skull was severed, leaving the brain exposed. Life was apparently not extinct, for the limbs moved convulsively'.[33]

Sometimes this bungling could produce almost comedic details. At a public execution in France in 1901, 'one of the executioners slipped and fell in a pool of the man's blood'.[34] In a 'distressing triple execution scene' in Australia in 1906, '[a] warder fell into the pit as the bolt was pulled'.[35]

Stories also emphasised the inevitable pain of botched execution. The hanging of Mary Rogers in Arizona in 1905 was 'a wretched bungle', meaning she 'must have endured intense agony' whilst being 'slowly strangled to death'.[36] A 'Negro' executed in the United States had to be hanged for a total of 13 minutes before he died, causing a 'painful scene'.[37] A hanging in Russia in 1908 went awry when 'the condemned man fell to the ground shrieking. The hangman silenced the man by pressing his foot on his neck'.[38] Blood, agony, shrieking and convulsions were core elements of heightening the entertain-ment value of a death penalty story.[39] Working-class and lower middle-class

31 Ibid., pp. 4–5.
32 'Scenes at an Execution: A Dreadful Struggle', *Gloucester Citizen*, 12 August 1902.
33 'Execution Horror', *Manchester Courier and Lancashire General Advertiser*, 23 January 1906.
34 'Public Execution in France', *Sheffield Evening Telegraph*, 12 November 1901.
35 Untitled, *The South Eastern Gazette*, 23 January 1906.
36 'Ghastly Execution Scene', *Manchester Courier and Lancashire General Advertiser*, 16 December 2005.
37 'A Bungled Execution: Painful Scene at the Hanging of a Negro', *Western Times*, 26 December 1905.
38 'Horrible Scene at an Execution', *Cornishman*, 17 December 1908.
39 See Chapter Three for a further discussion of execution as entertainment.

readerships in the early twentieth century did not yet live lives from which the blood, pain and bodily functions of others had been removed from everyday experience.[40] However, fascination with the gory details of execution was not restricted to the provincial press. The botched hanging of Mary Rogers was also reported in the *Manchester Guardian*.[41]

The reporting of foreign executions in *The Times* focused on the behaviour of the crowd at public executions. At an execution near Lille in 1909 the crowd was 'violent and almost hysterical'. This was, however, understandable as the local population were 'simple folk of primitive passions' and were relieved at the putting to death of 'murderous brigands'.[42] The newspaper only tended to provide details of execution itself under the guise of foreign political affairs, which enabled seemingly legitimate, non-sensationalist discussion of the moment of death. The Spanish anarchist, Francisco Ferrer, 'was shot standing erect with a bandage over his eyes'.[43] Press were admitted to the 'grim spectacle' of the execution of four traitors in France in 1920, one of whom was female. *The Times* reported that '[t]he woman was shot with her hands still clasped in prayer. One of the unhappy wretches still lived after the firing party had done its work, and had to be finished off with two revolver shots'.[44]

The greater efficiency in British execution practice established by the changes recommended by the Aberdare Committee, and the increased secrecy of the execution scene as journalists were excluded, made it harder for the twentieth-century press to report on the body in pain. However, the audience was invited to imagine the suffering body of the condemned via consumption of stories of foreign executions. These were one imaginary step removed, as the condemned were not members of the national community of sentiment. Nevertheless, the pain of slow strangulation, the horror of the guillotine and the nerves of the executioner were a reminder of the violence of the execution scene and of the body at its centre. These accounts in the popular press were also clearly intended to be sources of novelty and pleasurable entertainment for readers, open to elite criticism as serving the same 'primitive passions' as public execution. The presence of the body of the condemned in the 'quality' press demonstrated that high culture had not completely eschewed the sanguinary, but that due to the requirements of 'good taste', greater justification was often needed for its reporting, such as the context of a political situation.

The death of the condemned

Although detailed accounts of blood and gore were not possible in relation to twentieth-century British executions, the provincial press reported the final

---

40 See, for example, E. Roberts, *A Woman's Place: An Oral History of Working Class Women, 1890–1940*, Oxford: Blackwell, 1984.
41 'A Ghastly Execution', *Manchester Guardian*, 10 December 1905.
42 'Capital Punishment in France', *The Times*, 13 June 1909.
43 'Execution of Senor Ferrer', *The Times*, 14 October 1909.
44 'Execution of Traitors', *The Times*, 17 May 1920.

hours and moments of the condemned as far as possible. These stories blended different genres to incorporate attention to the banal details of waiting in the condemned cell, whether or not the prisoner took religious guidance, whether they made a last minute confession and, where possible, what happened to their body after it dropped. As such, stories were formulaic and retained the conventions of Victorian accounts.[45] The *Tamworth Herald*'s account of the last morning and hanging of Samuel Dougal in 1903 in Chelmsford was fairly typical of the mixing of the quotidian and transcendental that such reports contained:

> He succeeded in dressing without assistance, attiring himself in the blue serge suit he wore during his trial. His breakfast, consisting of bread and butter, tea, and one egg, was then brought in, and the doomed man ate with apparent relish.

After breakfast, '[p]rayers followed, the wretched man joining in with intense fervour'. Dougal's 'last scene was intensely dramatic' as he confessed to the murder 'acknowledging the justice of his sentence'. He did not disgrace himself, showing '[n]ot the slightest sign of nervousness' and held fast to his emotions, leading the journalist to comment 'the self control of this remarkable man was extraordinary'. Press were admitted to the execution so it was possible to report that after the drop '[a] shudder went round the crowded shed: all that could be seen was the quivering rope'. Finally, the story further underlined the point that justice had been done, explaining that 'the cruel fate of Miss Holland [the victim] was expiated'.[46]

This report emphasised Dougal's guilt and the rightness of his sentence, and as such strongly endorsed capital punishment. However, it also granted the condemned a measure of heroism, describing him as not only self-controlled, but also 'remarkable'. Dougal's courage on the scaffold meant that there was a sense of admiration for him in the story of his final moments. Of course, it is impossible to know how accurately journalists conveyed the reactions of the condemned to their predicament, but they were not all portrayed as heroic. Herbert Bennett, executed at Norwich prison in 1901 for murdering his wife, had 'lost altogether the admirable command of himself' shown during his trial and 'gave way to paroxysms of rage' in the condemned cell. He was not stoical at the end, rather 'before he reached the scaffold he seemed almost in a collapse'.[47] These judgments of bravery

---

45 In his analysis of the reporting of executions in Lincoln newspapers, Tulloch outlines the traditional scenes included in news stories as the last meal, the last visit, the condemned sermon, the procession to the scaffold and the drop, 'The Privatising', p. 438. Dyndor's study of capital punishment in the *Northampton Mercury* also emphasises the formulaic nature of press reporting, Z. Dyndor, 'Death Recorded: Capital Punishment and the Press in Northampton, 1780–1834', *Midland History*, 2008, 33(2): 179–95, p. 184.

46 'Execution of Dougal', *Tamworth Herald*, 18 July 1903.

47 'Execution of Bennett', *Yorkshire Evening Post*, 21 March 1901.

(or lack of it)[48] can be understood in the context of early twentieth-century norms of masculinity, which stressed self-control and courage as manly virtues.[49] However, women's bravery in the face of impending hanging was also noted approvingly. Baby farmers Ann Walters and Amelia Sach, executed at Holloway in 1903, 'displayed remarkable fortitude to the last'.[50]

By the 1920s, it was the convention for journalists to be excluded from the execution itself, meaning that descriptions of the body of the condemned disappeared from reports on British hangings. Whether there had been 'convulsive moments' after the drop,[51] or a 'momentary tremor of the muscles of the arms and legs' could no longer be recorded.[52] In 1921, the *Manchester Guardian* explained disapprovingly that journalists were to be admitted to an execution for 'the first time in a good many years'. The editorial pointed out that public executions were abolished 'because they merely pandered to a morbid and brutal curiosity' and that reports from the execution itself 'only ministered to an indecent curiosity in a less degree'.[53] From this high culture perspective, sensation was disavowed as savagery and further privatisation of the execution scene was to be welcomed.

Modernity, civilisation and change

Changing execution practices were sometimes a theme in execution stories. In the provincial press, emphasis was placed on shifts towards modernity, underlined via comparison with the past. A story from the *Coventry Evening Telegraph* on an execution in Warwick in 1902 pointed out that '[s]ome remember public execution in Warwick' when spectators would pay to secure a spot in a window with a good view. The execution which had taken place that morning was 'more in accordance with our civilisation and humanitarianism'. Officials endeavoured 'to keep the execution as private as possible' (press had not been admitted) and although the crowd outside the gaol waited expectantly for the black flag, it was in vain because this practice had been discontinued.[54] The hanging of Thomas Allaway at Winchester Prison in 1922 was cause for the

48 Such judgments were part of the well-established formula of reporting hangings, see Tulloch, 'The Privatising', p. 439.
49 There were, of course, multiple masculinities in the late nineteenth and early twentieth centuries, with domesticity also featuring as an aspect of manliness. However, 'heroic' masculinity was an important construction. See M. Francis, 'The Domestication of the Male? Recent Research on Nineteenth and Twentieth Century Masculinity', *The Historical Journal*, 2002, 45(3): 637–52 and S. Heathorn, 'How Stiff Were Their Upper Lips? Research on Late Victorian and Edwardian Masculinity', *History Compass*, 2004, 2(1): 1–7.
50 'Execution of Two Women', *Shields Daily Gazette*, 3 February 1903. For a gendered analysis of this case, see A. Ballinger, *Dead Woman Walking*, Aldershot: Ashgate, 2000, pp. 81–89.
51 'Execution of Bennett'.
52 'Execution at Lincoln', *Lincolnshire Chronicle*, 31 July 1903.
53 'The Press at Executions', *Manchester Guardian*, 4 February 1921.
54 'Execution at Warwick this Morning', *Coventry Evening Telegraph*, 30 December 1902.

Western Gazette to comment that the posting of the execution notice 'now takes the place of the tolling of the prison bell and the hoisting of the black flag, which in the olden days people used to travel miles to witness'.[55] These practices had only ended twenty years previously, but the article created a sense of change and modernisation via comparison with 'the olden days'. The efficiency of contemporary hanging was stressed in some articles. Norman Thorne was executed at Wandsworth Prison in 1925 and a journalist from the Press Association was admitted, who described the hanging as 'one of the most expeditious on record. From the time that Thorne emerged from his cell door until the moment he passed into eternity only ten seconds elapsed'.[56] This kind of report was in contrast with the foreign execution blood and gore stories, and instead highlighted capital punishment as something which could be consistent with civilisation and modernity.

Relatives of the condemned and the emotional public sphere

Capital punishment as something which was emotionally traumatic was also a feature of twentieth-century news stories. This intensified in the 1940s and 1950s, but also appeared in earlier reports. Emotion could be added by the arrival of relatives of the condemned at the execution scene. When William Kennedy was executed at Wandsworth Prison in 1928 for the murder of a policeman, the crowd saw his wife arrive in a taxi. As the clock struck 9am, 'she broke down and falling forward into the taxi, burst into loud sobs and cries', at which point '[p]eople crowded round the taxi to gaze at Mrs Kennedy'.[57] According to the *Daily Mail*, of those who assembled for the executions of Edith Thompson and Freddie Bywaters, 'few questioned the justice of the sentences, but there was deep sympathy with the families of both Mrs Thompson and Bywaters'. There was a 'murmur of sympathy' when Thompson's parents arrived at Holloway to attend the inquest. Thompson's father, Mr Graydon, was 'ashen and broken' and 'fought hard to control his grief, and at times gave way to deep emotion'.[58] This story introduced a note of ambivalence about the death penalty, whereby justice was acknowledged to have been done, but at a cost to innocent others, such as the parents of those executed.

Friends, relatives and lovers of the condemned were a constituent part of the story of high-profile capital cases, especially in the popular press. This coverage humanised the condemned, placing them within a web of relationships. It also enabled access to their interior lives. When Alan Grierson awaited execution for the murder of his fiancee's mother in 1935, the press focused on his romance with Maxine Gann, the daughter of the woman he

55 'Execution of Allaway', *Western Gazette*, 25 August 1922.
56 'Execution of Norman Thorne', *Exeter and Plymouth Gazette*, 23 April 1925.
57 'Execution Scenes Contrasts', *Hull Daily Mail*, 31 May 1928.
58 'Ilford Murderers Hanged', *Daily Mail*, 10 January 1923.

had killed. As a 'last resort', Maxine allowed the *Daily Mirror* to publish letters he had written her from the condemned cell.[59] These 'pitiable and ... gallant' messages to Maxine told her '[y]ou are for the hearth and not the cloister' and described her as a 'wonderful little woman' and a 'great-hearted girl child'.[60] The *Mirror* also reported how Alan's 'sweetheart' and father 'kept a hopeless vigil' for him only to find no reprieve had been granted.[61]

This focus on the emotional drama (and trauma) experienced by the condemned's loved ones grew stronger in subsequent decades.[62] Partly, this can be explained by the development of the popular press and its news values. As Bingham highlights, newspapers such as the *Daily Mirror* and *Daily Express* thrived in the 1940s and 1950s, with large readerships. The editorial mix strongly featured human interest stories, which negotiated constructions of gender, sexuality and family life,[63] and this approach figured in coverage of capital cases. Press attention to emotion can also be interpreted in relation to transformations in the British public sphere to include greater emotionalism.[64] As Langhamer argues, emotion was reconfigured in this era 'within an expanded public sphere' and capital punishment was one of the issues around which this reconfiguration took place.[65] Finally, mid-twentieth century shifts in understandings of the self were also significant, whereby the notion of an authentic interior life had deepened.[66]

Newspapers were not the only cultural form to link emotional trauma with capital punishment. Dorothy L. Sayers' 'golden age' detective, Peter Wimsey, was a man tormented both by shellshock and his role in sending the guilty to the gallows. In the final Wimsey novel, *Busman's Honeymoon*, the detective asks forgiveness from the murderer the night before he is to be executed. The next morning, Wimsey breaks down before his new wife, Harriet, who 'huddl[es] his head in her arms that he might not hear the eight o clock strike'.[67] Through Wimsey's guilt, Sayers introduced emotion into detective

59 'He Dies on Wedding Eve: Love Letters from Condemned Cell', *Daily Mirror*, 28 October 1935.
60 '"Seek Love": Last Message of Man about to Hang', *Daily Mirror*, 31 October 1935.
61 'A Lover's Vigil', *Daily Mirror*, 30 October 1935.
62 Newspapers went to lengths to secure exclusives with relatives, S. Chibnall, *Law-and-Order News*, London, Tavistock, pp. 57–8.
63 Bingham, *Gender* and *Family Newspapers?*
64 M. Francis, 'Tears, Tantrums and Bared Teeth: The Emotional Economy of Three Conservative Prime Ministers, 1951–63', *Journal of British Studies*, 2002, 41(3): 354–87. Francis identifies a shift in mid-1950s Britain away from emotional restraint and towards a 'new culture of sensation', which valued self-expression, p. 358.
65 C. Langhamer, '"The Live Dynamic Whole of Feeling and Behaviour": Capital Punishment and the Politics of Emotion, 1945–57', *Journal of British Studies*, 2012, 51(2): 416–41, p. 421.
66 See C. Steedman, 'State Sponsored Autobiography', B. Conekin, F. Mort and C. Waters (eds), *Moments of Modernity: Reconstructing Britain, 1945–1964*, London: Rivers Oram, 1999 and F. Mort, 'Social and Symbolic Fathers and Sons in Postwar Britain', *Journal of British Studies*, 1999, 38(3): 358–84.
67 D. L. Sayers, *Busman's Honeymoon*, London: Gollancz, 1937, p. 397.

fiction.[68] She also highlighted the moral ambivalence of the detective's role, in which he is implicated 'in the violence that he ostensibly opposes'.[69] Wimsey's work induces identity crisis[70] – he continues to be in a 'death-dealing profession' as he was in the War.[71] He exists in an 'ambiguous and unsettling world', left traumatised by the First World War.[72] In *Busman's Honeymoon* his guilty conscience and, therefore, his inner life, is revealed to the reader.[73] Primarily addressing themes of justice, power and social class, Graham Greene's *It's a Battlefield* provides insight into the tortured existence of Conrad Drover, whose brother, Jim, faces execution for the murder of a policeman.[74] Conrad's inner life is vividly portrayed as a 'modern man crushed under the fear of political power',[75] who is also in love with Jim's wife and carrying the burden of his brother's incipient hanging by the state.

The significance of relatives to enhancing the emotionalism of a death penalty story, and to providing access to the inner life of the condemned, can be seen from newspaper coverage of the case of Derek Bentley. Bentley was only 19 and his impending execution in early 1953 was highly controversial for two main reasons: he had not shot PC Miles, for whose murder he was convicted, and he appeared to be of low intelligence. Incredibly painful accounts of the anguish experienced by his parents, William and Lilian, and sister, Iris, and their attempts to secure a reprieve, appeared in the newspapers. The Sunday before he was executed, the *News of the World* depicted the home life of the Bentleys. This story quoted his mother as saying Derek was 'animal crazy' and informed readers that his pets included two lurchers, five cats and a tank of fish.[76] The following day, the Bentleys received a letter informing them that no reprieve was to be granted. Newspapers quoted William Bentley that '[t]his has come as a terrible blow'[77] and '[w]e shall still

---

68 K. C. Connelly, 'From Detective Fiction to Detective Literature: Psychology in the Novels of Dorothy L. Sayers and Margaret Millar', *Clues*, 2007, 25(3): 35–47, p. 38. The Wimsey novels represented the transition from logic-based detective stories to ones where the detective is a character with emotions and experiences, M. Lott, 'Dorothy L. Sayers, the Great War and Shell Shock', *Interdisciplinary Literary Studies*, 2013, 15(1): 103–26, p. 103.

69 A. Freedman, 'Dorothy Sayers and the Case of the Shell-Shocked Detective', *Partial Answers*, 2010, 8(2): 365–87, p. 375.

70 Connelly, 'From Detective', p. 38.

71 Freedman, 'Dorothy Sayers', p. 381.

72 Ibid., p. 366.

73 Connelly, 'From Detective', p. 38. Wimsey's breakdown also signals the redefinition of masculinity after the First World War – anti-rationality and tears are part of his make-up, Lott, 'Dorothy L', p. 104.

74 G. Greene, *It's a Battlefield*, London: Heinemann, 1934.

75 S. Sinha, 'Existential Motifs of Thought in Greene's Fiction', S. K. Paul and A. N. Prasad (eds), *Reassessing British Literature*, New Delhi: Sarup and Sons, 2007, p. 275.

76 'Bentley's Pets Join Family Circle as the 11th Hour Approaches', *News of the World*, 25 January 1953.

77 'Bentley is Refused Reprieve', *Evening Standard*, 26 January 1953.

fight for Derek's reprieve. My wife is terribly distressed. I had to call the doctor'.[78]

Abolitionist Labour MP, Sydney Silverman, tabled a motion for the Home Secretary to reconsider his decision, which was signed by 50 MPs and the Bentleys cabled Churchill, who was aboard the Queen Mary ocean liner.[79] They also visited Derek in Wandsworth, where he spoke to them 'with tears in his eyes'.[80] Aneuran Bevan, in a last ditch attempt, led six Labour MPs to see Home Secretary Maxwell Fyfe and to present an appeal signed by 200 MPs, but all these efforts were to no avail.[81] The *Daily Mail* described the 'moving sight' of 'hundreds of people' coming to the House of Commons to 'urge their MPs to fight for Bentley'. When William Bentley received the final, hopeless news from MP Tom Driberg he 'moved away as though stunned'. In tears, he stated, '[w]e have tried everything and failed'.[82] Derek's final farewell to his parents was a heartrendingly understated 'Cheerio'.[83] On the day of his execution, the *Daily Mirror*'s front page carried a large photograph of Lilian and Iris Bentley sobbing, both covering their faces with their hands, under the sub-heading 'Their grief became nation's problem'.[84] The *Mirror* presented the Bentleys as belonging to the same community of sentiment as their readers, with the grief of Derek's family therefore being something that they, as citizens of the nation, needed to be concerned about. Punishment that was severe to the relatives as well as to the convicted criminal was, through this interpretation, becoming intolerable.

Later the same year, 21-year-old Michael Davies was sentenced to death for the murder of 17-year-old John Beckley on Clapham Common. Five other young men were charged with Beckley's murder but were instead convicted of common assault. The case raised some of the same themes of 'hooliganism' and the dangers of youth as the Craig/Bentley one. News stories focused on the figure of Maud Davies, Michael's mother, and her hopes for a reprieve. A letter from Maud to the *Sunday Pictorial* tugged at readers' heartstrings, as she remembered him as 'a small baby'. Appealing specifically to the mothers of sons, she asked for them to 'plead for the life of my youngest child'. Maud's authority derived from her motherhood – she knew 'nothing about the about the law ... I'm just a mother'.[85] Unlike Mr and Mrs Bentley, Maud was granted her wish. Various newspapers pictured her opening the telegram that carried news of reprieve and described her reaction. The *Daily Mail* journalist reported, '[s]he sobbed and collapsed on the carpet. With her

78 'Fyfe Decides: No Reprieve for Bentley', *The Star*, 26 January 1953.
79 See '11th Hour Bid to Save Bentley', *Birmingham Gazette*, 27 January 1953.
80 O. Summers, "Help Me ... I Didn't Plan to Kill" Cry', *Daily Sketch*, 27 January 1953.
81 'The Verdict: Bentley Hangs', *Daily Mail*, 28 January 1953.
82 'Father Holds Back News from his Wife', *Daily Mail*, 28 January 1953.
83 O. Summers, '200 MPs Plead in Vain to Save Bentley', *Daily Sketch*, 28 January 1953.
84 'Bentley Dies Today: No Last Minute Reprieve', *Daily Mirror*, 28 January 1953.
85 M. Davies, 'Condemned Boy's Mother Writes to the "Pic"', *Sunday Pictorial*, 19 January 1954.

27-year-old daughter, Joyce, I carried Mrs Davies to a settee'.[86] The *Daily Herald* stated that '[w]hen she recovered, she dabbed her eyes, "My prayers have been answered ... Now"'.[87] It was not only the popular press that recognised the human interest appeal of Maud Davies. The *Daily Telegraph* related how 'Davies's mother collapsed at her home in Turret Grove, Clapham'.[88]

Stories that focused on the relatives of the condemned were not necessarily part of the mid-twentieth century's burgeoning abolitionism. Newspapers such as the *Daily Mirror* and *Daily Herald* were abolitionist, the *Daily Mail* was not. However, all could recognise the human interest angle of suffering parents. Even though abolitionism was not coded into all of these reports, their stress on the anguish experienced by a 'boy's' parents formed an emotional public sphere around the issue of capital punishment. This is defined by Richards as 'the emotions which are involved in the political life of a nation', and which the news media are particularly involved in shaping.[89] The emotional public sphere which developed around the death penalty contributed to its ambivalence – whilst the rightness of hanging in terms of justice or deterrence was not necessarily troubled by these stories, the damage it caused to innocent relatives was highlighted. In the popular press at least, readers were invited to see certain families of the condemned, such as the Bentleys and Maud Davies, as fellow citizens with whom they could identify.

In 1957, William Bentley published a memoir entitled *My Son's Execution*, which was also serialised in the *Sheffield Telegraph*.[90] This vividly explained the severe emotional toll that Derek Bentley's arrest, conviction and execution had taken on the family – which had already weathered the death of Derek's twin at birth and of his older sister in the Blitz. When informed by a police officer that Derek had 'killed a man',[91] 'Lilian had collapsed on the settee. Iris lay in a heap beside her, sobbing'.[92] Bentley also discussed his inner emotional turmoil. After the guilty verdict was announced he 'stumbled out of

---

86 'Clapham Common Killer Reprieved', *Daily Mail*, 22 January 1954.

87 'Davies Reprieved after 91 Days', *Daily Herald*, 22 January 1954.

88 'Youth Not to be Hanged', *Daily Telegraph*, 22 January 1954.

89 B. Richards, 'News and the Emotional Public Sphere', S. Allan (ed.), *The Routledge Companion to News and Journalism*, London: Routledge, 2009, p. 346. Lunt and Stenner define the emotional public sphere as one that 'encourages, manages and reflects upon emotional conflict in a public context' P. Lunt and P. Stenner, 'The Jerry Springer Show as an Emotional Public Sphere', *Media, Culture and Society*, 2005, 27(1): 59–81, p. 63. Both of these conceptualisations are relevant, although the formation of an emotional public sphere around capital punishment was not only based on notions of emotional conflict, as the discussion of relatives of the condemned illustrates.

90 W. Bentley, *My Son's Execution*, London: W. H. Allen, 1957; W. G. Bentley, 'I told Craig: Keep away from here' and 'No-one in court thought he was a killer', *Sheffield Telegraph*, 31 July 1957; 'Police told me: Your son has killed a man' and 'Three Days of Agony', 1 August 1957 and 'Our last moment with him was the worst', 6 August 1957.

91 Bentley, *My Son's Execution*, p. 82.

92 Ibid.

court into the corridor, sobbing inwardly'.[93] He concluded that the law was a machine and 'has no heart'.[94]

The emotional resonance of execution's impact on relatives of the condemned is movingly portrayed in Frank Tilsley's 1955 novel *Thicker than Water*, in which a respectable working-class family, the Greensmiths, endure the arrest, conviction and hanging of 20-year-old Sid.[95] It traces the doubt, resentment and grief experienced by his siblings and parents. In the 1957 film, *Time Without Pity*, a father (played by Michael Redgrave) struggles with his alcoholism and his guilt about being an inadequate parent as he races against the clock to prove his son's innocence of murder to save him from the gallows.[96]

Derek Bentley and Michael Davies were both young, barely out of boyhood, and therefore from one of the social categories that heightened anxiety surrounding the death penalty. As a woman and, not only that, a mother, Ruth Ellis was from another.[97] Women were (and are) perceived more fully through their familial and friendship relationships than men. Ellis' story had a particularly strong human interest angle in terms of the torment of her friends and relatives during the countdown to her execution. Her best friend, Jacqueline Dyer, attempted to secure a reprieve by going to see the Home Secretary, Gwilym Lloyd George, the reporting of which contributed to the sense of emotional urgency surrounding the case.[98] The *Birmingham Post* reported that Dyer had sent Ellis flowers on the eve of her execution and 'said afterwards, speaking with great emotion: "Ruth is looking well, but she is obviously under terrible strain"'.[99] Similarly, Ellis' parents had taken her 'a bunch of red roses' and a 'last letter' on their final visit to her in Holloway.[100] Those close to Ellis published articles about her, explaining her life story and character to readers. Jacqueline Dyer recounted how she 'pleaded' with Ellis not to leave family and friends for a man 'who wasn't worth a penny'.[101]

As I have discussed elsewhere, articles in the press by Ellis' brother and mother related the physical abuse she had experienced from David Blakely and also her demeanour in the condemned cell.[102] The *Empire News* ran a further article by Dyer on the Sunday following Ellis' execution. It emphasised the special perspective that those close to Ellis had on the case, stating

93 Ibid., p. 120.
94 Ibid., p. 165.
95 F. Tilsley, *Thicker than Water*, London: The Popular Book Club, 1955.
96 J. Losey, *Time Without Pity* [Motion Picture], Harlequin Productions Ltd, UK, 1957.
97 Langhamer highlights the particular mobilisation of emotion around condemned women and young men, 'The Live Dynamic', p. 431.
98 'Girl Friend Fights to Save Ruth Ellis', *Empire News*, 26 June 1955.
99 'Parents Twice Visited Mrs Ruth Ellis', *Birmingham Post*, 13 July 1955.
100 'Dramatic New Move to Save Ruth Ellis', *Evening News*, 12 July 1955.
101 J. M. Dyer, 'Ruth Ellis – The Story She Would Not Tell', *Empire News*, 10 July 1955.
102 L. Seal, 'Ruth Ellis and Public Contestation of the Death Penalty', *Howard Journal*, 2011, 50(5): 492–504 and 'Ruth Ellis in the Condemned Cell: Voyeurism and Resistance', *Prison Service Journal*, 2012, 199: 17–19.

'I can understand so much – understand as the Home Secretary cannot, because he did not share so much of her life that led up to these tragic events – I can forgive her'.[103] Empathy and the importance of personal biography were stressed as crucial to understanding Ellis' actions, carving out a space for recognition of the value of emotional responses to capital cases, and of the importance of including those personally connected to the condemned in the public discussion.

Readers could therefore gain enough 'first hand' information about Ruth Ellis to form a personal identification with her, which I have argued was significant in the public contestation of capital punishment in relation to her case.[104] As well as being able to read articles by Ellis' family and friends, her four-part autobiography appeared in the *Woman's Sunday Mirror* on the three Sundays leading up to the execution, and the Sunday afterwards.[105] In itself, this was not unusual. There was an established tradition of newspapers competing for notorious murderers' (ghost written) own stories.[106] In 1953, the *Sunday Pictorial* published John Christie's story, which gave insight into his psychological disposition in relation to his murders.[107] Ellis' autobiography, however, can be understood as important to the creation of an emotional public sphere around her case. It discussed the injuries (including causing her to have a miscarriage) that she sustained from David Blakely's abuse, his willingness to spend her money and his unfaithfulness to her. Ellis acknowledged that she should have left Blakely but 'I wasn't sensible. I was a woman in love'.[108]

Crucial to the telling of Ellis' story was her gender and appeal to a female emotional public sphere. Her experiences were 'a warning [to] save some other woman from falling into the same trap as I did'.[109] This had a disciplinary aspect to it – the newspaper introduced the series as 'a lesson for every young girl from a respectable home who is attracted to the champagne and chandeliers of London after dark',[110] but also a voyeuristic aspect as it promised a peek into this subterranean world. Beyond this was the notion that '[o]nly a woman can fully understand her reasons', an argument that called into question whether Ellis had received justice from a male dominated criminal justice system. It also made the case for the importance of empathic insight into her motivation. The articles contained invocations of feminine understanding,

---

103 J. M. Dyer, 'Ruth Ellis: Pale and Calm at the Last Goodbye', *Empire News*, 17 July 1955.
104 Seal, 'Ruth Ellis and Public Contestation'.
105 This was ghost written by Robert Hancock, S. Tweg, 'Not the Full Story: Representing Ruth Ellis', *Biography*, 2000, 23(1): 1–28, p. 5.
106 Bingham, *Family Newspapers?* p. 147.
107 J. Christie, 'He Pins his Hopes on Mercy', *Sunday Pictorial*, 5 July 1953; 'Christie's Own Story: My Second Victim ... We Kissed and Cuddled', *Sunday Pictorial*, 12 July 1953. See Bingham, *Family Newspapers?* p. 147 and F. Mort, 'Scandalous Events: Metropolitan Culture and Moral Change in Post Second World War London', *Representations*, 2006, 93: 106–37.
108 R. Ellis, 'The Last Words of Ruth Ellis', *Woman's Sunday Mirror*, 17 July 1955.
109 R. Ellis, 'My Love and Hate', *Woman's Sunday Mirror*, 26 June 1955.
110 Ibid.

such as 'as every woman knows, you can feel passionate about a man without being in love'.[111]

Newspaper coverage of Ruth Ellis' case not only explored the emotional impact of the death penalty on her family and friends, but also her own emotional life. In doing so, it presented the reading public with a condemned woman with whom they could identify – and were especially invited to do so if they were also female. Ellis' inner life and the emotional turmoil that she had experienced were central to the construction of the case. Understanding her past was part of the key to unlocking her predicament. Of course, not all press coverage was sympathetic towards Ellis or contributed to the creation of an emotional public sphere. But her case demonstrated how a story with the right ingredients – an attractive young woman, a love story, the lure of the metropolitan underworld, an upper middle-class cad, a frenzied killing by gunshot – could, in the mid-1950s, epitomise the emotional battleground the death penalty had become.

Personal identification and the inner life of the condemned were also key elements of the novel and film versions of *Yield to the Night*, a fictional portrayal of glamorous, blonde murderess, Mary Hilton.[112] The novel is told from Hilton's first person perspective, including reflections such as 'I wonder how I'll be. I heard once that they had to call in the men officers to carry Mrs Thompson to … next door'.[113] As such, it creates a rich inner and emotional life. It finishes with her walking to the gallows, pinioned and hooded. The film adaptation has a voiceover from Hilton, which opens up her interior life to the viewer, her reason for committing the crime and her experiences of the condemned cell. Like the novel, it finishes as she is about to be hanged but does not show her pinioned and hooded.[114] Instead the camera focuses on her burning cigarette left in the ashtray. The novel was published before Ruth Ellis was executed so despite the parallels of a glamorous woman driven to kill by love,[115] it was not based on her case. The film, however, was released in 1956 and therefore, as Chibnall points out, those involved in its production would have been aware of the connections to be drawn between Mary Hilton and Ruth Ellis.[116] The narrator of the novel, *My Mother Was Hanged*, Reynold Marden,

---

111 R. Ellis, 'David Gasped: "I Can't Live Without You"', *Woman's Sunday Mirror*, 3 July 1955. This reference to sex without love supports Bingham's argument that in the 1950s, the popular press showed a greater willingness to discuss sex, alongside a decline in regarding it as 'dirty', *Family Newspapers?* pp. 144–6.
112 J. Henry, *Yield to the Night*, London: White Lion Publishers, 1954 and J. T. Lee, *Yield to the Night* [Motion Picture], Kenwood Productions, UK, 1956.
113 Henry, p. 115.
114 It is likely such a scene would have been censored if included – see Chapter Three's discussion of cuts made to 1958 Hollywood film *I Want to Live!*.
115 Mary Hilton shoots to death her lover's other lover, Lucy Carpenter, with whom he was obsessed and which led to his suicide.
116 S. Chibnall, 'The Anti Heroines of Holloway', P. Mason (ed.), *Captured by the Media: Prison Discourse in Popular Culture*, Cullompton: Willan, 2006, p. 179.

elucidates how his sense of self was rent by discovering that his mother – who appears to have been modelled on Ruth Ellis – was executed, leading him to, like her, commit murder and face hanging.[117]

Capital punishment as an emotional issue

In the 1950s, capital punishment was debated as an issue that was part of the nation's public emotional life and expression. There were editorials and articles that strongly rejected a 'sentimental' portrayal of the death penalty, but that it was an issue that stirred strong emotions became part of the discussion. Derek Bentley's execution exemplified this. It was 'a tragedy that has deeply distressed and sharply divided the public'[118] and had created 'unusually deep feelings on both sides'.[119] Some commentary acknowledged emotions would influence views on an execution like Bentley's. The *Western Morning News* argued that where feeling had been aroused by the case 'it cannot be suppressed'.[120] The *Manchester Guardian*, historically wary of 'sentimentality', stated that '[t]he arguments made for special consideration [for Bentley] make a powerful appeal to the emotions, and in so tragic a story it is right that they should'.[121] An opinion piece in the *Daily Express* agreed that emotion about Bentley's life was 'understandable' but argued that such appeals to the Home Secretary were based 'on nothing else'. It was his job 'not to yield to clamour'.[122] The *Newcastle Journal* dismissed the atmosphere surrounding the case as 'sentimentality' and argued that Fyfe's decision should not be swayed by it.[123] For the *Yorkshire Post*, the decision not to grant a reprieve was the right one, but the 'emotional background to the case' must have made it a particularly heavy one for Fyfe.[124] The *New Statesman and Nation*, in a leader criticising the execution, concluded that 'a few more days for the spontaneous revulsion of the public to gather momentum' would probably have resulted in a reprieve.[125] In the *Picture Post*, Kenneth Allsop reflected that with the hanging of Derek Bentley, 'a nation is in an emotional upset. I can recall only two other comparable occasions: Dunkirk and the King's death'. He emphasised the collective nature of the sentiment, with 'each of us momentarily entangled in a perturbation common to all' and, in

117 E. S. Willards, *My Mother Was Hanged*, London: Heinemann, 1958. An earlier novel, *Because I Must*, has a similar plot, whereby the traumatised daughter of a hanged woman grows up to commit murder (of her sister) and is hanged, H. Lewis, Cheltenham: Cheltenham Press Ltd, 1946.

118 'Bentley and the Law', *Daily Mirror*, 29 January 1953.

119 'Our London Correspondence', *Manchester Guardian*, 27 January 1953.

120 'Bentley', *Western Morning News*, 28 January 1953.

121 'Death Sentence', *Manchester Guardian*, 29 January 1953.

122 'Opinion: Emotion is a Bad Master', *Daily Express*, 29 January 1953.

123 'Commentary: The Bentley Case', *Newcastle Journal*, 27 January 1953.

124 'Justice Has Been Done', *Yorkshire Post*, 28 January 1953.

125 'The Case of Derek Bentley', *New Statesman and Nation*, 31 January 1953.

comparing the execution with landmark national events, made it extremely significant.[126]

There was no consensus on the appropriateness of the influence of emotional responses to capital cases, but that these responses were part of the public discussion of the death penalty was accepted in the 1950s. In abolitionist publications such as the *Mirror* and the *Picture Post*, emotionality and anxiety about capital punishment was constructed to include the whole nation as a community of sentiment, and was a means to implicitly advocate abolition. In his article on the emotional fallout from the Bentley execution, Allsop asserted that everyone felt some guilt after executions.[127] This was of course highly debatable, but coded the death penalty as not only a shared anxiety, but also a shared responsibility.

Viscount Templewood's (Samuel Hoare) anti-capital punishment *The Shadow of the Gallows* began with a chapter on his 'personal outlook'. This recalled his repulsion, as Home Secretary in the late 1930s, when confronted with 'mementoes of other people's deaths' such as notes on the calendar marking appeals and executions.[128] These were unnecessary as Home Secretaries were bound to dwell on hangings. The burden placed on the Home Secretary had become an established theme by the time Ruth Ellis was executed in 1955. The *Daily Sketch* argued that Lloyd George should not be 'assailed by emotional and partisan appeals' and had 'a right to be protected from half-hysterical public clamour'.[129] A letter to the *Birmingham Post* concurred, stating 'capital punishment deserves to be discussed unemotionally and in an atmosphere of the strictest objectivity'.[130] The centrality of feeling to the dilemma of the Ellis case was articulated by the *Daily Dispatch*, which aphorised '[e]motions demand that she should live. The law decrees that she should hang'.[131]

Prominent abolitionists made contrasting public arguments about the role of emotion in the case. Writing in *The Star*, Sydney Silverman contended 'emotion is not irrelevant, nor necessarily merely sentimental'. The 'essential human pathos' of Ruth Ellis' act of killing David Blakeley demonstrated to most people that she was 'all too human'.[132] Hugh Klare, Secretary of the Howard League, wrote to the *Manchester Guardian* to explain that 'rational penal policy ought not to be affected by sentiment'. Although there was 'an emotional outcry' for the 'young and pretty' Ellis, 'public feeling will be reversed' in the case of a 'less glamorous murderer'.[133] These divergent views show the discussion of the emotional public sphere that surrounded the death

126 K. Allsop, 'The People Didn't Think So', *Picture Post*, 14 February 1953.
127 Ibid.
128 Viscount Templewood, *The Shadow of the Gallows*, London: Victor Gollancz, 1951, p. 9.
129 'One Man and Ruth Ellis: "The Sketch Says"', *Daily Sketch*, 4 July 1955.
130 G. Statham, 'Capital Punishment', *Birmingham Post*, 20 July 1955.
131 'As We See It: Jealousy and the Law', *Daily Dispatch*, 1 July 1955.
132 S. Silverman, 'Ruth Ellis and the Death Penalty', *The Star*, 12 July 1955.
133 H. Klare, 'The Death Penalty', Letter to the Editor, *Manchester Guardian*, 17 July 1955.

penalty did not clearly break down across abolitionist and retentionist lines. Rather, it led to consideration of the proper place for the expression and influence of emotion in public discourse. In the 1950s, many abolitionists acknowledged the need to recognise, rather than dismiss, death penalty emotion. When Victor Gollancz and Arthur Koestler launched the National Campaign for the Abolition of Capital Punishment not long after the Ellis execution, they sought to engage outrage against injustice and to connect with emotional responses.[134] Ernest Gowers, who had chaired the Royal Commission on Capital Punishment, concluded that 'in the last resort, it is emotion rather than reason that will decide the issue'.[135]

Capital punishment did not suddenly become an emotional issue in the mid-twentieth century – it had historically stirred emotional public reactions, and disgust at bodily punishment had long been a marker of 'refinement'. However, by the 1950s the debate on the appropriate role of feeling in relation to capital cases meant that an emotional public sphere was constructed around the issue of the death penalty in the press. The popular press was especially important in terms of its attention to the inner lives of the condemned and of their relatives. Capital punishment became entwined with the negotiation of public emotional expression in Britain. A clear shift can be identified from the early twentieth-century stories in provincial newspapers, which maintained the publicness of execution by informing an audience about its operation, to the mid-twentieth-century emotional public sphere that formed around the death penalty.

Archival collections

The National Archives, Prison Commission (PCOM)

Newspapers and magazines

Birmingham Gazette
Birmingham Post
Cornishman
Coventry Evening Telegraph
Daily Dispatch
Daily Express
Daily Herald
Daily Mail

---

134 M. Scammell, *Koestler: The Indispensable Intellectual*, London: Faber and Faber, 2010, p. 444–5. Koestler and Rolph's 'Creed for Abolitionists' began by stating, '[o]ne should not deride what is sometimes called the "emotional" condemnation of the death penalty, for the emotions or inherent feelings can sometimes be a sure guide to what is right', A. Koestler and C. H. Rolph, *Hanged by the Neck,* London: Penguin, 1961, p. 142.

135 E. Gowers, *A Life for a Life*, London: Chatto and Windus, 1956, p. 138. The importance of emotion to retentionism was critically explored by Gardiner, who argued that fear and anger drove support for capital punishment, G. Gardiner, *Capital Punishment as Deterrent: And the Alternative*, London: Victor Gollancz, 1956, p. 81.

Daily Mirror
Daily Sketch
Daily Telegraph
Empire News
Evening News
Evening Standard
Exeter and Plymouth Gazette
Gloucester Citizen
Hull Daily Mail
Lincolnshire Chronicle
Manchester Courier and Lancashire General Advertiser
Manchester Guardian
Newcastle Journal
News of the World
New Statesman and Nation
Picture Post
Sheffield Evening Telegraph
Sheffield Telegraph
Shields Daily Gazette
Sunday Pictorial
Tamworth Herald
The South Eastern Gazette
The Star
The Times
Western Morning News
Western Times
Woman's Sunday Mirror
Yorkshire Evening Post
Yorkshire Post

Bibliography

Ballinger, A., *Dead Woman Walking: Executed Women in England and Wales, 1900–55*, Aldershot: Ashgate, 2000.

Bentley, W., *My Son's Execution*, London: W. H. Allen, 1957.

Bingham, A., *Gender, Modernity, and the Popular Press in Inter-War Britain*, Oxford: Clarendon Press, 2004.

——*Family Newspapers? Sex, Private Life, and the British Popular Press, 1918–1978*, Oxford: Oxford University Press, 2009.

——'Reading Newspapers: Cultural Histories of the Popular Press in Modern Britain', *History Compass*, 2012, 10(2): 140–50.

Bourdieu, P., *Distinction: A Social Critique of Judgment and Taste*, London: Routledge and Kegan Paul, 1984.

Chibnall, S., *Law-and-Order News*, London: Tavistock, xxxx.

——'The Anti Heroines of Holloway', P. Mason (ed.), *Captured by the Media: Prison Discourse in Popular Culture*, Willan: Cullompton, 2006, 172–90.

Connelly, K. C., 'From Detective Fiction to Detective Literature: Psychology in the Novels of Dorothy L. Sayers and Margaret Millar', *Clues*, 2007, 25(3): 35–47.

Dyndor, Z., 'Death Recorded: Capital Punishment and the Press in Northampton, 1780–1834', *Midland History*, 2008, 33(2): 179–95.

Evans, R., *Rituals of Retribution*, Oxford: Oxford University Press, 1995.

Fiske, J., *Understanding Popular Culture*, Abingdon: Routledge, 1989.

Francis, M., 'The Domestication of the Male? Recent Research on Nineteenth and Twentieth Century Masculinity', *The Historical Journal*, 2002, 45(3): 637–52.

——'Tears, Tantrums and Bared Teeth: The Emotional Economy of Three Conservative Prime Ministers, 1951–63', *Journal of British Studies*, 2002, 41(3): 354–87.

Freedman, A., 'Dorothy Sayers and the Case of the Shell-Shocked Detective', *Partial Answers*, 2010, 8(2): 365–87.

Friedman, L., *Crime and Punishment in American History*, New York: Basic Books, 1993.

Gans, H., *Popular Culture and High Culture: An Analysis and Evaluation of Taste*, New York: Basic Books, 1999, 2nd edition.

Gardiner, G., *Capital Punishment as Deterrent: And the Alternative*, London: Victor Gollancz, 1956.

Garland, D., 'The Problem of the Body in Modern Punishment', *Social Research*, 2011, 78(3): 767–98.

Gatrell, V. A. C., *The Hanging Tree: Execution and the English People, 1770–1868*, Oxford: Oxford University Press, 1996.

Gowers, E., *A Life for a Life*, London: Chatto and Windus, 1956.

Greene, G., *It's a Battlefield*, London: Heinemann, 1934.

Heathorn, S., 'How Stiff Were Their Upper Lips? Research on Late Victorian and Edwardian Masculinity', *History Compass*, 2004, 2(1): 1–7.

Henry, J., *Yield to the Night*, London: White Lion Publishers, 1954.

Koestler, K. and Rolph, C. H., *Hanged by the Neck*, London: Penguin, 1961.

Langhamer, C., '"The Live Dynamic Whole of Feeling and Behaviour": Capital Punishment and the Politics of Emotion, 1945–57', *Journal of British Studies*, 2012, 51(2): 416–41.

Lee, J. T., *Yield to the Night* [Motion Picture], Kenwood Productions, UK, 1956.

Lewis, H., *Because I Must*, Cheltenham: Cheltenham Press Ltd, 1946.

Linders, A., 'The Execution Spectacle and State Legitimacy: The Changing Nature of the Execution Audience, 1833–1937', *Law and Society Review*, 2002, 36(3): 607–56.

Losey, J., *Time Without Pity* [Motion Picture], Harlequin Productions Ltd, UK, 1957.

Lott, M., 'Dorothy L. Sayers, the Great War and Shell Shock', *Interdisciplinary Literary Studies*, 2013, 15(1): 103–26.

Lunt, P. and Stenner, P., 'The Jerry Springer Show as an Emotional Public Sphere', *Media, Culture and Society*, 2005, 27(1): 59–81.

Lynch, M., 'On-Line Executions: The Symbolic Use of the Electric Chair in Cyberspace', *POLAR*, 1999, 23(2): 1–20.

Madow, M., 'Forbidden Spectacle: Executions, the Public and the Press in Nineteenth-Century New York', *Buffalo Law Review*, 1995, 43(2): 461–562.

Masur, L., *Rites of Execution: Capital Punishment and the Transformation of American Culture, 1776–1865*, Oxford: Oxford University Press, 1991.

Mort, F., 'Social and Symbolic Fathers and Sons in Postwar Britain', *Journal of British Studies*, 1999, 38(3): 358–84.

——'Scandalous Events: Metropolitan Culture and Moral Change in Post Second World War London', *Representations*, 2006, 93: 106–37.

Potter, H., *Hanging in Judgment: Religion and the Death Penalty in England*, London: SCM Press Ltd, 1993.

Richards, B., 'News and the Emotional Public Sphere', S. Allan (ed.), *The Routledge Companion to News and Journalism*, London: Routledge, 2009, 301–11.

Roberts, E., *A Woman's Place: An Oral History of Working Class Women, 1890–1940*, Oxford: Blackwell, 1984.

Rowbotham, J. and Stevenson, K., 'Introduction', J. Rowbotham and K. Stevenson (eds), *Criminal Conversations: Victorian Crimes, Social Panic and Moral Outrage*, Columbus: Ohio State University Press, 2005, xxi–xxxii.

Sarat, A., *et al.*, 'Gruesome Spectacles: The Cultural Reception of Botched Executions in America, 1890–1920', *British Journal of American and Legal Studies*, 2012, 1(1): 1–30.

Sayers, D. L., *Busman's Honeymoon*, London: Gollancz, 1937.

Scammell, M., *Koestler: The Indispensable Intellectual*, London: Faber and Faber, 2010.

Seal, L., 'Ruth Ellis and Public Contestation of the Death Penalty', *The Howard Journal*, 2011, 50(5): 492–504.

——'Ruth Ellis in the Condemned Cell: Voyeurism and Resistance', *Prison Service Journal*, 2012, 199: 17–19.

Sinha, S., 'Existential Motifs of Thought in Greene's Fiction', S. K. Paul and A. N. Prasad (eds), *Reassessing British Literature*, New Delhi: Sarup and Sons, 2007, 266–78.

Steedman, C., 'State Sponsored Autobiography', B. Conekin, F. Mort and C. Waters (eds), *Moments of Modernity: Reconstructing Britain, 1945–1964*, London: Rivers Oram, 1999, 41–54.

Templewood, Viscount, *The Shadow of the Gallows*, London: Victor Gollancz, 1951.

Tilsley, F., *Thicker than Water*, London: The Popular Book Club, 1955.

Trotti, M., *The Body in the Reservoir: Murder and Sensationalism in the South*, Chapel Hill: University of North Carolina Press, 2008.

Tulloch, J., 'The Privatising of Pain: Lincoln Newspapers, "Mediated Publicness" and the End of Public Execution', *Journalism Studies*, 2006, 7(3): 437–51.

Tweg, S., 'Not the Full Story: Representing Ruth Ellis', *Biography*, 2000, 23(1): 1–28.

Willards, E. S., *My Mother Was Hanged*, London: Heinemann, 1958.

3 Trial and execution as entertainment

The previous chapter explored how press coverage of executions ensured that they remained public events, and how this increasingly became part of the reconfiguration of emotion in the public sphere. The contours of this reporting were shaped by what would be of interest to readers and so these stories can be also understood as entertainment. This chapter further develops the discussion of the interconnection between sensationalism, cultural distinction and capital punishment by exploring the death penalty as entertainment. As Friedman has argued, trials can be regarded as 'lexitainment' – legal process as entertainment.[1] Governments do not have a monopoly on trials as a 'didactic device',[2] meaning that a multiplicity of messages and meanings can be conveyed. The capital trial, and its written accounts, was one form of death penalty related lexitainment in twentieth-century Britain. Others included cultural representations of executions or the executed in theatres, waxwork shows and films. 'Bad taste' popular representations received criticism from the perspectives of high and official culture, but were successful with the public. This chapter discusses debates over the capital trial as entertainment in relation to the famous Crippen and Thompson/Bywaters cases, and reporting of the crowds that congregated outside the prison on execution morning. It goes on to explore other forms of capital punishment lexitainment, such as waxwork shows of the executed, performances by ex-hangmen and the depiction of execution on film.

Capital trials as entertainment

By the end of the nineteenth century, there 'had been a shift from the spectacle of public bodily punishment to the spectacle of the trial itself'.[3] From 1898, the accused could be examined in court, which enhanced the drama of the trial.[4] In capital cases, an extra frisson was added by the knowledge that a

---

1 L. M. Friedman, 'Lexitainment: Legal Process as Theater', *DePaul Law Review*, 2001, 50(2): 539–58.

2 Ibid., p. 544.

3 S. D'Cruze, '"The Damned Place was Haunted": The Gothic Middlebrow Culture and Inter-War "Notable Trials"', *Literature and History*, 2006, 15(1): 37–58, p. 38.

4 Ibid.

guilty verdict would result in the death sentence, and then perhaps in hanging. Sensational trials – often those involving stories of murder and infidelity amongst the middle classes – were consumed via the press as entertainment.[5] This was frequently criticised from the perspective of high culture, but this criticism should not be taken as an indication that consumers of high culture did not find capital trials entertaining, but rather that the crafting of an upper middle-class habitus entailed disavowing the vulgar sensationalism of the masses.[6] Such criticism was also made on the grounds that the publicity given to sensational cases worked against the privacy of execution. As Trotti argues in relation to early twentieth-century Virginia, murder became a staple of popular culture and fascination with 'lurid stories of crime and bloodshed' existed in contrast with efforts to fashion a civilised, modern society.[7] Since the mid-nineteenth century, 'the culture of modernity has been characterized by a volatile relationship between high art and mass culture',[8] which is illustrated by capital cases in particular.

Crippen

The sensational pursuit, capture and trial of Hawley Harvey Crippen in 1910 provided a vehicle for debate in *The Times* of the inappropriate theatricality and publicity surrounding such cases. Historically, *The Times* had been by no means immune from sensationalist crime reporting.[9] However, this newspaper exercised the most 'cultural authority' and was 'written for and read by the country's higher classes and controlling minority'.[10] It was conservative and

5 These were constituent elements of the 'perfect' English murder, as identified by George Orwell, that would entertain readers of the *News of the World* on a Sunday afternoon. He classed Crippen and Thompson/Bywaters as falling into this category. From the perspective of 1946, Orwell looked back nostalgically at such murders as the 'product of a stable society', G. Orwell, *Decline of the English Murder and Other Essays*, London: Penguin Books, 1965, p. 13.

6 Huyssen argues that modernist high culture developed via a conscious strategy of excluding the 'other' of mass culture and remained anxious at the prospect of contamination, A. Huyssen, *After the Great Divide: Modernism, Mass Culture, Postmodernism*, Bloomington: Indiana University Press, 1986, p. 1.

7 M. Trotti, *The Body in the Reservoir: Murder and Sensationalism in the South*, Chapel Hill: University of North Carolina Press, 2008, p. 6.

8 Huyssen, *After*, p. 1.

9 *The Times'* reporting of Victorian murders was sensationalist and influenced the 'sensation novels' of the 1860s, such as Collins' *The Moonstone* and Braddon's *Lady Audley's Secret*; P. Brantlinger, 'What is "Sensational" About the "Sensation" Novel', *Nineteenth Century Fiction*, 1982, 37(1): 1–28, p. 9. There was also similarity between crime coverage in *The Times* and more 'lowbrow' newspapers, such as *Reynolds News*, J. Rowbotham and K. Stevenson, 'Introduction', J. Rowbotham and K. Stevenson (eds), *Criminal Conversations: Victorian Crimes, Social Panic and Moral Outrage*, Columbus: Ohio State University Press, 2005, p. xxvi and N. Goc, *Women, Infanticide and the Press, 1822–1922*, Aldershot: Ashgate, 2013, p. 8.

10 K. E. Westman, '"For Her Generation the Newspaper was a Book": Media, Mediation and Oscillation in Virginia Woolf's *Between the Acts'*, *Journal of Modern Literature*, 2006, 29(2): 1–18, pp. 4, 5.

pro-Empire.[11] Reading *The Times* denoted education, social status and cultural distinction – an upper middle-class, masculine habitus, which entailed establishing (professed) distance from the sensational, popular and feminine, a habitus which in turn was reproduced in the newspaper's editorial line. Reading it was a routine, everyday way to receive 'training in knowing where you are and how best to do things there'.[12]

Crippen's trial was heralded as the most sensational of the new century. Hawley Crippen was arrested aboard a steamship as it docked in Quebec on 31 July 1910, for the murder of his wife, Cora. He and his lover, Ethel Le Neve, had sailed from Antwerp disguised as father and son. Unbeknownst to both of them, after recognising Crippen and Le Neve from newspaper stories, the captain of the ship had telegraphed Scotland Yard using new wireless technology. Cora Crippen had vanished in January of that year – according to her husband she had returned to their native United States and then sadly died there. Cora's friends were suspicious about her sudden disappearance and this deepened when Le Neve, a young woman who worked for Crippen, moved into his house in Hilldrop Crescent in Holloway and started to wear items of Cora's jewellery and clothing. Crippen and Le Neve left London for Belgium after he was interviewed and the house was searched by police. The police failed to find anything but searched the house several more times after Crippen and Le Neve disappeared, eventually discovering a section of human flesh. Due to a distinctive scar, this was believed to be the remains of Cora Crippen, and pathologists' tests revealed she had been poisoned.[13]

Ethel Le Neve was acquitted of being an accessory after the fact to murder, but Crippen was found guilty and sentenced to hang. Before his trial had commenced, *The Times* despaired of the fascination that the case had caused, especially as Crippen had not yet been convicted of a crime. In an editorial entitled 'Vulgar Curiosity', it argued '[w]e cannot, nowadays, look on bodily torture; but there is a large public that will go to any trouble to witness mental torture'.[14] When murders became a source of pleasure, interest in them could be considered 'perverse' and the 'murderer is so much regarded as an entertainer that people

11 Ibid., p. 5.
12 C. Mercer, 'Regular Imaginings: The Newspaper and the Nation', T. Bennett (ed.), *Celebrating the Nation: A Critical Study of Australia's Bicentenary*, London: Allen and Unwin, 1992, p. 31.
13 On the Crippen case, see K. D. Watson, *Poisoned Lives: English Poisoners and their Victims*, London: Continuum, 2004, pp. 62–6 and E. Larson, *Thunderstruck*, New York: Random House, 2007; on the case and understandings of modernity, see J. E. Early, 'Technology, Modernity, and the "Little Man": Crippen's Capture by Wireless', *Victorian Studies*, 1996, 39(3): 309–37; on the significance of understandings of class and gender, J. E. Early, 'Keeping Ourselves to Ourselves: Violence in the Edwardian Suburb', S. D'Cruze (ed.), *Everyday Violence in Britain, 1850–1950*, London: Longman, 2000. Modern DNA testing has cast doubt on Crippen's guilt as it shows that the flesh found in Hilldrop Crescent was from a man, S. Nelson, 'CSI Proves Dr Crippen was Innocent: DNA Tests Reveal Remains in the Cellar were "Not his Wife"', *MailOnline*, 27 January 2011: www.dailymail.co.uk/news/article-1347642/CSI-proves-Dr-Crippen-innocent-DNA-tests-reveal-remains-cellar-wife.html.
14 'Vulgar Curiosity', *The Times*, 2 September 1910.

under suspicion of murder are offered engagements at theatres or music-halls'. Such behaviour was in clear bad taste. This was especially demonstrated by the editorial's invocation of music hall, which was a target of middle and upper middle-class disapproval and seen as representative of 'low' culture.[15] The article scolded, '[v]ulgar curiosity is a besetting sin of our time, because we now hear so much about everything that happens'.[16] Here, the more connected, informed mass society made possible by modernity was a source of ambivalence as it gave reign to sensationalism, vulgarity and cruelty. The recurrent criticism of popular culture as harmful to civilisation that Gans identifies was evident.[17]

A further editorial published at the end of Crippen's trial returned to this theme of the damaging nature of legal theatricality. *The Times* sternly asserted that '[a] Criminal Court is not a show room, nor is such a trial of the nature of a matinee' and reminded its readers that it had urged reducing the extent of preliminary proceedings in capital trials 'on the ground that the public mind was needlessly saturated with foul details'.[18] This stance, and what it meant in terms of the public nature of capital trials, was debated in the letters to the editor page. Barrister W. E. Cameron, who had been involved with the trial, decried the practice of allotting tickets for entry as 'monstrous bad taste', which had led to a trial in which '[a]ll the appurtenances of the popular music-hall were present'. He argued that only press should be admitted to murder trials and also suggested that the 'hideous trappings and archaic formalities' of the death sentence, such as donning the black cap, should be removed.[19] Barrister and legal scholar, Harry Poland, countered Cameron's view, describing an English murder trial as 'dignified, solemn, and pathetic'. He cautioned, 'let not an effusive display of sentiment lead your readers astray on this subject'.[20]

This charge of sentimentality exposed a fissure in high culture responses to capital punishment and its accoutrements. In Cameron's disgust at the trial's 'bad taste' and vulgarity, which included the theatrical nature of intoning the death sentence, Poland saw weakness and a lack of patriotism, recalling the Victorian criticism of abolitionism as 'effeminate' (although Cameron was not advocating abolition).[21] This debate over taste and sentimentality continued

15 Music hall was 'born from below' and a 'vital element in working class culture', D. Kift, *The Victorian Music Hall: Culture, Class and Conflict*, Cambridge: Cambridge University Press, 1996, p. 2. See also P. Bailey, 'Conspiracies of Meaning: Music-Hall and the Knowingness of Popular Culture', *Past & Present*, 1994, 144: 138–70.

16 'Vulgar Curiosity'.

17 H. Gans, *Popular Culture and High Culture: An Analysis and Evaluation of Taste*, New York: Basic Books, 1999, 2nd edition.

18 'The Crippen Trial', *The Times*, 24 October 1910. Like music hall, other forms of popular theatre were also understood as emblematic of working-class culture, see P. Joyce, *Visions of the People: Industrial England and the Question of Class, c.1848–1914*, Cambridge: Cambridge University Press, 1993, pp. 305–29.

19 W. E. Cameron, 'The Crippen Trial', Letter to the Editor, *The Times*, 26 October 1910.

20 H. B. Poland, 'The Crippen Trial', Letter to the Editor, *The Times*, 28 October 1910.

21 See J. Gregory, *Victorians Against the Gallows*, London: I. B. Tauris, 2012, pp. 163, 186.

after Crippen's execution. Academic Arthur C. Benson argued that it was 'horrible to reflect' that the Crippen case had 'given to thousands of people the keenest excitement'. Implicating the press, he contended that it had 'nowadays recovered a good deal of the publicity which the suppression of public executions temporarily removed'. In particular, he objected to the persistence of hanging, which was an 'awful ceremony', whereas poison or anaesthetic would 'have some touch of privacy and decorum'.[22]

Benson's discomfort with the death penalty's continuing elements of publicity and its attachment to ritual in the 'awful ceremony' of hanging was consistent with what have been diagnosed as elite desires for a clean, modern, civilised version of capital punishment.[23] He also found hanging to be in bad taste, as it lacked 'decorum'. Benson's letter provoked a flurry of responses, which demonstrated the lack of consensus on the 'best' form of execution. Herbert Stephen, barrister and legal scholar, retorted that poison or anaesthetic would 'be prompted not by any regard for the condemned man, but by an unmanly shrinking, on the part of those responsible, from the actual facts of the situation'. There was no point 'in glossing over the process so as to make it seem as polite as possible'.[24] Again, the charge of 'effeminacy' was levelled at the suggestion that hanging was too brutal. As discussed, this was a well-established critique of perceived shrinking from the realities of hanging and one that mobilised early twentieth-century norms of masculine stoicism. The letters page debate illustrated the ambivalences in high culture about how best to carry out capital punishment – with tensions between muscularity and refinement.

Other responses tackled the theme of publicity. Carl Heath, secretary of the National Peace Council, did not want to 'rush ... into any kind of sentimentalism', but nevertheless stated that the 'sensational Press' had effected 'the practical return to public executions', a situation which could only be made worse 'with the highly effective aid of wireless telegraphy, photography, and the cinematograph'.[25] Heath's fears mirrored *The Times'* own stated anxieties about the corrupting influence of popular culture on mass society. Crippen's case was especially apposite, given the role of wireless telegraphy in his capture. Filson Young, journalist and penal reformer,[26] spoke up for abolition and sought to counter the inevitable charge of sentimentality. He argued 'it is really the sentimental people, the gentle, refined, sentimental people, who

22 A. C. Benson, 'Executions', Letter to the Editor, *The Times*, 30 November 1910.
23 In relation to the prominence of these sentiments in the United States, see T. Kaufman-Osborn, *From Noose to Needle*, Ann Arbor: University of Michigan Press, 2002 and D. Garland, 'The Problem of the Body in Modern Punishment', *Social Research*, 2011, 78(3): 767–98. On Britain, France and Germany, see A. Hammel, *Ending the Death Penalty: The European Experience in Global Perspective*, Basingstoke: Palgrave MacMillan, 2010.
24 H. Stephen, 'Executions', Letter to the Editor, *The Times*, 6 December 1910.
25 C. Heath, 'Executions', Letter to the Editor, *The Times*, 7 December 1910.
26 And subsequently author of the volume on Crippen for the Notable British Trials series, F. Young, *The Trial of Hawley Harvey Crippen*, Notable British Trials, London: Hodge, 1920.

hang men and women, and who then find the subject so unpleasant that they would rather not discuss it'. This meant that the condemned 'goes to his death, not out in the world or in the presence of any friend, but like a rat in a corner'.[27] Young articulated the abolitionist concern that the privatisation of execution had ensured its survival, as the 'refined' did not have to dwell on its brutality. Sir Henry Smith, former Commissioner of City of London Police, agreed that privacy was not necessarily desirable, but from a different standpoint. He asked 'why all this secrecy?' and suggested that journalists should be more frequently allowed to attend and report on executions. The public would then know 'what they have a right to know'. He recognised limits – 'sensational and gruesome details' would not be required.[28] 'K E B' was willing to admit to 'sensitiveness or sentimentality, or both' in sharing Benson's discomfort with the 'gruesomeness' of the current situation. He questioned the need to publish the execution date and objected to having seen posters advertising the date of Crippen's demise. It would be preferable for 'silence and mystery' to 'shroud the rest till the end is over'.[29]

The editorials in *The Times* and the accompanying debates in the letters page provide access to early twentieth-century high culture conceptualisations of the death penalty, and reveal the importance of questions of taste and the appropriate display, or lack of display, of public emotion. For the most part, the discussion was not about retention versus abolition but about the correct way to carry out and portray capital punishment. This demonstrates the extent to which consideration of the death penalty was a discussion of cultural distinction. Sensationalism and theatricality were in bad taste and unashamed curiosity about trials and execution was vulgar. As Bourdieu argues, '[t]aste classifies and it classifies the classifier'.[30] *The Times* did not argue that it was wrong to be interested in Crippen's trial. The crucial distinction that it drew was in deriving 'pleasure' from that interest, which was 'perverse'. Implicitly, the newspaper justified its own detailed and extensive coverage of the case as serious and informative, and therefore not merely for entertainment.

The readers' letters can be understood as part of the negotiation of an upper-middle-class, masculine, British habitus in relation to the issue of capital punishment, and provide access to varied understandings of how this habitus should be constructed. This negotiation was similar to the performance of civilisation that Martschukat discusses in relation to the death penalty in nineteenth-century Germany.[31] Letter writers accepted that the

27 F. Young, 'Executions', Letter to the Editor, *The Times*, 8 December 1910.
28 H. Smith, 'Executions', Letter to the Editor, *The Times*, 16 December 1910.
29 K. E. B., 'Executions', Letter to the Editor, *The Times*, 19 December 1910.
30 P. Bourdieu, *Distinction: A Social Critique of Judgment and Taste*, London: Routledge and Kegan Paul, 1984, p. 6.
31 J. Martschukat, 'Nineteenth-Century Executions as Performances of Law, Death and Civilization', A. Sarat and C. Boulanger (eds), *The Cultural Lives of Capital Punishment*, Stanford, CA: Stanford University Press, 2005.

sensationalism of mass culture, with its penchant for the gruesome, was an undesirable means of portraying the issue. Beyond that, there was a variety of opinions as to how far execution should be public, how it should be carried out, and on the tensions between modernity and civilisation. Crippen's case was particularly pertinent to these debates. The use of wireless telegraphy to effect his capture and the importance of pathologist Bernard Spilsbury's expert evidence in gaining his conviction showcased the technological and scientific advances of modernity, and their potential for bringing criminals to justice.[32] But, as the concerned letter writers pointed out, widespread public fascination with the case, fed by up to the minute press reporting, highlighted another aspect of modernity – the popular culture of the masses with its attendant sensationalism and vulgarity. An important cultural classifier was the avoidance of sentimentality. Sentimentality was commonplace, mass, fake and vulgar – it was working-class and lower-middle-class. It was also feminine. Two clear polluting elements, the lower class and the feminine, were therefore identified in this process of classification.[33] Lying underneath this discussion was the assignation of sentimentality to foreign and less advanced cultures.[34] In the early twentieth century, the derogation of sentimentality remained an important aspect of high culture responses to the death penalty. Whilst 'sentimentality' retained its pejorative meanings, the emotionality of the death penalty, as the previous chapter explored, became accepted as inevitable in the mid-twentieth century.

The criticism of public interest in murder trials for entertainment as vulgar curiosity and sensationalism became a well-established and enduring press narrative in the twentieth century, with the in-built, unacknowledged irony that such curiosity could not be sustained without the press. That too much obvious enjoyment of a murder trial was in bad taste became a line that was

32 Early, 'Technology', highlights how the lower-middle-class 'little man' became symbolic of modern, mass society in the Edwardian era. Due to his evidence to the Crippen trial, Spilsbury became Britain's first celebrity pathologist, see I. Burney and N. Pemberton, 'The Rise and Fall of Celebrity Pathology', *British Medical Journal*, 2010, 341: 1319–21. See also J. Robins, *The Magnificent Spilsbury and the Case of the Brides in the Bath*, London: John Murray, 2010, Ch. 4.

33 Sentimentality, the display of emotional excess, was other to early twentieth-century conceptions of masculine, and British, restraint, M. Francis, 'Tears, Tantrums and Bared Teeth: The Emotional Economy of Three British Prime Ministers, 1951–63', *Journal of British Studies*, 2002, 41(3): 354–87, pp. 359–60. The emotional mob was conceptualised as feminine from the perspective of developing modernist high culture, Huyssen, *After*, p. 47 and sentimental cultural products, such as popular fiction and sentimental melodrama, were associated with women, S. Crozier-De Rosa, 'Popular Fiction and the Emotional Turn: The Case of Women in Late Victorian Britain', *History Compass*, 2010, 8(12): 1340–51 and J. Burrows '"Melodrama of the Dear Old Kind": Sentimentalising British Action Heroines in the 1910s', *Film History*, 2006, 18(2): 163–73.

34 On discourses of British manliness in Victorian children's literature, with an emphasis on heroism, leadership and the defence of civilisation, see R. Knuth, *Children's Literature and British Identity: Imagining a People and a Nation*, Plymouth: Scarecrow Press, 2012, pp. 49–72.

pursued in both 'quality' and popular newspapers. As the Crippen case demonstrated, the combination of extramarital sex and murder was a particularly winning one in terms of newsworthiness.

Thompson/Bywaters

In late 1922, the 'Ilford Murder' captured the headlines. This was the case of Edith Thompson and Frederick Bywaters, lovers who had supposedly conspired to kill Edith's husband, Percy. Bywaters had, in fact, caused Percy's death by stabbing him in the street but Edith was also convicted of murder on the basis of letters she had sent to Bywaters which related her attempts to kill Percy by putting poison and ground up glass in his drinks.[35] The *News of the World* summed it up best, stating that no trial 'has gripped the public imagination with such intensity as that which is the outcome of the Ilford tragedy, pitched as it is in an atmosphere of love, passion, and intrigue'.[36] Stories highlighted the willingness of sensation-seekers, including 'elegantly dressed women', to queue from the early hours to secure a place for the day's trial proceedings.[37] Enterprising unemployed people sold places in the queue for sums reportedly ranging from £2 to £5.[38]

Most newspaper editorials criticised this interest as unhealthy and in bad taste, with sentimentality figuring as a particular *bête noire*. According to the *Daily Mirror*, those who queued outside the Old Bailey 'were affected by the glamour of false sentimentality and feverish drama thrown over the vulgar facts'.[39] For the *Daily News* a 'disgusting atmosphere of cheap sentiment ... clouded the whole case like a bad scent'.[40] The *Manchester Guardian* particularly disapproved of those who queued for admission to the last day, when they would hear the death sentence proclaimed. An editorial opined '[c]ivilisation makes little progress towards abandoning goggling at monsters as an entertainment' and that although people 'no longer form merry parties to attend executions ... we seem in these latter years to be increasingly willing

35 For doubts on the soundness of Edith Thompson's conviction, see R. Weis, *Criminal Justice: The True Story of Edith Thompson*, London: Hamish Hamilton, 1988. On the significance of gender to her conviction and execution, see A. Ballinger*, Dead Woman Walking*, Aldershot: Ashgate, 2000, pp. 221–32. On Thompson as a 'modern' woman, see L. Bland, 'The Trials and Tribulations of Edith Thompson: The Capital Crime of Sexual Incitement in 1920s England', *Journal of British Studies*, 47(3): 624–48. On the sense of self that Thompson constructed in her letters to Bywaters, see M. Houlbrook, '"A Pin to See the Peep Show": Culture, Fiction and Selfhood in Edith Thompson's Letters', *Past & Present*, 2010, 207(1): 215–49.

36 'Ilford Murder Trial: Unparalleled Scenes at Old Bailey', *News of the World*, 10 December 1922.

37 Ibid. Bland highlights how disapproval of female audiences was part of castigating the 'cheap thrill' that murder trials offered, and that similar criticisms were made in the Victorian press, 'The Trials', pp. 642–3.

38 See 'What We Think', *Daily News*, 12 December 1922 and 'The Ilford Murder', *Evening Standard*, 12 December 1922.

39 'Love and Crime', *Daily Mirror*, 12 December 1922.

40 'The Ilford Murder', *Daily News*, 12 December 1922.

to sit on camp stools overnight'.[41] *The Times* described interest in the case as 'prurient' and claimed not to understand why 'the entrance to the Court was besieged day by day by men and women'.[42] The points about civilisation and the echoes of public execution in fascination with the trial were taken up in current affairs weekly, *The Nation and the Athenaeum*, in order to make the case for abolition. Capital punishment turned the trial 'into a beastly melodrama' and caused 'horrible crowds'. Its abolition would 'stay the infection it breeds through the carriers of the Press'.[43]

Such editorials demonstrated the anxieties generated by the sometimes competing demands of civilisation and modernity. Nationwide 'goggling at monsters' was made possible by the expanded readership of the modern press. In 'high culture' publications, there was a rounding on sensationalist popular culture as fostered by newspapers[44] and criticism of the usually 'wholly uninterested masses', who had been roused by a sensational execution story.[45] As discussed in the previous chapter in relation to blood and gore, it is important to scrutinise these jeremiads with regard coverage of capital cases in 'quality' newspapers. *The Times* may have decried the interest of the 'masses' in the Ilford Murder as 'prurient', but had reported for its readers that Freddie Bywaters was 'improperly familiar with Mrs Thompson' and had quoted from the letters Thompson had written to Bywaters, which were read out as evidence in court and which referred to their sex life.[46]

A different tack was taken in the *Daily Mail*, which noted that people's interest in the case was such that they were willing to queue all night for the Old Bailey to open, but stated that it did

> not feel inclined to stigmatise this curiosity as something to be ashamed of. It is very natural and human after all, that exceptional emotion should be evoked by a disaster which has overwhelmed three lives in common ruin.[47]

This difference can be explained by the distinct news values of the *Daily Mail*, which sought to engage female readers and so did not automatically deride the expression of emotion to shore up a masculine habitus.[48] The *Daily*

---

41 'An Ordinary Charge', *Manchester Guardian*, 12 December 1922.
42 'The Ilford Murder Trial', *The Times*, 12 December 1922.
43 'Justice and the Ilford Case', *The Nation and the Athenaeum*, 30 December 1922.
44 'An Ordinary Charge'.
45 'The Ilford Murder Trial'.
46 See 'Ilford Inquest Verdict', *The Times*, 24 October 1922 and 'Ilford Murder Charge: Mrs Thompson's Letters', *The Times*, 25 November 1922.
47 'The Right Verdict', *Daily Mail*, 12 December 1922. This quotation demonstrates that the narrative of the death penalty as an emotional issue, explored in the previous chapter, could be found before the 1950s. It became more prominent, and more related to the issue of capital punishment itself, in the 1940s and 1950s.
48 A. Bingham, *Gender, Modernity, and the Popular Press in Inter-War Britain*, Oxford: Clarendon Press, 2004, p. 26.

Telegraph acknowledged that '[h]uman nature would have been changed out of knowledge if such a case had not drawn crowds to the Old Bailey' but was sure to point out that it was a case that appealed 'to the imagination of the ordinary man and woman',[49] in other words, not the man and woman of distinction.

Like the Crippen case, the Ilford Murder provided the press with the opportunity to discuss and define the distinctions of culture, and also the appropriate limits of the public sphere.[50] Where Crippen was a modern man, Edith Thompson was a modern woman – they could both be understood as representing elements of mass society's moral and cultural decay.[51] From the perspective of an upper-middle-class habitus, interest in the case was warranted, but intense fascination for the purpose of entertainment was vulgar and disgusting. Markers of class and gender were significant – it was the 'masses', the working and lower middle classes that displayed unhealthy curiosity in the drama of sex and death. This curiosity was connected to an emotional identification with the case that was 'repugnant'[52] and should have no place in a masculine public sphere. The inappropriateness of voyeuristic enjoyment of the case was a line taken in the majority of newspapers, with the quality press tending to blame the popular press for its cultivation – whilst also reporting the trial in minute detail.

Deploring the queues for admittance to sensational trials continued to be an editorial staple in relation to high-profile capital cases in the mid-twentieth century. As discussed in the previous chapter, an emotional public sphere developed in relation to capital punishment, which admitted a place for emotional identification with the condemned. However, the press censure of vulgar curiosity continued. In 1946, *The Observer* sighed, '[t]o any sensitive person the Heath trial at the Old Bailey, with its all-night queues, as it were for a ring-side seat at the arena, and its morning and evening columns of description in detail was odious and depressing'.[53] Neville Heath was tried and executed for the murder of Margery Gardner, and was also charged with killing another woman, Doreen Marshall. Central to his case seemed to be his ability to charm women. News stories explained that queuing would be necessary for those seeking admission to the Old Bailey,[54] and that hundreds of people were expected.[55] The trope of trial as theatre was employed by the *Daily Mirror*, which showed two photographs, one of people queuing for the Heath trial outside the Old Bailey, and the other of queues outside the Old

49 'The Ilford Murder', *Daily Telegraph*, 12 December 1922.
50 Bland argues that designating the case the 'Ilford Murder' signalled the lower-middle-class, suburban cultural context of the case, 'The Trials', p. 637.
51 Ibid. and Early, 'Technology'.
52 'The Ilford Murder', *Evening Standard*, 12 December 1922.
53 'Arena', *The Observer*, 29 September 1946.
54 '35 Seats at Heath Trial', *Manchester Dispatch*, 17 September 1946.
55 See 'Heath: Big Guard at Old Bailey', *Daily Mail*, 23 September 1946 and 'Heath Queue Today', *Daily Express*, 23 September 1946.

Vic for the opening of King Lear, under the headline 'They Waited at 2am for Two Dramas'.[56]

In particular, the press predicted the attendance of women at the Heath trial. In *The People*, Stanley Buchanan foresaw 'a gallery of goggle eyed women' indulging their 'morbid curiosity' in Heath.[57] Women's supposed fascination with him was imputed to have a sexual element to it, but the femininity of capital trial audiences was highlighted in relation other cases, continuing a well-established gendered narrative.[58] In 1953, Louisa Merrifield was tried along with her husband, Alfred, for the murder of Sarah Ricketts, an old woman with whom they lived and also cared for. The jury could not agree on Alfred's guilt and he was acquitted, but Louisa was found guilty and hanged. A queue waited for admission to the thirty-second Magistrate's hearing in Blackpool, of which those who were let in were 'nearly all middle-aged women in light summer clothes'.[59] When Louisa Merrifield was sentenced to death two-and-a-half months later, '[a] woman held up her young child as the Judge came out in his wig and red and black robe and then hurried round the back to hold her up again as a black police van took Mrs Merrifield away'.[60] The curiosity of women, particularly where it involved the corruption of their children, was an especial marker of the 'low' nature of the capital trial as entertainment.[61]

---

56 *Daily Mirror*, 24 September 1946. This theatrical metaphor was established in the nineteenth century to draw parallels between the audiences for public hangings and those at the theatre, R. Crone, *Violent Victorians: Popular Entertainment in Nineteenth-Century London*, Manchester: Manchester University Press, 2012 [Kindle Edition], Ch. 3: 'Legendary murderers and material culture'.

57 S. Buchanan, 'World-wide Interest in the Heath Trial', *The People*, 15 September 1946.

58 Bland, 'The Trials', pp. 642–3. Gatrell explains that, in the nineteenth century, women were repeatedly said to have 'attended executions more avidly than men', V. A. C. Gatrell, *The Hanging Tree: Execution and the English People, 1770–1868*, Oxford: Oxford University Press, 1996, p. 68. The attendance of women at public executions had been used to support privatising capital punishment. Madow explores how the privatisation of execution in nineteenth-century New York led to the exclusion of women from the execution scene but not men, who could gain admission through an appointment system, M. Madow, 'Forbidden Spectacle: Executions, the Public and the Press in Nineteenth-Century New York', *Buffalo Law Review*, 1995, 43(2): 461–562, p. 516. When women were admitted, male reporters disapproved, J. D. Bessler, *Death in the Dark: Midnight Executions in America*, Boston, MA: Northeastern University Press, 1997, p. 69. The mob, which was both lower class and feminine, was the site of dangerous, volatile emotions, J. Martschukat, 'A Horrifying Experience? Public Execution and the Emotional Spectator in the New Republic' J. C. E. Gienow-Hecht (ed.), *Emotions in American History: An International Assessment*, Oxford: Berghahn Books, 2010, p. 191. Female spectators were a problem as their attendance signalled their lack of respectability. The appearance of a woman in public was associated with prostitution, A. Linders, 'The Execution Spectacle and State Legitimacy: The Changing Nature of the American Execution Audience, 1833–1937', *Law and Society Review*, 2002, 36(3): 607–56, p. 622.

59 '"Thank You" Says Mrs Merrifield', *Manchester Evening News*, 8 May 1953.

60 'Death Sentence on Mrs Merrifield', *Manchester Guardian*, 1 August 1953.

61 High culture was coded as masculine, Huyssen, *After*, p. 47.

The spectating crowd

The presence (or not) of a crowd at the prison was a constituent part of execution stories. Like the queues for admission to capital trials, the gathering of the crowd on execution morning was a residue of public execution. Once the hoisting of the flag had been abolished, the crowd collected to see the execution notice posted. Press reports frequently gave and commented on (presumably estimated) figures for the size of the crowd. Only around 70 or 80 people were outside Winchester Prison on the morning of Thomas Allaway's execution in 1922 – 'not as much as might be expected'.[62] In contrast, the executions of Edith Thompson and Freddie Bywaters attracted extremely large crowds of 4000 and 5000 respectively, undaunted by the 'downpour of a fine rain'.[63] These may well have been gross overestimates to enhance the drama of the story, but crowds of this size would have matched those for public executions in the late eighteenth and early nineteenth centuries.[64]

The behaviour of the crowd and its composition was a feature of news stories, particularly as there were often quite a few women present. Demonstrations of emotion made the crowd's presence more newsworthy. When Arthur Birkett was hanged at Strangeways in 1912, at the tolling of the bell 'many women and girls in the crowd of about 500 persons outside the gates burst into tears, and one or two became hysterical'.[65] Unruliness was also worthy of comment, such as amongst the 'crowd of nearly 200 women and girls' at Walton Gaol in Liverpool in 1933 at the execution of Richard Hetherington. They 'jeered at a white-haired man who knelt in silent prayer' and then a 'rabble of girls surged into the road-way' when the death notice was posted.[66] As with court audiences, the femininity of the crowd was highlighted. Outside Holloway the day before Ruth Ellis' execution in 1955, the *Daily Express* reported that a crowd of 200 had formed by lunchtime, which included '[w]omen with prams and shopping bags … and children sucking ice cream'.[67] Ruth Ellis' execution was highly controversial and stirred protest on her behalf. However, as the quote about women and their shopping bags illustrates, perceived lack of solemnity on the part of the crowd was represented with disapproval. According to the *Daily Mirror*, an atmosphere of levity existed amongst the 500 people present outside Louisa Merrifield's execution: 'Not one of the 300 women in the crowd showed any emotion. No man doffed his hat. Women, with children in their arms, stood chatting, and teenagers giggled in the crowd'.[68] This appeared within a story that was primarily about

---

62 'Execution of Allaway', *Western Gazette*, 25 August 1922.
63 'Ilford Murderers Hanged', *Daily Mail*, 10 January 1923.
64 Gatrell states that a crowd of 3000–7000 attendees was standard 1770–1830, *The Hanging Tree*, p. 7.
65 'Hymns at an Execution', *Western Gazette*, 26 July 1912.
66 'Execution Scenes: Women Jeer at Praying Man', *Western Gazette*, 23 June 1933.
67 'Ruth Ellis – Jail Crowd Chant, Shout', *Daily Express*, 13 July 1955.
68 'Move On the Merrifield Ghouls', *Daily Mirror*, 19 September 1953.

the 'gloating sightseers' who gathered by the garden wall of the Blackpool bungalow in which the murder of Sarah Ricketts had taken place. By the 1950s, the *Daily Mirror* pursued a strongly abolitionist line, which contextualises the story's criticism of 'ghoulish' sightseers and the emotionless crowd.

The reporting of the presence of the crowd outside executions meant that there was a continued sense of public participation in hanging as an event, however limited this was. Although hanging took place behind prison walls, it was not out of view culturally as the previous chapter established. Some press reports, such as the one about Louisa Merrifield, underlined the crowd's apparent approbation for hanging the condemned (in this case to find this attitude callous). A celebratory atmosphere was reported outside Pentonville for the execution of John Christie in 1953. Two hundred people watched the notice be posted, while they 'gossiped, laughed and joked'.[69]

Press reports cannot be unproblematically accepted as evidence of the execution crowd's composition and behaviour. Certain recurrent themes, such as the presence and behaviour of women, indicate that these were formulaic tropes with which to tell the story (and reveal much about understandings of the disruptiveness of femininity in public space). By the 1950s, crowds were regularly reported as being 200 strong, indicating that this was a standard figure rather than a journalist's best estimate of the size of the crowd. However, the crowd's reactions were not always reported as being the same, and the type of murder and perceptions of the social identity of the condemned seem to have been significant to how the crowd responded. Of course, attending the prison on execution morning was not necessarily a form of entertainment, as the next chapter explores through consideration of popular protests.

Sightseers and daytrippers

Another form of 'lexitainment', and a means to come face-to-face with the executed, was to visit waxwork exhibitions, the most prominent of which was the Chamber of Horrors in Madame Tussaud's in London. This was one of its most popular displays from the nineteenth century onwards.[70] Waxwork shows were regarded as a 'spectacular', rather than 'aesthetic' form of entertainment, relying on the visual (rather than contemplative) and the presence of a crowd.[71] As such, they were 'low' or popular culture, aimed at a diverse public.[72] A sense of the Chamber of Horrors as family entertainment was communicated by a *Times* article on bank holiday visitors to Madame Tussaud's in 1910: 'Most visitors went to see the portrait model of "Dr" Crippen

---

69 'Prison Crowd Jokes as Christie Dies', *Western Morning News*, 16 July 1953.

70 A. V. Seaton, 'Guided by the Dark: From Thanatopsis to Thanatourism', *International Journal of Heritage Studies*, 1996, 2(4): 234–44, p. 243.

71 M. E. Bloom, *Waxworks: A Cultural Obsession*, Minneapolis: University of Minnesota Press, 2003, p. 14.

72 Ibid., p. 16.

in the dock'.[73] This witnessing of Crippen's form, post-execution, was connected to 'spectacle at the gallows and with gallows culture',[74] drawing on erstwhile traditions of public execution.[75]

In the nineteenth century, waxworks exhibitions were a hugely popular form of entertainment but, after the First World War, their appeal waned. Bloom states that 'silent film diminished the appeal of wax museums because of its more consistent and compelling illusion of movement'.[76] An article in the *Manchester Guardian* in 1922 lamented the decline of waxworks in favour of the 'kinema' and the stage, and noted that even 'the display of the identical rope with which some famous murderer was hanged fails to create any interest in a jaded mind'.[77] In 1923, the same newspaper reported the closure of Reynold's Waxwork Show in Liverpool after 80 years of business. It was the second largest after Tussaud's. The piece commented that there was not much hope of selling off the murderers 'when sixpence will introduce you any evening to an assassin who slaughters with every appearance of reality'. Waxworks had become 'a quaint and rather amiably old-fashioned spectacle'.[78]

Despite this contraction in the popularity of waxwork shows, they did not disappear and in the mid-twentieth century remained a means of witnessing notorious executed murderers. After the Second World War, large crowds visited Tussaud's to see the models of Neville Heath, John Haigh and John Christie.[79] Seaside waxworks exhibitions also displayed models of sensational murderers. Continuing the theme of women's fascination with Heath, the *Yorkshire Observer* reported that 'hundreds of women are paying to see a life-size model of Heath, attired in sports jacket and flannel trousers in a Brighton waxworks exhibition'.[80] Audiences for waxwork models of the executed were gratified quickly. According to Pilbeam, Heath's waxwork was installed in Tussaud's Chamber of Horrors 20 minutes after his execution[81] and the *Daily Mirror* reported that John Christie's effigy appeared in the Chamber of Horrors within an hour of his hanging.[82]

Spectators also pursued their own, non-organised sight-seeing in relation to high-profile cases.[83] The *Manchester Guardian* reported that neighbours

73 'Bank Holiday in London: Madame Tussaud's', *The Times*, 27 December 1910.
74 B. Melman, *The Culture of History: English Uses of the Past, 1800–1953*, Oxford: Oxford University Press, 2006, p. 39.
75 Ibid., p. 31.
76 Bloom, *Waxworks*, p. 21.
77 A. Bowes, 'The Decline in Waxworks', *Manchester Guardian*, 7 August 1922.
78 'A Last Appearance', *Manchester Guardian*, 20 March 1923.
79 P. Pilbeam, *Madame Tussaud and the History of Waxworks*, London: Continuum, 2006, p. 210.
80 'Heath Model at Waxworks Show', *Yorkshire Observer*, 15 October 1946.
81 Pilbeam, *Madame*, p. 212.
82 'Killer Christie Joins the Waxworks', *Daily Mirror*, 16 July 1953.
83 This desire to visit the crime scene was a continuation of Victorian-era sightseeing and souvenir hunting after high-profile murders, see Crone, *Violent Victorians*, 'Legendary murderers and material culture'.

claimed 'never a day goes by without its quota of "pilgrims"' in the Notting Hill cafe where Christie had tea with his victims.[84] As mentioned above, visitors clustered outside the Blackpool bungalow where Louisa Merrifield killed Sarah Ricketts, leading the mayor to ask the police to protect it.[85] Seaton argues that the increased geographical specificity in press reporting of well-known murders since the nineteenth century increased public interest and promoted tourism.[86] Public fascination with high-profile capital cases could be a source of revenue for those involved. Louisa Merrifield's husband, Alfred, was paid £200 for his waxwork to be exhibited alongside hers in Blackpool's Chamber of Horrors.[87] An interview with him by Lionel Crane for the *Daily Mirror* situated Alfred's eccentric behaviour within the context of Blackpool[88] where '[f]reaks are ten a penny and the weird and wonderful happens every day'. Alfred Merrifield was currently Blackpool's 'greatest one man draw'. According to the profile at least, Alfred expressed pride in the popularity of Louisa's effigy, claiming 'they've had 1,000 an hour going through since they put Louisa in there. Come and have a look'.[89]

Working-class seaside resorts like Blackpool had long signified mass leisure, and the Golden Mile symbolised the tawdry pleasures of 'low' culture. The story of the waxworks of Louisa and Alfred Merrifield was a harmless, if eccentric, novelty. Whilst the 'ghouls' who crowded round the bungalow were to be disparaged for their lack of taste and sensitivity, the sideshow was not a threat. Louisa was 'never an attractive woman – plump, with untidy hair, thick woollen stockings, dowdy clothes and spectacles'.[90] Consequently, she could be a figure of amusement and ridicule, as could her publicity-seeking husband. Ruth Ellis was a different matter. Her spectacular femininity, as Grant argues in relation to the execution of women, exposed the violence underlying the state's action.[91] When her effigy appeared in the Blackpool Chamber of Horrors clad in 'a low-cut, black evening gown and black tuile stole' there

84 'Sightseers at Pentonville: Christie Executed', *Manchester Guardian*, 16 July 1953.
85 'Move on the Merrifield Ghouls'.
86 Seaton, 'Guided', p. 242. Such sightseeing can be conceptualised as 'thanatourism', defined by Seaton as 'travel to a location wholly, or partially, motivated by the desire for actual or symbolic encounters with death, particularly … violent death', p. 240.
87 'Mr Merrifield is Among the Horrors', *Daily Express*, 2 October 1953.
88 The most popular destination for northern working-class holidaymakers, Blackpool was emblematic of working-class leisure and extravagance, see G. S. Cross, *Time and Money: The Making of Consumer Culture*, London: Routledge, 1993, pp. 114, 124. The 'freaks' could be found on the Golden Mile, where Tussaud's Chamber of Horrors was located. Cross and Walton argue that Blackpool crowds were viewed as harmless by elites but received criticism from socialists and the organised working class, G. S. Cross and J. K. Walton, *The Playful Crowd: Pleasure Places in the Twentieth-Century*, New York: Columbia University Press, 2005, p. 98.
89 L. Crane, '"Watch 'em Looking at Me" Said Mr Merrifield', *Daily Mirror*, 6 October 1953.
90 'The One Charm of Mrs Louisa Merrifield', *Daily Mirror*, 1 August 1953.
91 C. Grant, *Crime and Punishment in Contemporary Culture*, Abingdon: Routledge, 2004, p. 126. On Ruth Ellis' 'spectacular femininity' see J. Rose, 'Margaret Thatcher and Ruth Ellis', *New Formations*, 1988, 6: 3–29.

were calls to have it banned.[92] For the *Daily Herald*, the waxwork was 'a revolting tribute to the revolting emotions which have been fed by her execution'.[93]

In Parliament, Labour MP Tom Price asked Gwilym Lloyd George, the Home Secretary, if the exhibition of waxworks of convicted murderers could be outlawed.[94] Public opinion had been 'shocked and scandalised by the gross commercialism' of the Ruth Ellis effigy displayed in Blackpool, which had appeared only one day after she was hanged. This was 'degrading Britain in the eyes of many foreign visitors and also demoralising young people who are taken into these disgusting exhibitions'. Lloyd George replied that it was not possible to legislate for 'every departure from good taste' and that if public opinion was really shocked, it could be remedied by the public refusing to visit the show. Labour MP Emrys Hughes asked why Lloyd George talked of 'execrable taste' when he was 'less enlightened and humane than his colleague the Secretary of State for Scotland, who reprieves people and does not execute them?'.[95] Thus, the Labour MPs used the issue of taste and the Ruth Ellis waxwork to make an abolitionist point.

Stage and screen

Stage plays of famous murder cases, which culminated in the execution of the murderer, were another means for the public to engage in imagining capital punishment for the sake of entertainment. Increased verisimilitude could be achieved by employing an actual hangman to carry this out. In December 1927, John Ellis, a retired Chief Executioner who had hanged Hawley Crippen and Edith Thompson, appeared at the Grand Theatre in Gravesend playing the Victorian hangman, William Marwood, in *Charles Peace*, a play about the life and times of the famous burglar and murderer. The *Daily Herald* described how 'Peace, in convict's clothes, was pinioned by Ellis and the rope drawn around his neck. Then the lever was pulled dramatically and he vanished through a trap-door with realistic suddenness'.[96] Newspapers disapproved of the theatre audience's delight in witnessing the rituals of capital punishment. They 'seemed thoroughly to enjoy the trial scene and laughed at the judge when he donned the black cap and pronounced sentence'.[97] The *Daily Express* reported that the hanging was carried out 'in the full sight of

---

92 'Row over Ruth Ellis Effigy as 3000 Queue to See it', *Daily Express*, 15 July 1955. The *Express* reported that a local councillor and Methodist minister had asked for the waxwork to be banned.

93 'What we think: Aftermath', *Daily Herald*, 14 July 1955.

94 The disapproval of the waxwork from the *Daily Herald* and Labour MPs illustrates Cross and Walton's point that criticism of frivolous working-class pleasures was not confined to establishment elites. The development of mass society, with its attendant consumerism and shallow pleasures, was also the subject of left wing disapproval, *The Playful Crowd*.

95 Hansard, HC Deb, 21 July 1955, vol. 544, cols 546–7.

96 'Executioner as Actor', *Daily Herald*, 13 December 1927.

97 'Execution Scene on the Stage', *Daily News*, 13 December 1927.

an enthusiastically excited audience with the promptness and expedition that comes from long practice'.[98]

John Ellis' presence made the hanging scene uncomfortably realistic – and was also the reason to go and see the play. The executioner's appearance was 'the signal for a burst of applause from the audience'[99] and '[t]he whole attraction of the melodrama is obviously the hanging, with Ellis taking the part as the hangman. The people who came to the theatre tonight wanted to see Ellis and the way he did his work'.[100] The *Daily News* expressed the opinion that the public should have boycotted the show[101] and reported a resolution passed by the Executive Committee of the Variety Artists' Federation condemning Ellis' appearance as an 'attempt to pander to morbid-minded people'.[102] The *Daily Herald* quoted Labour MP Philip Snowden that the play was 'an outrage upon public decency' and also Conservative Sir Henry Brittain, who stated that 'even the Grand Guignol ... would draw the line at having the Public Executioner of France to perform on the stage'.[103] The Lord Chamberlain interviewed the stage manager at the Grand Theatre but no cuts were made to the play and no action was taken against Ellis.[104]

The appearance of a real hangman on stage, rather than the depiction of execution, was the problem. Execution scenes were frequently praised in reviews of theatre productions, or viewed as harmless fun. The *Daily Mirror*'s dramatic critic found the execution scene in a 1928 stage version of Thackeray's *The Rose and the Ring* 'especially effective'.[105] The *Manchester Guardian* described a 1927 production of *Maria Marten* at the Royal Osborne Theatre as 'one of the greatest of last century's barnstorming classics' and reported that 'good, hearty laughter was the reaction to the terrific fight that preceded the murder in the barn, and to the execution'.[106] *The Times* noted with approval that in the opera, *Schwanda*, staged in Covent Garden, 'the execution scene ... brings the climax of the first act in a riot of colour'.[107] Realism was also a

98 'Hangman Acts in Play', *Daily Express*, 13 December 1927.
99 'Execution Scene on the Stage'.
100 'Hangman Acts in Play'.
101 'The "Hangman" Play', *Daily News*, 16 December 1927.
102 'Executioner Play', *Daily News*, 16 December 1927. This resolution was also covered in the *Manchester Guardian*, which explained the Federation felt that an execution play with a real hangman was not 'an edifying spectacle as an entertainment', 'The Hanging Scene', 16 December 1927.
103 'Hangman-cum-Showman: Storm of Protest', *Daily Herald*, 14 December 1927.
104 'The "Hangman" Play' and 'Executioner in Play', *Daily Mirror*, 16 December 1927.
105 'Rose and the Ring', *Daily Mirror*, 21 November 1928.
106 'Maria Marten', *Manchester Guardian*, 11 October 1927. This play was a melodrama based on the famous 'Red Barn' murder of 1828 and the first versions of it were performed in 1840, aimed at working-class audiences, K. Leaver, 'Victorian Melodrama and the Performance of Poverty', *Victorian Literature and Culture*, 1999, 27(2): 443–56. It became one of the most popular melodramas of the nineteenth century, Crone, *Violent Victorians*, Ch. 4: 'Murder Melodramas'.
107 'Covent Garden Opera', *The Times*, 12 May 1934.

virtue – reviewing the Strauss opera, *Till Eulenspiegel*, at the Munich Music Festival, *The Times* praised the climax as being 'as vivid and thrilling as a real trial and execution scene on the stage'.[108] These theatrical productions offered execution as entertainment from the safe distance of history, in the case of *The Rose and the Ring* and *Maria Marten*, or were reassuringly highbrow in the case of the operas. John Ellis was a real hangman who had executed people only three or four years before he appeared on stage in *Charles Peace* operating a real gallows. This dangerously attached entertaining spectacle to modern capital punishment – and eroded its prized secrecy.

Home Secretary, William Joyson-Hicks, explained in the House of Commons that he could not prevent public performances such as *Charles Peace*, especially as Ellis was retired from his role as hangman. He agreed that 'these exhibitions are not seemly' but stated they could not be banned.[109] The same principle held in 1932, when Ellis toured fairgrounds 'with a show demonstrating an actual hanging'.[110] Despite objections from Liberal MP, Geoffrey Mander, Home Secretary, Herbert Samuel, opined that he had no power to stop Ellis.[111] Discomfort at Ellis' public appearances was not universally the reaction of the parliamentary elite. Scottish Conservative MP, Frederick Macquisten, joked that Ellis' show could 'prevent serious crime' and as such could be offered to Chicago after he had completed his tour.[112] Like certain of the correspondents to *The Times* about Crippen, Macquisten saw a place for the pedagogy of the scaffold in securing deterrence.

Cinema was another means of portraying execution for the purposes of entertainment. By the 1950s and 1960s, British and American films tackled capital punishment as a social issue through debating the morality of its use and highlighting the problem of executing the innocent.[113] Sometimes this also involved the depiction of execution itself. The biopic *I Want to Live!* portrayed the case of Barbara Graham, a Californian woman found guilty in 1953, along with two men, of murdering a 62-year-old woman. She was executed in the gas chamber at San Quentin in 1955.[114] In the film, Graham is in fact

108 'Munich Music Festival', *The Times*, 4 August 1931.
109 Hansard, HC Deb, 21 July 1927, vol. 212, col. 409.
110 'The "Fun" of the Fair', *Western Daily Press*, 20 April 1932.
111 Hansard, HC Deb, 19 April 1932, vol. 264, col. 1398–99.
112 'The "Fun" of the Fair' and HoC Debates, 19 August 1932.
113 *Yield to the Night*, as discussed in the previous chapter, has a strong anti-capital punishment theme, J. L. Thompson [Motion Picture], Kenwood Productions, UK, 1956. *Time Without Pity* explores wrongful conviction and a father's race against the clock to save his condemned son, J. Losey, [Motion Picture] Harlequin Productions Ltd, UK, 1957. *Beyond a Reasonable Doubt* takes up the issue of doubts about the safety of capital punishment through the story of a journalist who voluntarily frames himself for murder – with the twist in the tale that he is guilty, F. Lang [Motion Picture] Bert E. Friedlob Productions, USA, 1956.
114 R. Wise, *I Want to Live!* [Motion Picture] Figaro, USA, 1958. On the film as women's biography, see D. Bingham, 'I Do Want to Live!: Female Voices, Male Discourse, and Hollywood Biopics', *Cinema Journal*, 1999, 38(3): 3–26, and for an historical analysis of the Graham case's importance (including discussion of the film), see K. A. Cairns, *Proof of Guilt:*

innocent of the crime but seals her fate when she is tricked into making a false confession to an undercover police officer. *I Want to Live!* makes much of its verisimilitude, with a caption at the beginning proclaiming 'You are about to see a factual story', asserted to be based on news articles and letters by Graham.

Public fascination with Graham as a celebrity murderess and the glare of the media spotlight are key themes of the film. Newspaper headlines are frequently shown and Graham has a group of devoted teenage fans who follow her from court to the prison gates. This publicity extends to the gas chamber itself. The preparation of the cyanide eggs is depicted in detail, as is Graham's final night in the condemned cell. She is highly aware of her celebrity status, commenting wryly on her death cell attire – scarlet silk pyjamas – 'I wouldn't want to disappoint my public'. Journalists cram into the gas chamber to witness her execution. Even as her life is extinguished, she remains in the public eye and the cinema audience is implicated in this spectacle. *I Want to Live!* was a hit film and Susan Hayward won both a Golden Globe and an Oscar for her portrayal of Graham.

In Britain, the film 'r[a]n into difficulties with the censorship' and four minutes were cut from the execution scene,[115] demonstrating elite reservations about 'realistic' portrayals of the death penalty. However, as the review of *I Want to Live!* in *The Times* pointed out, the 'solemn documentary approach when it comes to the technical preparations for the execution is the keynote of the whole' as this conveyed the horror of the procedure.[116] The film's release was delayed from February to July 1959 after wrangling between United Artists and the British Board of Film Censors over the cuts. This controversy was covered in the press, with a *Reynolds News* journalist travelling to Amsterdam to watch and report on the film.[117] The BBFC removed scenes which depicted Graham in the gas chamber and some of the execution preparation on the grounds that these would appeal to 'people with a morbid curiosity'.[118] In an interview with the *Sunday Express*, John Trevelyan, Secretary of the BBFC, explained that if it were to allow the details of execution to be shown on film, 'the next thing we know there will be a camera going into Wandsworth to show a chap being swung'.[119]

Barbara Graham and the Politics of Executing Women in America, Lincoln: University of Nebraska Press, 2013.

115 'I Want to Live: A Camera in the Condemned Cell', *The Times*, 22 July 1959.

116 'I Want to Live: A Camera in the Condemned Cell'. *The Quare Fellow*, an adaptation of a Brendan Behan play, depicts preparations at an Irish prison for a hanging, including prisoners digging the grave of the condemned the night before. It shows the noose being placed around the neck of the hooded 'quare fellow' although cuts away from the moment of the drop itself – A. Dreifuss, *The Quare Fellow* [Motion Picture] Liger Films, UK, 1962. *3 Clear Sundays*, an episode of the BBC's 'Wednesday Play', shows the preparations of the hangman and his assistant, including the practice hanging of a dummy – D. Potter, *The Wednesday Play: 3 Clear Sundays* [Television Episode], BBC, UK, 1965.

117 A. Aldgate and J. C. Robertson, *Censorship in Theatre and Cinema*, Edinburgh: Edinburgh University Press, 2005, p. 171.

118 Ibid., p. 172.

119 Ibid. The full version was released in Britain on video in 1998.

Conclusion

Execution as lexitainment persisted in twentieth-century Britain and retained many continuities with elements of Victorian popular entertainment. The press was crucial to turning certain capital cases into sensations that could be consumed for pleasure, and was also the primary means for a conversation about both the nature of press reporting and of public fascination with the death penalty. The disavowal of the lower class and the feminine was an important way to distinguish high culture from mass culture, and to exclude these contaminating influences from an upper-middle-class, masculine habitus. That the popular press also frequently disparaged 'goggling' at the condemned demonstrates that to be seen to embrace sensationalism was a marker of disreputability into the mid-twentieth century. However, whether 'quality' or popular, newspapers were sure to relate the sensational details of high-profile cases to their readers.

In relation to other forms of death penalty lexitainment, the danger of coming too close to the reality of bodily punishment was a source of cultural anxiety from high culture and elite perspectives, whether it was witnessing a real hangman operate a real gallows, or seeing the waxwork of a condemned woman too soon after she was hanged. To be entertained in such circumstances was 'morbid' – it was unhealthy and uncivilised, sounding an unwelcome echo of the execution crowd. The movie camera threatened an even greater level of 'reality', whereby the audience could be present in the gas chamber and see for themselves exactly what was involved in death penalty preparations – raising the danger of using this technology to show actual executions. Unlike John Ellis' shows or Ruth Ellis' seaside waxwork, the execution scene of *I Want to Live!* could be censored and brought under paternalistic control. If anything, the BBFC's cuts were designed to blunt the film's abolitionist message, which demonstrates how it is important not to straightforwardly interpret the mid-twentieth century as an era when elites strove to counter the bloodthirsty retentionism of the masses. In relation to elite responses to capital punishment culture, questions of 'seemliness' and 'appropriateness' (and their unarticulated connection with the privacy of state power) could take precedence over issues of morality and justice.

Newspapers, news websites and magazines

Daily Express
Daily Herald
Daily Mail
Daily Mirror
Daily News
Daily Telegraph
Evening Standard
MailOnline

Manchester Dispatch
Manchester Evening News
Manchester Guardian
News of the World
The Nation and the Athenaeum
The Observer
The People
The Times
Western Daily Press
Western Gazette
Western Morning News
Yorkshire Observer

Bibliography

Aldgate, A. and Robertson, J. C., *Censorship in Theatre and Cinema*, Edinburgh: Edinburgh University Press, 2005.

Bailey, P., 'Conspiracies of Meaning: Music-Hall and the Knowingness of Popular Culture', *Past & Present*, 1994, 144: 138–70.

Ballinger, A., *Dead Woman Walking: Executed Women in England and Wales, 1900–55*, Aldershot: Ashgate, 2000.

Bessler, J. D., *Death in the Dark: Midnight Executions in America*, Boston, MA: Northeastern University Press, 1997.

Bingham, A., *Gender, Modernity, and the Popular Press in Inter-War Britain*, Oxford: Clarendon Press, 2004.

Bingham, D., 'I Do Want to Live!: Female Voices, Male Discourse, and Hollywood Biopics', *Cinema Journal*, 1999, 38(3): 3–26.

Bland, L., 'The Trials and Tribulations of Edith Thompson: The Capital Crime of Sexual Incitement in 1920s England', *Journal of British Studies*, 47(3): 624–48.

Bloom, M. E., *Waxworks: A Cultural Obsession*, Minneapolis: University of Minnesota Press, 2003.

Bourdieu, P., *Distinction: A Social Critique of Judgment and Taste*, London: Routledge and Kegan Paul, 1984.

Brantlinger, P., 'What is "Sensational" About the "Sensation" Novel', *Nineteenth Century Fiction*, 1982, 37(1): 1–28.

Burney, I. and Pemberton, N., 'The Rise and Fall of Celebrity Pathology', *British Medical Journal*, 2010, 341: 1319–21.

Burrows, J., '"Melodrama of the Dear Old Kind": Sentimentalising British Action Heroines in the 1910s', *Film History*, 2006, 18(2): 163–73.

Cairns, K. A., *Proof of Guilt: Barbara Graham and the Politics of Executing Women in America*, Lincoln: University of Nebraska Press, 2013.

Crone, R., *Violent Victorians: Popular Entertainment in Nineteenth-Century London*, Manchester: Manchester University Press, 2012 [Kindle Edition].

Cross, G. S., *Time and Money: The Making of Consumer Culture*, London: Routledge, 1993.

Cross, G. S. and Walton, J. K., *The Playful Crowd: Pleasure Places in the Twentieth-Century*, New York: Columbia University Press, 2005.

Crozier-De Rosa, S., 'Popular Fiction and the Emotional Turn: The Case of Women in Late Victorian Britain', *History Compass*, 2010, 8(12): 1340–51.

D'Cruze, S., '"The Damned Place was Haunted": The Gothic Middlebrow Culture and Inter-War "Notable Trials"', *Literature and History*, 2006, 15(1): 37–58.

Dreifuss, A., *The Quare Fellow* [Motion Picture] Liger Films, UK, 1962.

Early, J. E., 'Technology, Modernity, and the "Little Man": Crippen's Capture by Wireless', *Victorian Studies*, 1996, 39(3): 309–37.

——'Keeping Ourselves to Ourselves: Violence in the Edwardian Suburb', S. D'Cruze (ed.), *Everyday Violence in Britain, 1850–1950*, London: Longman, 2000, 170–84.

Francis, M., 'Tears, Tantrums and Bared Teeth: The Emotional Economy of Three British Prime Ministers', 1951–63, *Journal of British Studies*, 2002, 41(3): 354–87.

Friedman, L. M., 'Lexitainment: Legal Process as Theater', *DePaul Law Review*, 2001, 50(2): 539–58.

Gans, H., *Popular Culture and High Culture: An Analysis and Evaluation of Taste*, New York: Basic Books, 1999, 2nd edition.

Garland, D., 'The Problem of the Body in Modern Punishment', *Social Research*, 2011, 78(3): 767–98.

Gatrell, V. A. C., *The Hanging Tree: Execution and the English People, 1770–1868*, Oxford: Oxford University Press, 1996.

Goc, N., *Women, Infanticide and the Press, 1822–1922*, Aldershot: Ashgate, 2013.

Grant, C., *Crime and Punishment in Contemporary Culture*, Abingdon: Routledge, 2004.

Gregory, J., *Victorians Against the Gallows*, London: I. B. Tauris, 2012.

Hammel, A., *Ending the Death Penalty: The European Experience in Global Perspective*, Basingstoke: Palgrave MacMillan, 2010.

Hansard, HC Deb, 21 July 1927, vol 212, col. 409.

——HC Deb, 19 April 1932, vol 264, col. 1398–99.

——HC Deb, 21 July 1955, vol 544, cols 546–7.

Houlbrook, M., '"A Pin to See the Peep Show": Culture, Fiction and Selfhood in Edith Thompson's Letters', *Past & Present*, 2010, 207(1): 215–49.

Huyssen, A., *After the Great Divide: Modernism, Mass Culture, Postmodernism*, Bloomington: Indiana University Press, 1986.

Joyce, P., *Visions of the People: Industrial England and the Question of Class, c 1848–1914*, Cambridge: Cambridge University Press, 1993.

Kaufman-Osborn, T. V., *From Noose to Needle*, Ann Arbor: University of Michigan Press, 2002.

Kift, D., *The Victorian Music Hall: Culture, Class and Conflict*, Cambridge: Cambridge University Press, 1996.

Knuth, R., *Children's Literature and British Identity: Imagining a People and a Nation*, Plymouth: Scarecrow Press, 2012.

Lang, F., *Beyond a Reasonable Doubt* [Motion Picture] Bert E. Friedlob Productions, USA, 1956.

Larson, E., *Thunderstruck*, New York: Random House, 2007.

Leaver, K., 'Victorian Melodrama and the Performance of Poverty', *Victorian Literature and Culture*, 1999, 27(2): 443–56.

Linders, A., 'The Execution Spectacle and State Legitimacy: The Changing Nature of the Execution Audience, 1833–1937', *Law and Society Review*, 2002, 36(3): 607–56.

Losey, J., *Time Without Pity* [Motion Picture] Harlequin Productions Ltd, UK, 1957.

Madow, M., 'Forbidden Spectacle: Executions, the Public and the Press in Nineteenth-Century New York', *Buffalo Law Review*, 1995, 43(2): 461–562.

Martschukat, J., 'Nineteenth-Century Executions as Performances of Law, Death and Civilization', A. Sarat and C. Boulanger (eds), *The Cultural Lives of Capital Punishment*, Stanford, CA: Stanford University Press, 2005, 49–68.

——'A Horrifying Experience? Public Execution and the Emotional Spectator in the New Republic', J. C. E. Gienow-Hecht (ed.), *Emotions in American History: An International Assessment*, Oxford: Berghahn Books, 2010, 181–200.

Melman, B., *The Culture of History: English Uses of the Past, 1800–1953*, Oxford: Oxford University Press, 2006.

Mercer, C., 'Regular Imaginings: The Newspaper and the Nation', T. Bennett (ed.), *Celebrating the Nation: A Critical Study of Australia's Bicentenary*, London: Allen and Unwin, 1992, 26–46.

Orwell, G., *Decline of the English Murder and Other Essays*, London: Penguin Books, 1965.

Pilbeam, P., *Madame Tussaud and the History of Waxworks*, London: Continuum, 2006.

Potter, D., *The Wednesday Play: 3 Clear Sundays* [Television Episode], BBC, UK, 1965.

Robins, J., *The Magnificent Spilsbury and the Case of the Brides in the Bath*, London: John Murray, 2010.

Rose, J., 'Margaret Thatcher and Ruth Ellis', *New Formations*, 1988, 6: 3–29.

Rowbotham, J. and Stevenson, K., 'Introduction', J. Rowbotham and K. Stevenson (eds), *Criminal Conversations: Victorian Crimes, Social Panic and Moral Outrage*, Columbus: Ohio State University Press, 2005, xxi–xxxii.

Seaton, A. V., 'Guided by the Dark: From Thanatopsis to Thanatourism', *International Journal of Heritage Studies*, 1996, 2(4): 234–44.

Thompson, J. L., *Yield to the Night* [Motion Picture], Kenwood Productions, UK, 1956.

Watson, K. D., *Poisoned Lives: English Poisoners and their Victims*, London: Continuum, 2004.

Weis, R., *Criminal Justice: The True Story of Edith Thompson*, London: Hamish Hamilton, 1988.

Westman, K. E., '"For Her Generation the Newspaper was a Book": Media, Mediation and Oscillation in Virginia Woolf's Between the Acts', *Journal of Modern Literature*, 2006, 29(2): 1–18.

Wise, R., *I Want to Live!* [Motion Picture] Figaro, USA, 1958.

Young, F., "The Trial of Hawley Harvey Crippen", *Notable British Trials*, London: Hodge, 1920.

4   Popular protest against execution

Entertainment was not the only reason for crowds to gather outside the prison on execution morning. Occasionally, cases sparked spontaneous popular protests. Perceptions of unequal treatment were central to this and highlighted a persistent weakness of capital punishment – that, depending on certain factors, it could appear to be disproportionate and cruel. Spontaneous protests were not necessarily instances of the upwelling of abolitionism, which opposed the death penalty on principle. Rather, they were in response to perceived injustice in relation to particular cases and were linked to cases in which attempts to secure a reprieve had failed. Specific capital cases could become vehicles for debating public understandings of justice. This chapter discusses protests against the execution of certain individuals in the early and mid-twentieth century. It goes on to examine Violet van der Elst's long running campaign against the death penalty.

The execution of Ernest Kelly at Strangeways in 1913 was one such inflammatory case of perceived injustice. Kelly, 20, was accomplice to Edward Hilton, 18, in the murder of an Oldham bookseller. Hilton was reprieved on the grounds that he was a 'mental defective', and on the basis of his youth. As Hilton was the one believed to have actually killed the victim by clubbing him to death, and as Kelly was also a young man, efforts were made for Kelly's reprieve. In addition to sending a petition to the King, a local deputation consisting of MPs, the Chief Constable and the Mayor was denied a meeting about the case with the Home Secretary.[1] In a statement to the press, the deputation expressed its view that 'such treatment is wrong to their constituents, an injustice to Kelly, and discourteous to themselves'.[2] A meeting in Oldham in support of a reprieve was the site of '[s]cenes of disorder'.[3]

The news that a reprieve had been denied was met in Oldham with 'a great outburst of popular indignation'.[4] Violent protest broke out and '[w]indows in tramcars, fire stations, and a police station were smashed, missiles were

---

1 'Oldham Murder: No Reprieve for Kelly', *Manchester Guardian*, 17 December 1913.
2 Ibid.
3 'Oldham Murder: Agitation on Behalf of Kelly', *Manchester Guardian*, 16 December 1913.
4 'Execution of the Oldham Murderer', *The Times*, 18 December 1913.

thrown at the police'.[5] Cries of '"Rescue Kelly"' and '"March to Manchester and rescue Kelly!"' preceded a ten-mile march of 10,000 people from Oldham to Strangeways Prison in Manchester.[6] Once there, they hurled sticks and stones at the police.[7] Newspapers emphasised that the protest was a popular, working-class one. Whilst stating that there were many female demonstrators, the *Manchester Guardian* described the majority of the crowd as 'young men of the operative class'.[8] More evocatively, the *Western Gazette* described how 'they tramped the ten miles to Manchester, their clogs clattering on the city's pavement flags'.[9] News reports highlighted the unusual nature of the Oldham protest, which was 'without precedent in modern times'.[10]

The Oldham protest was a localised response to perceived unfairness of treatment, which demonstrated the ambivalence that was woven into the application of the death penalty. As Hilton appeared to be the more culpable of the two young men, reprieving him and executing Kelly seemed like an injustice, even though the decision, which had taken into account Hilton's 'mental defectiveness', was consistent with established practice and criminal justice thinking.[11] Although not a prominent national issue at the time, capital punishment had stirred local opposition. Reports of the dismissive reception the Home Office gave to the Oldham delegation no doubt helped to stoke unrest in a region with a tradition of popular radicalism.[12]

The possibly class-based implications of reprieve decisions were brought into sharp relief by the hanging of Henry Jacoby in 1922. Jacoby was only 18, making his execution contentious. A pantry boy in a London hotel, he had battered to death a guest, 66-year-old Lady Alice White, during the course of an attempted robbery. The jury at his trial 'strongly recommended him to mercy on the ground of his youth, and because they believed he had no intention of killing when he entered the room'.[13] Even so, Jacoby was hanged and his youth was a pressure point creating ambivalence about his execution. Still hoping for a reprieve, a *Manchester Guardian* editorial commented that 'a decision to carry out the sentence in this case would be a step back to a barbarous past'.[14] *The Times*, on the other hand, emphasised that Jacoby was

5 'Amazing Scene at an Execution', *Cornishman*, 25 December 1913.
6 'March to an Execution', *Western Gazette*, 19 December 1913.
7 'Amazing Scenes at an Execution'.
8 'Oldham Murder: Execution of Kelly at Strangeways', *Manchester Guardian*, 18 December 1913.
9 'March to an Execution'.
10 'Oldham Murder: Execution of Kelly at Strangeways'.
11 On views and practices in relation to reprieve for the young and the insane, see R. G. Chadwick, *Bureaucratic Mercy: The Home Office and the Treatment of Capital Cases in Victorian England*, unpublished PhD thesis, Rice University, 1989, pp. 271–338.
12 See J. E. King, '"We Could Eat the Police": Popular Violence in the North Lancashire Cotton Strike of 1878', *Victorian Studies*, 1985, 28(3): 439–71 and M. H. Blewett, 'Traditions and Customs of Lancashire Popular Radicalism in Late Nineteenth-Century Industrial America', *International Labour and Working Class History*, 1992, 42: 5–19.
13 'Jacoby Sentenced to Death', *Manchester Guardian*, 29 April 1922.
14 'The Case of Jacoby', *Manchester Guardian*, 5 June 1922.

'almost nineteen' and congratulated the Home Secretary, Edward Shortt, for resisting 'the appeal of sentimentality'.[15]

Jacoby's execution became more controversial when, two days after he was hanged, Shortt reprieved Ronald True, who had been found guilty of the murder of a young woman in her flat. True was rumoured to be 'well connected' and there was lively debate in the press as to whether the hanging of Jacoby, who was 'not well connected' and the reprieve of True, highlighted unequal justice.[16] The *Daily Mail* described the reprieve as 'a great miscarriage of justice' and questioned whether Shortt should remain in office, describing the decision to reprieve True as a 'blow at public confidence in the fairness of British justice'.[17] Dismay at True's reprieve did not necessarily signal abolitionist views – the *Yorkshire Post* stated that 'neither of the convicted persons should have been reprieved'.[18] The *Manchester Guardian* noted that, as True was deemed insane, the Home Secretary had no option but to reprieve him and that his case was not an example of the discretionary exercise of the royal prerogative of mercy.[19] However, the *Daily News* questioned why 'a panel of experts [had not] been called in to decide upon the state of Jacoby's mind'.[20] Although it was legally sound, True's reprieve for a crime not dissimilar to Jacoby's raised the contentious issue of unfairness in the application of the death penalty. This had the potential to inflame criticism in a way that abstract issues concerning the morality of retaining capital punishment did not. The issue of Jacoby's execution and True's reprieve dogged Shortt when he appeared at regional political meetings in subsequent months. In Bolton, he 'was greeted with a cry of "Now, boys, remember Jacoby and Ronald True"'[21] and in Newcastle he was obliged to reply to the accusation that he had acted 'under high and important influence' in reprieving True by stating that both cases had been treated the same.[22]

Reactions to perceived inequity in the treatment of Jacoby and True reflected ambivalence about the application of the death penalty, but primarily in relation to class-based understandings of injustice rather than the wider issue of the use of capital punishment. This was in keeping with the burgeoning political power and influence of labour in the 1920s.[23] By the 1950s, capital punishment itself was contentious and certain cases made a deep cultural impression. Continuity with pre-existing ambivalences was exhibited in

---

15 'Murder and Its Punishment', *The Times*, 8 June 1922.
16 'Criticism of Home Secretary: Public Astonished at Reprieve', *Western Gazette*, 16 June 1922.
17 'The True Scandal', *Daily Mail*, 12 June 1922.
18 Ibid.
19 'True's Reprieve', *Manchester Guardian*, 10 June 1922.
20 'Storm of Public Protest', *The Times*, 13 June 1922.
21 'A Lively Meeting for Mr Shortt', *Manchester Guardian*, 14 November 1922.
22 'Mr Shortt Replies to his Traducers', *Manchester Guardian*, 15 September 1922.
23 This was, of course, the point at which the franchise had been extended to incorporate nearly all working-class men, trade unions had grown in strength and the Labour Party was ascendant. See M. Pugh, *Speak for Britain: A New History of the Labour Party*, London: Vintage, 2011.

popular protests against executions that seemed unfair and/or unjust. The hanging of Derek Bentley in 1953 was a prime example. This case had strong parallels with that of Ernest Kelly in 1913, in that an extremely young man, perceived as the less responsible out of a pair, was executed while his co-convicted escaped the death penalty. Unlike the Kelly case, the hanging of Derek Bentley did lasting damage to the legitimacy of capital punishment and retained a place in cultural memories of execution.

In November 1952, Derek Bentley, 19, and Christopher Craig, 16, attempted to break into a warehouse in Croydon. When the police arrived, Craig shot and injured an officer who had restrained and arrested Bentley, and Bentley informed the officer that Craig was armed with a revolver and had further ammunition. The police claimed that Bentley shouted, 'Let him have it, Chris', just before Craig shot another officer in the head, killing him. Bentley's defence, however, denied that he said this. Both young men were found guilty of murder but as a minor Craig was ineligible for the death penalty. Despite attempts to secure a reprieve for Bentley, including those by his family discussed in Chapter Two, he was hanged. There were a number of factors that made Derek Bentley's hanging especially disputed and emotive. As explored previously, the anguish that his family experienced after he was sentenced to death was reported in the newspapers. He was still a teenager and also said to be 'backward'. There were concerns that his defence during the trial had been inadequate. Crucially, Bentley appeared to not only be the less responsible party in the crime, but to perhaps not even be guilty. He was under arrest when the murder happened and whether he had urged Craig to shoot was disputed.

Derek Bentley was executed on 28 January 1953. On the evening of the 27th, demonstrations against his hanging took place in Piccadilly, Trafalgar Square and Whitehall.[24] Around 150–200 people gathered outside the House of Commons to demonstrate against his execution.[25] They shouted 'Bentley must not die'[26] and marched from there to the Home Office in order to petition Home Secretary, David Maxwell Fyfe, for a last-minute reprieve. The police prevented them from being able to enter the building. At 2am, the crowd went to Downing Street in an attempt to communicate with Eden, the Prime Minister, although the police stopped them from accessing either Downing Street or the residence of the Deputy Prime Minister. A police report described the crowd as orderly, apart from 'shouts of "We want Bentley" and "We want justice"'.[27] This demonstration was not organised by the Howard League, which did not use direct action techniques, but rather consisted of what the police report described as 'young persons'. It was not part of a sustained anti-capital punishment campaign, but rather a last ditch effort to save Bentley.

24 O. Summers, '200 MPs Plead in Vain to Save Bentley', *Daily Sketch*, 28 January 1953.
25 Report, 'Demonstration Resulting in Slight Disorder', TNA/HO291/225, 28 January 1953.
26 '2am – Bentley Crowds March', *Daily Express*, 28 January 1953.
27 'Demonstration Resulting in Slight Disorder'.

There was a crowd outside Wandsworth prison by 8.45am, which at 9am began singing the hymn 'Abide with Me'. Booing greeted the posting of the execution notice, and a section of the crowd became 'restive',[28] 'unruly'[29] and 'angry'.[30] There were shouts of 'murderer' and coins were thrown.[31] The *Manchester Guardian* reported fighting amongst the crowd – flailing fists, a kick administered by a woman to a policeman's shin and another officer received a punch on the nose.[32] A man named John Rees smashed the glass covering the notice, shouting 'Come on, let's get the murderers', and another man, John McEwan, further whipped up the crowd. These men were arrested and later appeared at the Magistrates' Court, charged with 'using insulting words and behaviour'.[33] Both in their twenties, they were also both working-class – Rees was a checker and McEwan a labourer.

The execution crowd was described as 'queerly assorted' by the *Manchester Guardian*,[34] and as containing 'women with young children' by the *Evening Standard*[35] and 'a group of girls and a group of workmen with bicycles' by *The Star*.[36] The *Manchester Guardian* made the point that not all of the crowd was there to protest the death penalty – some of its members approved of the hanging of what they perceived as a dangerous 'cosh boy'.[37] However, the protesting crowd that demonstrated on behalf of Derek Bentley and attended Wandsworth on execution morning represented an example of popular protest against the death penalty in his case, with a spontaneous eruption of anger when the notice was posted. Newspaper descriptions indicated that the crowd outside the prison was, as usual, mainly working-class.

In February, a 'Bentley Execution Protest Meeting' was held at St Pancras Town Hall, featuring as speakers Donald Soper, the abolitionist Methodist minister, Frank Dawtry from the Howard League and Sydney Silverman. In their report on the meeting, the Metropolitan Police estimated there were 'at least' 200 attendees.[38] The meeting passed a resolution that the Home Secretary's lack of attention to the 'overwhelming pressure of public opinion and the Jury's recommendation to mercy' in the Bentley case further underlined the need for abolition.[39] This was to be sent to the Home Secretary, Judges of the Court of Criminal Appeal, the Chief Justice and the Associated Press. The meeting and resolution represented a different style of protest from the

28 Report, 'Execution – Derek Bentley', HO291/225, 28 January 1953.
29 'Bentley Executed at Wandsworth', *The Times*, 29 January 1953.
30 '"Murder" Cries at Bentley Hanging', *Daily Worker*, 29 January 1953.
31 'Execution – Derek Bentley'.
32 'Execution of Bentley', *Manchester Guardian*, 29 January 1953.
33 'Bentley Executed at Wandsworth'.
34 'Execution of Bentley'.
35 'Telephone Protests to Home Office', *Evening Standard*, 28 January 1953.
36 'Derek Bentley Executed', *The Star*, 28 January 1953.
37 'Execution of Bentley: Scene Outside the Prison', *Manchester Guardian*, 29 January 1953.
38 Metropolitan Police, Special Branch report, HO291/225, 18 February 1953.
39 Ibid.

marching and chanting of the night leading to Bentley's hanging and the unrest amongst the execution crowd. However, both showed the increasingly fraught nature of capital punishment in the 1950s, and the significance of a case like Derek Bentley's that seemed both unjust and unfair.

The execution of Ronald Marwood, a 25-year-old scaffolder, in 1959 was the next time when physical violence broke out amongst a protesting section of the crowd. Out drinking on the occasion of his first wedding anniversary, Marwood had stabbed and killed a policeman in the street. His crime took place after the Homicide Act 1957, but was a capital one because he had murdered a police officer. Sympathy existed for Marwood because the killing was clearly spur of the moment (he was carrying a knife) and happened when he was drunk. He was also married to a woman only 20 years old. What made Marwood's death sentence even more contentious was the fact that he was convicted mainly on the basis of his own confession, which it was alleged by the defence had been made after several hours of questioning by the police. At this time, concerns about police corruption and use of brutality were intensifying, with scandals emerging that led to a Royal Commission on the Police in 1960.[40] Also relevant were previous capital cases that, to some, illustrated the bad behaviour of the police. The Evans case highlighted the danger of hanging someone based on their own confession, especially one which appeared to have been cajoled out of them, and there was active debate on whether the 'Judge's rules' for taking evidence needed greater codification.[41]

Two local priests, Rev. Jenner and Rev. Hulhoven, one Anglican and one Catholic, led the campaign for Marwood's reprieve, drawing up a pre-printed petition form for distribution, talking to the press and visiting the Home Office. As a child, Marwood had attended clubs at both of their churches and his wife worshipped at Hulhoven's church.[42] The priests emphasised the doubt over his confession, wider problems with taking evidence and also that Marwood was hard working and well liked within his community. The case for reprieve was also supported by Christian Action, the National Council for the Abolition of the Death Penalty and 150 MPs (mainly Labour).[43]

---

40 Police scandals in the late 1950s included corruption in Brighton and Nottingham, and a public tribunal into the conduct of Caithness police resulting from the case of the 'Thurso Boy', a 15-year-old boy assaulted by two officers. See C. A. Williams, 'Britain's Police Forces: Forever Removed from Democratic Control?', *History and Policy*, 2003, www.historyandpolicy.org/papers/policy-paper-16.html and 'Police Governance: Community, Policing, and Justice in the Modern UK', *Taiwan in Comparative Perspective*, 2011, 3: 50–65, pp. 56–9. On the 'Thurso Boy' see also A. Bartie and L. A. Jackson, 'Youth Crime and Preventive Policing in Post-War Scotland', *Twentieth Century British History*, 2011, 22(1): 79–102, pp. 96–7.
41 See 'Confessions and the Law', *The Observer*, 12 April 1959. This article highlighted that India had had an Evidence Act since 1872.
42 G. Kenihan, 'Priests Launch Marwood Petition', *Daily Mail*, 21 April 1959 and '2 Priests Fight for Marwood', *Daily Mirror*, 21 April 1959.
43 'The Case of Ronald Marwood', 29 April 1959, HO291/242 and '150 MPs Sign Appeal for Marwood', *The Times*, 30 April 1959.

The news that a reprieve had been denied was met with protest inside and outside Pentonville Prison. According to *The Guardian*, people in the crowd 'knelt in prayer for Marwood' while prisoners threw burning paper from cell windows and shouted for more than an hour.[44] *The Times* described a crowd of over 500, comprising 'mostly women and young people', which became increasingly 'demonstrative' as the burning paper floated to the ground.[45] Pentonville experienced an unusual level of disturbance on the eve of Marwood's hanging.[46] As well as throwing burning paper out of the windows, some prisoners broke furniture and windows.[47] The execution crowd swelled to around 1000 by 9am, the time Marwood was to hang. Pathé news footage shows people bearing placards reading 'Save Marwood' and 'Don't Murder Marwood'.[48] *The Guardian* described a 'mob', which 'went wild – punching, kicking, screaming, and cursing', but was stilled by the clock striking nine. A man was dragged from the throng and carried away by five officers, provoking boos and cries of 'savages', 'beasts' and 'murderers'.[49] The crowd was pushed back by a line of foot police and sections were charged by mounted police.[50]

Not all of the thousand strong crowd outside Pentonville was there to protest against Marwood's hanging. As with the execution of Bentley, *The Guardian* reported the presence of 'curiosity seekers', who had 'arrived in a state of macabre anticipation'.[51] This was a value heavy appraisal of the crowd, in an article that also claimed the morning of Marwood's execution had provided insight into the 'mentality of the festive crowds that used to line the route to Tyburn',[52] but it served to underline the point that by no means all of the public outside the prison were there to protest. Nevertheless, the emotional response to Marwood's hanging demonstrated how the Homicide Act had, if anything, deepened some of the ambivalences that surrounded capital punishment. The murder of police had been granted special status, but a drunken, unplanned murder of the kind that Marwood had committed was not especially heinous in comparison with many other murders that were no longer subject to the death penalty. An editorial in *The Times* criticised 'strident mass pressure against application of the law' but conceded that Marwood's case was 'a cautionary lesson'. It stated, '[w]hat the courts decide is not necessarily always equitable – as civilized contemporaries see equity – and it is not even

44 'Marwood: No Reprieve', *The Guardian*, 8 May 1959.
45 'Attempts to Save Marwood Fail', *The Times*, 8 May 1959.
46 T. Morris, *Pentonville*, London: Routledge and Kegan Paul, 1963, p. 121.
47 R. A. Butler, 'Pentonville Prison (Incidents)', Hansard, HoC Debate 14 May 1959, vol. 605, cols 172–173W.
48 'Marwood Hanged', *British Pathé*, 1959, www.britishpathe.com/video/marwood-hanged-print-complete.
49 'Crowd Shout Outside Gaol', *The Times*, 9 May 1959.
50 Ibid. and 'Police Charge Riot Crowd', *Daily Mirror*, 9 May 1959. See also 'Marwood Hanged', which shows the man being carried from the crowd and the mounted police charging.
51 'Mob Violence Outside Prison Gates'.
52 Ibid.

invariably right'.[53] Seventy abolitionist MPs announced a new campaign, with Sydney Silverman tabling a motion on the 'anomalies in the hanging laws' that Marwood's execution exemplified.[54] They were 'an abiding offence to the intelligence, the sense of justice, and the good sense of the community'.[55] Ripples of popular protest continued. *The Times* reported an incident where '50 to 70 youths rushed Tower Bridge police station', shouting 'Revenge for Marwood' and 'Let's get the Marwood killers'.[56]

The eruption of spontaneous popular protest against certain executions was rare in Britain. However, cases such as Ernest Kelly, Derek Bentley and Ronald Marwood showed that strong objections could be provoked when the application of the death penalty seemed unfair or excessive. Youth in the condemned was also a significant factor in making capital punishment appear unacceptable. Reactions against the hanging of Ernest Kelly and Derek Bentley demonstrated how the punishment could be perceived as unjust if the less culpable (or, even, innocent) party in a murder was executed when their co-accused escaped the gallows. Henry Jacoby and Ronald Marwood's cases showed how perceived failure to apply the death penalty equitably could arouse strong feeling. Of course, many examples of the inconsistent use of capital punishment passed without receiving the same level of public attention and reaction – although the particular details of the Kelly and Bentley cases, and the extreme youth of Jacoby, made their cases exceptional. The reaction at Marwood's execution scene was a clearer indication of the potentially fraught nature of capital punishment by the late 1950s, and the envelopment of mistrust of the police into this issue. Such popular protest, which accompanied more organised efforts for reprieve, was not necessarily abolitionist. To be incensed by unwarranted, unjust or inconsistent application of the death penalty was not the same as believing that it should be abolished altogether. What such reactions did show, however, was that capital punishment could be highly contentious and was increasingly so by the mid-twentieth century, especially in relation to understandings of justice.

Violet van der Elst and popular abolitionism

The protests discussed above were additional to organised efforts for reprieve but were not examples of a targeted movement against the death penalty. Organisations such as the Howard League and the National Council for the Abolition of the Death Penalty campaigned for abolition, but did so with the aim of making rational, scientific arguments against capital punishment that could be supported by evidence. Wealthy self-made businesswoman, Violet van der Elst, took a different approach. In 1935, she launched her populist campaign

53 'Capital Murder', *The Times*, 9 May 1959.
54 'New Move to End Hanging', *Daily Mirror*, 13 May 1959.
55 'Crowd Shout Outside Gaol'.
56 'Youths Rushed Police Station', *The Times*, 16 May 1959.

in opposition to the death penalty. Influenced by the militancy of the suffragettes, she adopted noisy, performative direct action techniques to register protest at executions, alongside other measures such as writing leaflets, publishing a magazine, compiling petitions and writing to the Home Secretary.[57] Violet sought to engage press and public attention, and initially hoped to bring about abolition within six months of launching her campaign.[58]

Born Violet Dodge in 1882, the daughter of a coal porter, Violet as a young woman built a successful business selling face cream. Along with her first husband, who was an engineer, she also manufactured shaving cream and by the 1930s, she employed around a hundred people. When her second husband, Jean van der Elst, died in 1934 she became a spiritualist, believing that she could contact him with the assistance of mediums. She decided to launch a campaign to abolish the death penalty as this was a cause in which both she and Jean had believed.[59] As a self-made woman from a working-class background, Violet contrasted with the patrician abolitionists of her day from the National Council for the Abolition of the Death Penalty. Whereas they expressly sought to keep emotions at bay in the debate over capital punishment,[60] Violet employed a tactical repertoire that aimed to induce outrage amongst the public against hanging.[61] She was not always successful in this endeavour, but frequently provoked reactions, both supportive and unfavourable, from the execution crowd.

Violet launched her campaign with a press release in March 1935, which stated her intention to stage a demonstration against the execution of George Harvey outside Pentonville. This announced that 'a band will play, and leaflets will be distributed, putting forward the arguments of the society against the death penalty'.[62] Some of Violet's plans for the demonstration were foiled by the police, who would not allow her 25-strong brass band to perform, or her 30 men wearing sandwich boards bearing anti-capital punishment slogans to march through Hyde Park. She was forced to dismiss the band and send the sandwichmen on an alternative route along Piccadilly and Regent Street.[63]

---

57 As Mercer notes, women's suffrage organisations such as the Women's Social and Political Union utilised propaganda alongside militancy. J. Mercer, 'Media and Militancy: Propaganda in the Women's Social and Political Union's Campaign', *Women's History Review*, 2005, 14(3&4): 471–86.
58 C. N. Gattey, *The Incredible Mrs van der Elst*, London: Leslie Fremin, 1972, pp. 41–2.
59 Ibid., pp. 20–37.
60 E. O. Tuttle, *The Crusade Against Capital Punishment in Britain*, London: Stevens and Sons, 1961, pp. 47–8.
61 'Tactical repertoire' refers to the strategies, tactics and styles of protest adopted by a campaign. See for example H. J. McCammon, '"Out of the Parlors and into the Streets": The Changing Tactical Repertoire of the US Women's Suffrage Movements', *Social Forces*, 2003, 81(3): 787–818.
62 'Band Outside Prison While Man Dies', *Evening Standard*, 12 March 1935.
63 Metropolitan Police Telegram, 13 March 1935, TNA/HO144/21831.

The demonstrations were calculated to be a spectacle and, as such, were highly newsworthy. The execution of Leonard Brigstock at Wandsworth in early April was an occasion. Violet hired three aeroplanes to fly over the prison, trailing banners that read 'Stop the death sentence!'. Sandwichmen marched on a half-mile long procession wearing boards stating 'Stop Capital Punishment'. Vans with loudspeakers drove through the streets around the prison playing the hymns 'Rock of Ages' and 'Abide with Me'. Violet arrived in her chauffeur driven Rolls Royce and addressed the crowd, shouting 'They are hanging an innocent man. We have got last-minute evidence to prove it'.[64] She was dressed entirely in black 'except for the heavy sable collar of her coat'.[65] At the time of the execution, a woman 'dropped on her knees and recited the Lord's Prayer'.[66]

Violet also put energies into gathering signatures for petitions. For Leonard Brigstock and Percy Anderson, a lorry with loudspeakers drove round London, stopping at street corners so that the men and women travelling in it could get signatures.[67] A petition signed by 85,000 was compiled for Brigstock, although Violet was not granted an audience with the Home Secretary, John Gilmour.[68] Instead, she presented the petition to abolitionist Labour MP, Clement Attlee, who delivered it for her.[69] She wrote letters to the Home Office on behalf of the condemned and would offer, as in the case of Brigstock, to pay for expert psychiatric examination so that their insanity could be established (with the aim of saving them from the gallows).[70]

Other tactics in the campaign were the publication of anti-capital punishment leaflets, and also her own weekly magazine, *Humanity*, which set out her abolitionist views as well as advertising her face cream. In 1937, Violet published *On the Gallows*, her treatise against the death penalty, the manuscript of which she had dictated to her secretary and was subsequently revised by a journalist.[71] This set out a variety of arguments against the death penalty, some of which drew on criminological understandings of the causes of crime. Above all, Violet argued that capital punishment was uncivilised and had a harmful effect on society.[72] Positivist explanations for crime, such as that it was caused by biological inheritance, mental disease or living in a poor environment, were advanced to contend that the death penalty was therefore not a deterrent.[73] In

---

64 'Amazing Execution Scenes', *Evening Standard*, 2 April 1935. See also 'Airplanes, Loud-Speaker Vans and Praying Women', *Evening Standard*, 2 April 1935.
65 'Execution Protest', *Western Morning News*, 3 April 1935.
66 'Propaganda at Execution', *Daily Mail*, 3 April 1935.
67 Special Branch Report, 21 March 1935, HO144/21831.
68 Letter to Home Office from Violet van der Elst, 29 March 1935, HO144/19935.
69 V. van der Elst, *On the Gallows*, London, The Doge Press, 1937, p. 139.
70 Letter to Home Office.
71 An advert in the *Daily Express* drew on Violet's fame and proclaimed that the book included 'a Striking Photograph of the Author', Advertisement for *On the Gallows*, 26 January 1939.
72 Elst, *On the Gallows*, p. 17.
73 Similar arguments were made in Violet's propaganda leaflets, for example, 'Capital Punishment Should be Abolished', undated, HO144/21831.

particular, Violet recommended the work of criminal anthropologists such as Lombroso, Ferri and Garofalo for understanding the role of heredity in criminality.[74] She also paid attention to social justice, stating that murder was more likely to be committed by the very poor as, unlike the rich, they could not afford doctors to cure them of the diseases that led to violence. Once in court, the poor did not have access to the kind of skilled legal defence that would be able to counter the arguments of the experienced prosecution barrister. *On the Gallows* was not detailed on Violet's spiritualist beliefs, but these could be detected in her assertion that 'evil vibrations in the atmosphere' influenced the committing of crimes.[75]

The other main tactic that Violet employed was to stand for Parliament, which she did twice under different affiliations. In October 1935, she was Independent Conservative candidate in Putney and lost her deposit. In 1940, she contested Southwark as Independent Labour candidate, although again failed to poll many votes.[76] She had switched to Labour in 1936, believing that her interest in unemployment and advocacy for nationalisation of the coal industry was more in keeping with socialism. She also perceived that socialists were greater supporters of abolitionism.[77] Violet's candidacy was a broader representation of her interest in social issues, and in Southwark she ran on 'increased old age pensions, better homes at better rents and increased health services', setting herself up as a champion of the poor.[78]

Violet's campaign against the death penalty was a long one – she protested against the executions of Derek Bentley and Ruth Ellis, and was interviewed by the *Picture Post* in 1953 for her views on the Report of the Royal Commission on Capital Punishment.[79] However, she gained the most press attention for her cause and her personality in the 1930s. Many of her demonstrations were reported in the press and it was noteworthy if she did not attend an execution.[80] She was the subject of some admiring profiles and reporting. The *Sunday Referee* discussed her attempts to save Percy Anderson in 1935 and noted '[h]er methods of focusing public attention on the question of abolition are reminiscent of the tactics adopted by suffragettes in their campaign for the franchise before

---

74 Elst, *On the Gallows*, p. 177. This remained an influence. In 1949, she wrote to the Home Secretary on behalf of Daniel Raven, whose case is discussed in the next chapter. In the letter, Violet recommended reading Lombroso and Christ, as both were opposed to the death penalty, Letter from V. van der Elst, Kingston, 21 December 1949, HO45/24497.

75 Ibid., p. 33.

76 Gattey, *The Incredible*, p. 182.

77 Ibid., p. 110.

78 T. Luckhurst, 'It is Thrown Against me that I have a Castle', *Journalism Studies*, 2012, 13(1): 107–23, p. 119. See this article more generally on the Central Southwark by-election of 1940.

79 'They Won't Stop me Till They Stop Hanging', *Picture Post*, 10 October 1953.

80 'Love Token Execution', *Nottingham Evening Post*, 16 July 1935: This story explained that a crowd of around 100 people outside Durham Prison for the execution of George Hague expected to see a demonstration by Violet, but she 'was not present, nor was she represented'.

the war'.[81] In *Everybody's Weekly*, Violet was dubbed 'the most remarkable woman in England', who was 'giving Scotland Yard sleepless nights' with her demonstrations. The profile explained that Violet was very rich and described her home with its '[j]ewelled idols, old masters, huge tapestries, gilded halls and thick carpets'.[82] In an article for *Picture Post* in 1939, she told 'the story of her remarkable life'. This explained that she was both an 'astute business woman' and interested in the occult and it featured photographs of her home at the time, Grantham Castle, with its Chippendale furniture and chandeliers, as well as a close up of Violet's jewelled hands.[83]

Flying planes over prisons, employing battalions of sandwichmen and rousing the execution crowd to song were in themselves newsworthy activities and, as a wealthy businesswoman, Violet suited contemporary news values. As Bingham argues, newspapers focused disproportionate attention on the unusual and Violet, an eccentric millionairess with a cause, was certainly that. Her successful business ventures meant that she could be understood as a 'modern woman', trailblazing the expansion of women's roles.[84] The fact that Violet for a time lived in a castle, wore expensive jewels and owned antique furniture enabled profiles about her to contain a strong 'lifestyle' element. Her activities also received international attention. The *New York Times* reported how she 'make[s] the names of little known killers front-page news' and referred to her expensive fur coats and large collection of books on 'black magic and witchcraft'.[85] *Time* magazine described her as 'an irrepressible lady', who lived in a 'swank Kensington home' and held spiritualist meetings.[86]

In reporting Violet's exploits the press gave both her and the cause of abolition much needed publicity. As well as successful modern businesswoman, she could be fitted into the stock character of 'wealthy English eccentric', and the latter emerged from the tone of the American reporting, with *Time* designating Violet one of the 'luxuries' that Britain could enjoy.[87] Although it was possible to represent Violet as a curiosity and self-publicist, she successfully brought her cause and the cases on which she campaigned to public attention in a way that existing abolitionists did not, as the *New York Times* highlighted. Violet's popular abolitionism was perfectly suited in the 1930s to the idiom of the expanding popular press. Her display of her grand homes, furs and jewels could of course have been interpreted as vulgar and arriviste, but this was not the tone adopted in popular press lifestyle features about her.

81 'Mrs van der Elst's Offer to the Home Secretary', *Sunday Referee*, 14 April 1935.
82 D. Bardens, 'England's Amazing Millionairess', *Everybody's Weekly*, 10 April 1935.
83 V. van der Elst, 'My Struggle', *Picture Post*, 2 September 1939.
84 A. Bingham, *Gender, Modernity, and the Popular Press in Inter-War Britain*, Oxford: Clarendon Press, 2004, p. 64. Bingham argues that the 'modern woman' was a more prominent figure in newspapers in the 1920s, but did not disappear in the 1930s, p. 79.
85 'Gives $20,000 a Week to Fight Hanging', *New York Times*, 5 May 1935. See also 'Planes Flaunt Protest as Briton is Hanged', *New York Times*, 3 April 1935.
86 'Foreign News: Crusade Against Death', *Time*, 15 April 1935.
87 Ibid.

Public reactions to the campaign

News stories did not usually explicitly endorse or criticise Violet's demonstrations, although they frequently reported negative reactions from the
crowd. The *Manchester Guardian* observed that at the execution of John
Bridge at Strangeways Prison in May 1935, Violet received 'little response
from the crowd except occasional booing',[88] although on the preceding day
she had held a public meeting of 1800 at Manchester Free Trade Hall.[89] The
Hull Daily Mail reported her demonstration for Percy Anderson at Wandsworth,
stating that '[a]bove the cries of "Hear, hear" was heard a voice asking:
"What about the victim …   What would you do if it had been your daughter?"'.[90] The impression gained from this article, however, is that the crowd
was broadly supportive of Violet on this occasion.

For the most part, the crowd's reaction to Violet's demonstrations must be
gleaned from news stories. These representations may, of course, have been
influenced by the editorial line on capital punishment taken by the paper in
question, although there was variation in the reactions reported, indicating
that they do reveal something of the mood of the crowd. As the *Hull Daily
Mail* story quoted above suggests, Violet's demonstrations could meet with
differing reactions from the same crowd. Depending on the identity of the
condemned and the type of murder they had committed, Violet could
encounter varying degrees of sympathy and hostility. At the execution of
Dorothea Waddingham at Winson Green Prison in 1936, many people joined
in with the hymns from Violet's loud-speakers and women in the crowd
sobbed. 'Nurse Waddingham' was the mother of five children, one of whom
was a small baby. The execution of women was frequently contentious and
ambivalent, especially if they were mothers. Violet's sandwichmen wore
placards reading 'Stop this terrible crime of hanging the mother of five children'
and a sign on her Rolls Royce stated 'This barbaric age would hang a mother
of five children'.[91]

The execution of Buck Ruxton, also in 1936, presented Violet with a hostile,
bordering on violent, crowd. Ruxton was a general practitioner who had
killed his wife and his children's nanny, and then dismembered their bodies in
order to dispose of them.[92] Unlike Dorothea Waddingham, he did not attract
public sympathy. Violet attempted a demonstration outside Strangeways and
was hooted and jeered at.[93] When she began to speak, a woman shouted

88 'Disturbance Outside a Prison', *Manchester Guardian*, 31 May 1935.
89 'Mrs van der Elst's Campaign', *Manchester Guardian*, 30 May 1935.
90 'Woman Opponent of Executions in Another Scene Outside Prison', *Hull Daily Mail*, 16 April 1935.
91 'Nurse Waddingham's Execution', *Western Gazette*, 17 April 1936.
92 On the Ruxton case and gender, race and class in 1930s Britain, see S. D'Cruze, 'Intimacy,
   Professionalism and Domestic Homicide in Interwar Britain: The Case of Buck Ruxton',
   Women's History Review, 2007, 16(5): 701–22.
93 'Mrs van der Elst Arrested', *The Times*, 13 May 1936 and 'Police Draw Batons as Crowd Press
   Forward', *Evening News*, 12 May 1936.

'How would you like your daughter cut up?'[94] The window of Violet's car was broken and the police, who had drawn their batons on the crowd, ordered her to remove it.[95] Violet refused and was physically dragged out of her Rolls Royce, sustaining heavy bruises as a result.[96] She was arrested and later fined three pounds at Manchester Stipendiary Magistrates' Court for refusing to stop her car. Her defence argued that she had misjudged the atmosphere of the crowd, not realising that due to the 'horrible murder' committed by Ruxton it would be unfriendly.[97] The Magistrate agreed that Violet had misunderstood that the crowd 'had very little sympathy with' Ruxton and 'were indignant at the murder of which [he] had been convicted'.[98]

As a committed abolitionist, Violet's opposition to capital punishment was unconditional – the particular details of a case did not alter her stance. This contrasted with mainstream opinion, which tended to favour reprieve due to extenuating circumstances. With some cases, Violet could draw on local sympathy, in others she met with incomprehension, ridicule and even hostility. As the Ruxton execution demonstrated, she was not afraid to face down the police and the crowd. Ten years after Buck Ruxton was hanged, Mass Observation sent an investigator to Pentonville Prison on the morning of Neville Heath's execution. The crowd comprised mainly people in their twenties and thirties stopping on their way to work. The general opinion was that Heath 'deserved what he got' but there was 'a general feeling of pity for his parents'.[99] The investigator conveys the sense of anticipation for Violet's arrival, stating 'everybody's on their toes expecting Mrs van der Elst who's generally referred to as "she"'. The investigator found the members of the crowd rather distasteful, commenting that people gathered around Violet's car 'in much the same way as spectators at the zoo gaze at the animals in their cages' and were happy to be 'the actors in a cheap vulgar set-up'. Violet was a novelty, at whom the crowd stared 'as if she were some abnormal creature', but some expressed admiration for her ability to challenge authority and 'pull a fast one over the police'. When the police forcibly dragged her into her car, there was booing, with one person retorting 'Leave her alone you bloody rotters' and another saying 'if the police didn't protect her from the mob they'd lynch her that's what they'd do straight'.[100]

Violet and the police

At the beginning of her anti-capital punishment campaign, Violet's activities were the subject of CID and Metropolitan Police Special Branch reports. This

94 'Police Draw Batons'.
95 Ibid. and 'Mrs van der Elst Arrested'.
96 'Mrs van der Elst in Court', *Evening News*, 20 May 1936.
97 '"Struck Bad Patch" Over Ruxton Execution', *Daily Express*, 21 May 1936.
98 'Execution Scenes', *Western Morning News*, 21 May 1936.
99 'Heath's Execution', LB, Capital Punishment Survey, 1938–56, 15 October 1946, MOA/TC72.
100 Ibid.

was in order to determine whether the campaign was linked to communism.[101] A Special Branch report sent to Under Secretary of State at the Home Office in June 1935 covered a meeting held by Violet in London, which was attended by around 450 people, 'almost all of whom were respectably dressed'. It described Violet as not well educated 'and occasionally using bad grammar' but conceded that 'a discreet perusal of the signed petition forms in the hall did not reveal the name of any known communist'.[102] Their reports on her campaign ceased.

Violet had regular run-ins with the police at demonstrations, which led to court appearances. Some of these were for public order offences such as repeatedly hooting the horn of her Rolls Royce or causing an obstruction.[103] Her refusal to respect police cordons and her propensity for simply driving straight at officers who attempted to halt her, causing them to leap out of the way and possibly sustain injury, also landed her in court. At the execution of Alan Grierson at Pentonville in 1935, she drove at a line of police guarding the entrance to the prison, slightly injuring the hand of a policeman who attempted to hold out his arm to stop her.[104] At Wandsworth, for Percy Anderson's execution, she hit an officer on the right hip and leg as he attempted to jump out of the way of her Rolls Royce.[105]

As a Metropolitan Police progress report from 1935 acknowledged, Violet welcomed attempts to prosecute her as it enhanced publicity for her campaign.[106] As far as the Metropolitan Police were concerned, Violet's demonstrations made her 'a bit of a nuisance'.[107] Certainly, they endured her taunting, such as when she refused to remove her car from Pentonville Prison at Alan Grierson's execution and shouted 'You cowards. Why don't you arrest me?'[108] When giving evidence against her at Magistrates' hearings, senior police officers sometimes attempted to discredit Violet by questioning her sanity. In July 1936, she was fined £5 at Exeter Magistrates' Court for obstructing a policeman in the course of his duty at the execution of Charlotte Bryant. The Chief Constable asked for her to be remanded, stating 'I think the woman is mental, and should be seen to', a charge which Violet described as

101 On the state's concerns about political extremism and public disorder in the 1920s and 1930s see R. C. Thurlow, 'The Straw that Broke the Camel's Back: Public Order, Civil Liberties and the Battle of Cable Street', *Jewish Culture and History*, 1998, 1(2): 74–94. On surveillance and suspected communist activity in the 1930s, see J. Smith, 'The Radical Literary Magazine of the 1930s and British Government Surveillance: the Case of *Storm* Magazine', *Literature and History*, 2010, 19(2): 69–86.
102 Special Branch report, 26 June 1935, TNA/HO144/21831.
103 See 'Summonses Against Mrs van der Elst', *Evening Standard*, 8 January 1936.
104 PC L. Jolley, Metropolitan Police Telegram, 30 October 1935, MEPO3/2444.
105 Process Report, Earlsfield, 16 April 1935, MEPO3/2444.
106 Process Report, 23 March 1935, MEPO3/2444.
107 Metropolitan Police report, Leman Street, 7 April 1935, HO144/21831.
108 Witness statement, Arthur Hawkins, Sub divisional Inspector, 1 November 1935, MEPO3/2444.

'scandalous' and argued had been made because she was a reformer.[109] When she was fined after Buck Ruxton's execution two months previously, Violet asserted that an officer had threatened 'You will get prison this time. We are going to have you medically examined'.[110] Although Violet was clearly given to exaggeration on occasion, the reported insinuation in the *Evening News* from Superintendent Page that she 'seemed dazed' and should be examined by the prison doctor lends support to her claims.[111] In *On the Gallows*, Violet reflected that the police had made similar allegations of mental imbalance against the suffragettes, but she asserted 'I am a reformer, and reformers are always ready to take great risks'.[112]

These reactions from the police show that Violet was not simply regarded by the authorities as a harmless eccentric. This was well illustrated in 1943, when she managed to gain possession of confidential medical reports of prisoners hanged at Wandsworth. According to her biographer, Violet received these from an ex-prisoner who salvaged them after the prison was bombed.[113] She gave to them to a photographer, with the intention of circulating copies for publication, but he passed the records to the police. They contained details such as how long the pulse beats after hanging, the attitude of the condemned to their sentence, and post-mortem reports. That Violet had gained access to this information was taken seriously by the Deputy Under Secretary of State at the Home Office, Frank Newsam, who expressed concern that 'publication of the information would almost certainly revive public interest with the vexed question of capital punishment and would give considerable impetus to the movement for abolition' – something which was to be avoided as it would prevent the execution of spies and traitors.[114] Violet was subsequently fined £10 for receiving the secret records.[115] The potential for explicit details of hanging to stir abolitionism was not brushed off lightly.

Violet's campaigning tactical repertoire was very different from the Howard League and the National Council for the Abolition of the Death Penalty which, as discussed, emphasised rationality in the capital punishment debate as essential and stressed the need for arguments to be based on scientific research. These organisations also largely avoided intervening in specific cases – something

109 'Mrs van der Elst Objects to "Insult"', *Daily Express*, 16 July 1936.
110 'Execution Scenes', *Western Morning News*, 21 May 1936.
111 'Police Draw Batons'.
112 Elst, *On the Gallows*, p. 204. Writing to Home Secretary, John Gilmour, on behalf of Leonard Brigstock, Violet assured him, 'I am a practical woman, known in commerce as a woman that has built up a huge business on my intelligence. I am not an hysterical woman. I look on facts and justice'. She was clearly aware that she would be portrayed as 'hysterical' and unstable, Letter from V. van der Elst, London, 29 March 1935, HO144/19935.
113 Gattey, *The Incredible*, p. 183.
114 F. Newsam, 11 February 1943, HO144/21831.
115 'Mrs van der Elst had Prison Secrets of Death Cell', *Derby Daily Telegraph*, 26 March 1943 and 'Mrs Van der Elst Fined: She Had Jail Secrets of Murders', *Daily Express*, 27 March 1943.

which was at the heart of Violet's activism – in order to underline their indiscriminate opposition to the death penalty. The 'official' abolitionist campaign was 'troubled ... by undesirable support'[116] and Roy Calvert worried lest the 'case for abolitionism should become associated in the public mind with hysterical emotionalism' of the kind he perceived Violet to peddle.[117] However, as Potter notes, Violet's campaign overshadowed that of the National Council for the Abolition of the Death Penalty in the 1930s, gaining far more press and public attention.[118] Her campaign did seek to engage the public's emotions and in this sense Violet's activism adumbrated the emotional public sphere that developed in relation to the death penalty after the Second World War. Her description in the *Picture Post* in 1953 of the Royal Commission's Report on Capital Punishment as a 'cold-blooded document' (accompanied by a photo of her tearing it up) illustrated how she had an enduring understanding of the inescapably emotional nature of execution that many of her contemporary abolitionists had lacked or repudiated.[119]

The genuinely subversive nature of Violet van der Elst's campaign, which gained a high profile through the use of direct action techniques, is important to recognise. Although clearly viewed as an eccentric, she was much more than a curiosity. As a woman who, like the suffragettes, broke the rules of polite protest[120] she claimed the role of active citizen during a period when women were becoming increasingly present in the public sphere and in public space.[121] Violet was not only present in public, but sought to both disrupt and gain control of the execution scenes that she attended and shaped. This was

---

116 Tuttle, *The Crusade*, p. 47.
117 Calvert in the abolitionist journal, *Penal Reformer*, 1, 4, April 1935 quoted in H. Potter, *Hanging in Judgment*, London: SCM Press, 1993, p. 125.
118 Ibid.
119 'They Won't Stop Me'. As discussed in Chapter Two, by the 1950s there was a stronger acknowledged link between emotionalism and capital punishment. Nevertheless, Violet was also 'kept at arm's length' by the National Campaign for Capital Punishment in the 1950s in case her 'exhibitionism' was 'detrimental to the cause', N. Twitchell, *The Politics of the Rope*, Bury St Edmunds: Arena, 2012, p. 61. The novel, *Thicker than Water*, satirises a wealthy female abolitionist who drives a Rolls Royce and induces false hope in May, the mother of the condemned, F. Tilsley, London: The Popular Book Club, 1956.
120 On the militancy of the suffragettes, see H. L. Smith, *The British Women's Suffrage Campaign, 1866–1928*, Harlow: Pearson Education Ltd, 2007, 2nd edition, Ch. 4.
121 Women were more visible in the public sphere in the 1930s than they had been before the First World War, and had greater access to professions and education, as well as greater property rights. They had also received the vote. Brooke argues that women's public place was 'fraught with complexity' – the 1930s was also the era when working-class women bore the brunt of the poverty wrought by unemployment', S. Brooke, '"A New World for Women?": Abortion Law Reform in Britain During the 1930s', *American Historical Review*, 2001, 106(2): 431–59, p. 438. Expansions in retailing meant that by the 1930s, women in cities and smaller towns could shop in the chain and department stores of the high street, which also offered employment opportunities beyond domestic service for working-class women, J. Giles, 'Class, Gender and Domestic Consumption in Britain, 1920–50', E. Casey and L. Martens (eds), *Gender and Consumption*, Aldershot: Ashgate, 2007, 15–32, pp. 18–19.

extremely challenging to authority. As the earlier part of this chapter discussed, execution crowds did not always play the part that state control of capital punishment mandated. However, Violet pursued a sustained campaign that sought to subvert the bureaucratic facelessness of twentieth-century hanging. She re-appropriated the elements of spectacle and carnival that had historically accompanied public execution and turned them to abolitionist ends. Particularly in the 1930s when she had plentiful resources, Violet's demonstrations put on a show for the watching crowd and, at one remove, newspaper readers. She combined elements of the carnivalesque with staged public mourning in the form of prayer and singing hymns. In this sense, her protests also incorporated aspects of solemnity and the funereal, adding a strong moral dimension to the performance.

Violet was a liminal figure in mid-twentieth-century Britain, a woman who crossed boundaries of class, gender and propriety. In carrying out her protest, she commanded, or attempted to command, public space. She assumed primacy in waging a personally motivated campaign on a topic that had been traditionally regarded as unsuitable for women.[122] She showed off her wealth, wearing diamonds and furs, driving a Rolls Royce and living in grand homes. Far from downplaying her riches, Violet used her status as a self-made businesswoman to generate publicity for herself and the campaign. On the one hand, this chimed with interwar notions of the 'modern woman', who could run a business and consume luxury goods.[123] On the other, it transgressed conventions of upper and upper-middle-class social codes of refinement – according to which she could never have been acceptable anyway. Violet's spiritualism (as well as her campaigning style) made her intolerable to abolitionists like Roy Calvert who advocated an intellectual approach. However, spiritualism grew in popularity with working and lower-middle-class people during the 1930s and appealed to the 'contemporary democratic values' of the 'average man', fitting with Violet's anti-establishment ethos.[124]

Her vulgar and showy campaigning activities were an embarrassment to officialdom, both because they violated 'good taste' but also because they shone a spotlight on execution itself. Violet was quick to highlight the troubling aspects of certain cases, such as whether the mental health of the condemned was in doubt. This did not always win wider support, particularly in cases where the murder seemed especially shocking or cruel. However, the discomfort that she caused to the Home Office in 1943 when she came into

122 J. Gregory, *Victorians Against the Gallows*, London: I. B. Tauris, 2012, p. 90.
123 On the modern woman and consumption, see P. Tinkler and C. K. Warsh, 'Feminine Modernity in Interwar Britain and North America: Corsets, Cars and Cigarettes', *Journal of Women's History*, 2008, 20(3): 113–43.
124 J. Hazelgrove, *Spiritualism and British Society Between the Wars*, Manchester: Manchester University Press, 2000, p. 19. Hazelgrove contends that spiritualism, which was linked to radicalism in the nineteenth century, was well suited to interwar discourses of egalitarianism and the 'man on the street'. There was also an established link between spiritualism and abolitionism, Gregory, p. 234.

possession of medical records of the hanged demonstrated that the state was highly anxious about the corporeal details of execution becoming public. Making capital punishment more public in an era when the tenets of civilisation and modernity required that it take place in private disrupted the state's veiled and restricted execution performance. Violet explicitly criticised the death penalty as uncivilised and, as a modern woman, implicitly opposed it as incompatible with modernity. Press attention may not have focused closely on Violet's abolitionist arguments but by itself newspaper coverage meant that the secrecy of hanging was reduced and the performance of execution as a civilised ritual was called into question.

Violet's biographer, Gattey, quotes Clement Attlee as stating that she 'had strong claims to be regarded as the woman who did more than anyone else to secure the abolition of capital punishment in Britain'.[125] How far she managed to change minds and win people over to abolitionism is difficult to know. It seems that she met with a more positive reception in cases where sympathy for the condemned already existed amongst the public and a more hostile one when it did not. However, Violet's campaign can be understood as illuminating the ambivalent nature of capital punishment in twentieth-century Britain, showing how this practice sometimes directly contradicted popularly understood notions of justice. As a liminal figure herself, Violet was well placed to highlight this ambivalence. Before the death penalty became a more high profile and contested issue following the Second World War, Violet's campaign was one of the primary means through which it came to public attention.

Violet van der Elst continued to actively oppose the death penalty into old age. She was interviewed when she was 65 by the *Mirror* about the first conviction for capital murder, of Patrick Dunbar, after the Homicide Act 1957.[126] By then, her wealth was much reduced and she had been overshadowed in the debate over capital punishment by the greater prominence of parliamentary abolitionism and Victor Gollancz's National Campaign for the Abolition of Capital Punishment.[127] The journalist described how '[t]he mighty voice of protest was almost silent' as poor health left Violet unable to raise her voice above a whisper. Nevertheless, she retained 'a spark of the old defiance'.[128] Violet van der Elst lived to see the achievement of abolition in 1965 and died in a nursing home in Kent in 1966.

125 Gattey, *The Incredible*, p. 7.
126 Dunbar killed an 82-year-old woman after breaking into her home to rob her. This was murder in the furtherance of theft, and therefore capital. His conviction was reduced to manslaughter on appeal.
127 Even so, a Pathé news broadcast from 1958, which suggested murders had risen since the Homicide Act, showed a brief clip of Violet outside a prison, describing her as 'that tireless campaigner, Mrs Van der Elst', 'Is Murder Increasing?', *British Pathé*, 1958, www.britishpathe.com/video/is-murder-increasing/query/van+der+elst.
128 J. Rolls, 'A Whisper', *Daily Mirror*, 4 June 1957.

Archival collections

British Pathé, *www.britishpathe.com*
Mass Observation (MOA)
The National Archives, Home Office (HO)
TNA, Metropolitan Police Office (MEPO)

Newspapers and Magazines

Cornishman
Daily Express
Daily Mail
Daily Mirror
Daily Sketch
Daily Worker
Derby Daily Telegraph
Evening News
Evening Standard
Everybody's Weekly
Hull Daily Mail
Manchester Guardian
New York Times
Nottingham Evening Post
Picture Post
Sunday Referee
The Observer
The Star
The Times
Time
Western Morning News
Western Gazette

Bibliography

Bartie, A. and Jackson, L. A., 'Youth Crime and Preventive Policing in Post-War Scotland', *Twentieth Century British History*, 2011, 22(1): 79–102.

Bingham, A., *Gender, Modernity, and the Popular Press in Inter-War Britain*, Oxford: Clarendon Press, 2004.

Blewett, M. H., 'Traditions and Customs of Lancashire Popular Radicalism in Late Nineteenth-Century Industrial America', *International Labour and Working Class History*, 1992, 42: 5–19.

Brooke, S., '"A New World for Women?": Abortion Law Reform in Britain During the 1930s', *American Historical Review*, 2001, 106(2): 431–59.

Chadwick, R. G., *Bureaucratic Mercy: The Home Office and the Treatment of Capital Cases in Victorian England*, unpublished PhD thesis, Rice University, 1989.

D'Cruze, S., 'Intimacy, Professionalism and Domestic Homicide in Interwar Britain: the Case of Buck Ruxton', *Women's History Review*, 2007, 16(5): 701–22.

Elst, van der, V., *On the Gallows*, London: The Doge Press, 1937.

Gattey, C. N., *The Incredible Mrs van der Elst*, London: Leslie Fremin, 1972.

Giles, J., 'Class, Gender and Domestic Consumption in Britain, 1920–50', *Gender and Consumption*, E. Casey and L. Martens (eds), Aldershot: Ashgate, 2007, 15–32.

Gregory, J., *Victorians Against the Gallows*, London: I. B. Tauris, 2012.

Hansard, HoC Debate 14 May 1959, vol. 605, cols 172–173W.

Hazelgrove, J., *Spiritualism and British Society Between the Wars*, Manchester: Manchester University Press, 2000.

King, J. E., '"We Could Eat the Police": Popular Violence in the North Lancashire Cotton Strike of 1878', *Victorian Studies*, 1985, 28(3): 439–71.

Luckhurst, T., 'It is Thrown Against me that I have a Castle', *Journalism Studies*, 2012, 13(1): 107–23.

McCammon, H. J., '"Out of the Parlors and into the Streets": The Changing Tactical Repertoire of the US Women's Suffrage Movements', *Social Forces*, 2003, 81(3): 787–818.

Mercer, J., 'Media and Militancy: Propaganda in the Women's Social and Political Union's Campaign', *Women's History Review*, 2005, 14(3&4): 471–86.

Morris, T., *Pentonville*, London: Routledge and Kegan Paul, 1963.

Potter, H., *Hanging in Judgment*, London: SCM Press, 1993.

Pugh, M., *Speak for Britain: A New History of the Labour Party*, London: Vintage, 2011.

Smith, H. L., *The British Women's Suffrage Campaign, 1866–1928*, Harlow: Pearson Education Ltd, 2nd edition, 2007.

Smith, J., 'The Radical Literary Magazine of the 1930s and British Government Surveillance: the Case of *Storm* Magazine', *Literature and History*, 2010, 19(2): 69–86.

Thurlow, R. C., 'The Straw that Broke the Camel's Back: Public Order, Civil Liberties and the Battle of Cable Street', *Jewish Culture and History*, 1998, 1(2): 74–94.

Tilsley, F., *Thicker Than Water*, London: The Popular Book Club, 1956.

Tinkler, P. and Warsh, C. K., 'Feminine Modernity in Interwar Britain and North America: Corsets, Cars and Cigarettes', *Journal of Women's History*, 2008, 20(3): 113–43.

Tuttle, E. O., *The Crusade Against Capital Punishment in Britain*, London: Stevens and Sons, 1961.

Twitchell, N., *The Politics of the Rope*, Bury St Edmunds: Arena, 2012.

Williams, C. A., 'Britain's Police Forces: Forever Removed from Democratic Control?', *History and Policy*, 2003, www.historyandpolicy.org/papers/policy-paper-16.html.

——'Police Governance: Community, Policing, and Justice in the Modern UK', *Taiwan in Comparative Perspective*, 2011, 3: 50–65.

5 Public responses to capital punishment

Historical public responses to the death penalty are elusive, even those from the well-documented twentieth century. The reported behaviour of execution crowds provides a sense of how the condemned provoked differing reactions, and examples of popular protest demonstrate that certain cases, especially those perceived as blatantly unfair, generated dissatisfaction with the application of the death penalty. However, this evidence does not give us access to more detailed understandings and perceptions of justice and injustice in relation to capital punishment.

Opinion polling on this issue in Britain began in the 1930s, the results of which can usefully shed light on how people responded to the issue of the death penalty in the abstract[1] – whether they thought it should be employed as a form of punishment, or whether they thought it should be abolished or suspended. Answers to abstract questions are important as they indicate how the issue is understood politically, but they do not illuminate deeper cultural understandings and they also do not show how views and responses shift according to the contextual details of particular cases. The impact of doubts over the soundness of a conviction or the presence of mitigating circumstances in relation to the crime are not captured by abstract closed questioning. More recent research on public attitudes towards punishment and sentencing finds that contextual information about the crime and the offender tends to lessen punitive responses, as does more information about sentencing options.[2] American data on public opinion of the death penalty shows that respondents' knowledge of the murderer's biographical details reduces the likelihood they will approve of execution in relation to that case.[3]

1 Gallup polls were collected on the issue in Britain from 1938. For an overview of mid-twentieth-century American and European results, which includes Britain, see H. Erskine, 'Capital Punishment: The Polls', *Public Opinion Quarterly*, 1970, 34(2): 290–307.
2 J. D. Unnever and F. T. Cullen, 'The Social Sources of Americans' Punitiveness: A Test of Three Competing Models', *Criminology*, 2010, 48(1): 99–129, p. 100.
3 S. R. Gross, 'American Public Opinion on the Death Penalty – It's Getting Personal', *Cornell Law Review*, 1998, 83(6): 1448–74.

British opinion polling on capital punishment in the mid-twentieth century found that approval fluctuated at certain points. This is consistent with the greater anxiety that surrounded the issue in the 1950s, although there remained a majority in favour of retention.[4] Recent American research on declining public support for the death penalty in the twenty-first century suggests that certain key factors, such as concern over execution of the innocent and apparent arbitrariness of application, are significant.[5] Direct comparison with mid-twentieth-century Britain is not possible as data on the particular impact of innocence and arbitrariness were not collected. However, there are qualitative sources, such as letters from the public and responses to open-ended survey questions, that do enable analysis of the significance of these issues in relation to specific cases. These sources, particularly the letters, also enable analysis of the symbolic meanings that people attached to capital punishment.

This chapter focuses largely on public responses to capital punishment in mid-twentieth-century Britain as they were articulated in letters and telegrams to the Home Secretary (or to the monarch or MPs that were forwarded to the Home Office). In addition, it also includes analysis of open-ended responses from one of the Mass Observation surveys on capital punishment carried out for the *Daily Telegraph* in 1955–56. The letters present a much fuller articulation of individuals' views than the survey answers and have the advantage of being non-engineered responses expressing whatever the author wished. They are not, of course, 'representative' sources of public opinion but allow analysis of meaning and significance in relation to capital cases.[6] Letters articulated the emotionally intense and multi-dimensional nature of people's views. Those who were motivated to write in response to a particular case were the exception,[7]

---

4 As would be expected, different polls produced different results. See L. R. England, 'Capital Punishment and Open-End Questions', *Public Opinion Quarterly*, 1948, 12(3): 412–16, H. Potter, *Hanging in Judgment*, London: SCM Press Ltd, 1993, p. 145 and B. Block and J. Hostettler, *Hanging in the Balance*, Winchester: Waterside Press, 1997, pp. 179, 266.

5 See M. L. Radelet and M. J. Borg, 'The Changing Nature of Death Penalty Debates', *Annual Review of Sociology*, 2000, 26: 43–61, S. R. Gross and P. Ellsworth, 'Second Thoughts: Americans' Views on the Death Penalty at the Turn of the Century', Public Law and Legal Theory Research Paper 00.05, University of Michigan, 2001: http://conium.org/~maccoun/LP_Gross%20Ellsworth2003.pdf, J. L. Kirchmeier, 'Another Place Beyond Here: The Death Penalty Moratorium Movement in the United States', *University of Colorado Law Review*, 2002, 73(1): 1–116 and F. R. Baumgartner, S. L. De Boef and A. E. Boydstun, *The Decline of the Death Penalty and the Discovery of Innocence*, Cambridge: Cambridge University Press, 2008.

6 M. Lynch, 'Capital Punishment as Moral Imperative: Pro Death Penalty Discourse on the Internet', *Punishment and Society*, 2002, 4(2): 213–36: Lynch analysed comments and discussion on pro-death penalty websites.

7 On letters as a source of public opinion, see T. Lee, *Mobilizing Public Opinion: Black Insurgency and Racial Attitudes in the Civil Rights Era*, Chicago, IL: University of Chicago Press, 2002, pp. 91–119. Lee argues that people who write to politicians are likely to be better educated. However, letters are a relatively democratic form as they are cheap to write and send, and also require only bare literacy, see M. Cross and C. Bland, 'Gender Politics: Breathing New Life into Old Letters', C. Bland and M. Cross (eds), *Gender and Politics in the Age of Letter Writing, 1750–2000*, Aldershot: Ashgate, 2004, pp. 5–6.

although they inevitably drew on (and reconstructed) wider cultural scripts. In particular, letter writers who were not personally connected to a case responded on the basis of what they had learned from newspaper reports.[8]

The survey responses comprise a much smaller dataset than the letters (in terms of number and length) but are valuable as they were from people who did not write to someone in authority about the issue or a case, but rather were asked about their views as they went about their day. Mass Observation sought to elicit 'self-expressionist' replies in their surveys by including questions on how people felt about certain issues.[9] The 1955–56 Capital Punishment Survey asked respondents whether they had seen, heard or read anything recently that had changed their opinion on capital punishment. This was included because there had been a 'good deal of discussion in the press and on the BBC'.[10]

In this chapter, these letters and survey responses are not discussed primarily in relation to the binary issues of retention and abolition. Until the Homicide Act 1957, all guilty verdicts for sane defendants in murder trials led to the death sentence. The judge and jury had no discretion in relation to the sentence but both could pass along a recommendation to mercy. The decision of whether or not to reprieve a condemned prisoner rested solely with the Home Secretary, although he was advised by his civil servants. Perceived inappropriate or unfair use of reprieve could provoke strong responses from the press and public. These responses could be tied to abolitionist views, but there was no inconsistency with either fully supporting the capital sentence as it operated but expressing dismay at certain reprieves or failure to reprieve, or in approving of the death penalty as a form of punishment but believing that it should be reformed or limited (which is what happened after the Homicide Act).[11] Turning the spotlight away from the issue of abolition alone allows us to more clearly see how contentious capital punishment became in the 1950s, without insisting that this contentiousness was only significant if it was attached to the movement for abolition.

Letters and petitioning for mercy

Many of the letters to the Home Office about capital prisoners continued the well-established tradition of petitioning for mercy. This was where

---

8 Bruckweh and Wood interpret letters sent to and about those accused of murder as forms of 'reader response' to news media. See K. Bruckweh, 'Fantasies of Violence: German Citizens Expressing their Concepts of Violence and Ideas about Democracy in Letters to Referring to the Case of the Serial Killer Jurgen Bartsch (1966–71)', *Crime, History and Societies*, 2006, 10(2): 53–82 and J. C. Wood, *The Most Remarkable Women in England*, Manchester: Manchester University Press, 2012, Ch. 9.

9 C. Langhamer, '"The Live Dynamic Whole of Feeling and Behaviour": Capital Punishment and the Politics of Emotion, 1945–57', *Journal of British Studies*, 2012, 51(2): 416–41, p. 418.

10 Report on Survey, Correspondence 1956 (Capital Punishment Survey 1956), MOA/72-2-A.

11 Related points have been made about the contemporary death penalty moratorium movement in the United States. Kirchmeier argues it 'is not an "anti-death penalty movement" because a large portion of the movement's supporters are not against the death penalty per se', 'Another Place', p. 21.

individuals made representation on behalf of the condemned with the hope of securing a reprieve. In the eighteenth century, in addition to the condemned and their relatives, respectable members of the local community, such as employers and landowners, would make petitions. These emphasised the condemned's qualities, such as hard work and respectability, and/or might stress mitigating factors, such as poverty.[12] The devastating impact that hanging the condemned would have on his or her family was also highlighted. In the nineteenth century, abolitionist campaigners also wrote to the Home Office on behalf of condemned prisoners and, in particular, would underline any reasons to doubt the safety of the conviction.[13]

This chapter explores letters sent to the Home Office in relation to capital cases in England and Wales in the mid-twentieth century and concentrates on those from the late 1940s onwards. It is derived from research carried out from case files of capital prisoners held in The National Archives into public responses to the death penalty 1930–65, the era of abolition. This means that only cases from England and Wales were included, although particularly after the Second World War, letters about these were received from all over the country (and further afield). All open files from the period were reviewed and 25 cases were selected for closer analysis according to volume of correspondence.[14]

In the late 1940s, there was a shift in responses from the public. In the 1930s and earlier 1940s, letters in relation to capital cases were mainly from people personally connected to the condemned, such as relatives, friends and neighbours. In keeping with the traditions of petitioning, letters were also sent by 'local notables'[15] like employers, former headmasters, vicars, the mayor and the local MP. They vouched for the respectability of the condemned, stressed the impact that execution would have on their families and highlighted any mitigating factors. A large number of letters in response to cases from this period was around thirty. In the late 1940s, letters became more numerous for certain high-profile cases and could run into the hundreds. In 1948, the death penalty became more politically salient than it had been previously, when a majority of MPs voted for abolition and it was suspended for most of the

12 See D. Hay, 'Property, Authority and the Criminal Law', D. Hay, P. Linebaugh, J. G. Rule, E. P. Thompson and C. Winslow (eds), *Albion's Fatal Tree*, London: Allen Lane, 1975, P. King, 'Decision-Makers and Decision-Making in the English Criminal Law, 1750–1800', *The Historical Journal*, 1984, 27(1): 25–58 and J. M. Beattie, 'The Royal Pardon and Criminal Procedure in Early Modern England', *Historical Papers*, 1987, 22(1): 9–22.

13 On nineteenth-century petitions, see V. A. C. Gatrell, *The Hanging Tree*, Oxford: Oxford University Press, 1996, pp. 198–220 and, on one particular case, M. J. Wiener, 'The Sad Story of George Hall: Adultery, Murder and the Politics of Mercy in Mid Victorian England', *Social History*, 1999, 24(2): 174–95. On letters sent by the Victorian Society for the Abolition of Capital Punishment, see J. Gregory, *Victorians Against the Gallows*, London: I. B. Tauris, 2012, pp. 212–14.

14 This selection was made according to what constituted a large volume at the time of the case. More letters were sent in relation to high-profile cases when capital punishment became more culturally and politically salient in the late 1940s.

15 Beattie, 'The Royal Pardon', p. 16.

year. Relatives, friends and 'local worthies'[16] did not stop writing, but their letters were far outweighed by those from people not personally connected to the condemned, and who were geographically dispersed. Unlike the Victorian Society for the Abolition of Capital Punishment, the National Council for the Abolition of the Death Penalty refrained from intervening in individual cases on the grounds that they opposed all capital punishment on principle. Violet van der Elst wrote letters to the Home Office in relation to capital cases throughout her campaign and Gerald Gardiner wrote as Chairman of the National Campaign for the Abolition of Capital Punishment.[17] By the 1960s, the Howard League sometimes did intervene in specific cases.[18] This chapter will concentrate on letters sent by the wider public.

The shift towards a wider constituency of letter writers in the late 1940s introduced the phenomenon of people writing to protest against reprieve.[19] These remained the minority as people were more likely to be motivated to write in order to help save someone than to ensure their demise, but these letters help to cast light on punitive rather than lenient responses. The most important, recurrent symbol utilised in the letters after the late 1940s was justice. This signalled the increased prominence of capital punishment as a national issue at this time and the intensification of anxiety that surrounded it. Correspondence in relation to capital cases therefore articulated popular understandings of justice and injustice, offering a window into how these symbols were constructed culturally beyond the legal system.

Five main objections to failure to reprieve, or to reprieve in itself, were articulated in public responses in relation to the justice symbol. The first was doubt about the safety of the conviction, whether for reasons of weak evidence, lack of motive or concern about the validity of the condemned's confession. The second was mitigation, whereby the author highlighted factors such as possible insanity, previous experience of mistreatment and living in poverty that did not appear to have received due attention. Mitigation was closely connected to the justice symbol because letter writers argued that to ignore these factors would be to perpetrate an injustice. The third was arbitrariness, where objection was raised either because it appeared the condemned would be executed for a lesser crime than those committed by reprieved prisoners, or

16 S. Garton, 'Managing Mercy: African Americans, Parole and Paternalism in the Georgia Prison System 1919–45', *Journal of Social History*, 2003, 36(3): 675–99, p. 682.
17 For example, Letter from Gerald Gardiner to the Home Office in relation to Ronald Marwood, London, 28 April 1959, TNA/HO291/242 and in relation to George Riley, 6 February 1961, HO291/250.
18 In a letter to the Home Office on behalf of George Riley (see Chapter Six), Elizabeth Howard, Acting Secretary of the Howard League, stated 'I feel obliged, on a point of principle, once again to break the usual rule of the Howard League that it does not intervene in individual cases', London, 5 February 1961, HO291/250.
19 This was not unprecedented – both Wiener 'Sad Story' and Gregory *Victorians* discuss pro-execution/anti-reprieve letters sent to the Home Office in the nineteenth century. However, such letters were not sent in the 1930s when the death penalty had lower salience.

conversely where the author feared they might be reprieved where lesser crimes had resulted in hanging. The fourth was inequity, where it seemed it was easier for certain types of people to secure a reprieve than others. This objection was mainly raised in relation to women and usually in order to argue that women stood less chance of being treated fairly. However, there were also objections that women were consistently treated too leniently. The fifth was a retributive objection which argued that reprieve would be a failure to secure justice for the victim, the victim's relatives or society more widely. More than one objection could be raised by the same letter writer. For example, insanity as a mitigating factor was closely related to doubt – an insane prisoner should have been ineligible for execution so insanity raised doubt over culpability.

Questioning justice was the predominant, but by no means the only, response to capital punishment expressed by letter writers and Mass Observation survey respondents. It is the focus of this chapter partly for reasons of brevity but also because, as discussed in previous chapters, the death penalty's perceived failure to be just was a compelling reason for its deepening ambivalence after the Second World War. Other important themes for those urging reprieve were the toll that hanging the prisoner would take on his or her relatives (a continuation of a well-established theme in 1930s cases), or a sense of empathy or personal identification with the condemned, on the grounds of which authors pleaded mercy.[20] The theme of the impact that execution would have on the condemned's relatives was related to notions of justice as, on a certain level, it argued that it was unfair to include innocent others in the punishment. However, most authors did not make the point in these terms but rather employed an emotional register to articulate the suffering that relatives would experience.[21] Those who deplored reprieve tended to emphasise the need for deterrence, a point that was closely related to concerns about safety from violence in a changing society.

Justice as symbol

Justice and punishment are not synonymous but 'justice' is a key symbol that can be deployed to validate the application of punishment. Punishment rests on legitimised coercion and violence. This is particularly apparent in relation to the death penalty but, as Cover argues, cooperation with other, lesser forms of punishment is also underpinned by the state's sanctioned use of violence.[22]

20 I have discussed personal identification with the condemned, especially if they were female, elsewhere, see L. Seal, 'Public Reactions to the Case of Mary Wilson, the Last Woman to be Sentenced to Death in England and Wales', *Papers from the British Criminology Conference*, 2008, 8: 64–84 and 'Ruth Ellis and Public Contestation of the Death Penalty', *The Howard Journal*, 2011, 50(5): 492–504.
21 See Seal, 'Ruth Ellis' – there was particular concern from letter writers about Ellis' children losing their mother, but also fears about the impact of the execution on her parents.
22 R. Cover, 'Violence and the Word', *Yale Law Journal*, 1986, 95(8): 1601–29, p. 1608.

A resistant prisoner would be forcibly taken to jail. 'Justice' is the symbol that legitimates the violence and coercion entailed by punishment. Via the legal system, meaning is created for the punishment event for those who benefit from it – supposedly members of the wider society. The capital sentence is unique in that it 'constitutes the most plain, the most deliberate, and the most thoughtful manifestation of legal interpretation as violence',[23] which cannot be fully obscured by 'the façade of civility'.[24] The special status of the death sentence means that it reveals more of the 'structure of interpretation' than other types of cases.[25] Cover, writing about American capital punishment, discusses this in relation to judicial interpretation. The possibility of the judge granting a stay of execution 'makes the deed an act of interpretation'.[26]

The British context was different in that the death sentence was an act of political, rather than judicial, interpretation as the power to reprieve lay with the Home Secretary. However, Cover's argument is also relevant to the system of reprieve – although the Home Office did not make reasons for reprieve public, the decision to grant or withhold it revealed something of the structure of interpretation that took place. For the most part, capital punishment works as a 'well co-ordinated form of violence'[27] but there is always 'a tragic limit to the common meaning that can be achieved'.[28] On this limit of common meaning 'falls the shadow of the violence of law, itself'.[29]

Cover's notion of the 'tragic limit' to shared meaning can be usefully applied to responses to capital punishment in mid-twentieth-century Britain. Whilst many capital prisoners had at least some letters sent to the Home Office on their behalf, few inspired the kind of geographically widespread responses that this chapter analyses. This is explicable as most capital cases – whether resulting in execution or reprieve (and imprisonment) – did not test the limits of common meaning. However, the 'shadow of the violence of law' increasingly fell on certain, high-profile capital cases in the 1950s. Although states need to legitimise their own violence in the name of justice, and attempt to 'dissociate their justice from human fallibility',[30] this attempt became stretched to the point of breaking in 1950s Britain.

As a general, abstract concept, 'justice' does not have one specific definition.[31] Rather, it is flexible. However, justice is a significant symbol, which through shared meanings, 'makes social communication and understanding possible'.[32] In responses to capital punishment, members of the public could draw on the

---

23 Ibid., p. 1622.
24 Ibid., p. 1623.
25 Ibid.
26 Ibid., p. 1624.
27 Ibid.
28 Ibid., p. 1629.
29 Ibid.
30 D. E. Curtis and J. Reswick, 'Images of Justice', *Yale Law Journal*, 1987, 96(8): 1727–72, p. 1733.
31 C. Burnett, 'Justice: Myth and Symbol', *Legal Studies Forum*, 1987, 11(1): 79–94, p. 79.
32 Ibid.

shared but flexible meanings of justice to 'increase [the] power of state-ments'.[33] This was especially applicable to letter writers, who were trying to influence the Home Secretary's decision of whether to reprieve the con-demned or not. The rest of the chapter analyses public responses to capital punishment that utilised the symbol of justice, and is organised around the five objections previously outlined.

Doubt

Doubt about the safety of murder convictions was an increasingly prominent concern in public responses to the death penalty from the late 1940s onwards. This was expressed as scepticism in relation to whether the prisoner had committed the crime or as an assertion that the legal process had not been conducted properly. These concerns about the integrity of the criminal justice system were exacerbated by the Timothy Evans case. However, unease was already building prior to the discovery of John Christie's crimes in 1953. Daniel Raven was a 23-year-old hanged for the murder of his in-laws, Leo-pold and Esther Goodman, on 6 January 1950, whilst his wife was in hospital recovering from the birth of their first child. According to the prosecution, he beat the Goodmans to death in their own home. When the police first spoke to him, they noticed that he was wearing a spotless linen suit, which struck them as unusual for clothes that had been worn all day in London. When they searched his home, they found blood stained trousers stuffed into the boiler.

Uncertainty about the safety of Raven's conviction centred on two main issues. The first was that he did not appear to have a motive for the murders. His explanation for the blood stained trousers – that he had discovered the Goodmans' bodies and fled their house in panic – was regarded by some as plausible. The other area for concern was his sanity. He had been ruled sane by the prison doctors but the defence argued that his epilepsy meant that if he had committed the murder, he was not legally responsible. Letter writers to the Home Office expressed scepticism about the safety of the evidence against him.

A female correspondent protested 'there isn't one iota of proof in this case' and was amazed that Raven had been 'found guilty on such slender evi-dence'.[34] A letter from Rainham, signed by eight people, explained '[w]e feel that the evidence put forward by the prosecution, as reported in the popular press, falls far short of the accepted standards in British Courts of Law'.[35] Raven's apparent lack of motive was troubling to others. A letter from Bridgnorth, signed by eleven people, explicitly employed the symbol of justice: 'He had no motive. We think that Justice if it is called so, in this case, is all

33 Ibid.
34 Letter from female author to the Home Office, Liverpool, 25 November 1949, TNA/HO45/ 24497. Names of letter writers are not given for reasons of confidentiality.
35 Letter signed by eight people to Home Office, Rainham, 29 December 1949, HO45/24497.

wrong'.[36] An After-care Officer from Keighley lamented 'I cannot think of any murder case, in recent times, where the prisoner appeared to receive so little "Justice"'.[37] A retired major from Folkestone warned 'there might possibly be a miscarriage of justice as there is no mention of fingerprints [in news stories]'.[38] The possibility that the murder had been committed by someone else and the bodies merely discovered by Raven nagged at other correspondents. A letter writer from Hampstead pointed out that there had been other cases where someone was covered in blood but innocent[39] and an author from Stamford Hill cautioned against 'draw[ing] conclusions from the actions and statements of a man at the time of his greatest state of shock'.[40] Favouring the alternative killer explanation, a husband and wife from Wokingham distinguished their doubts from abolitionism, stating 'we are certainly not "anti this or anti that" neither do we belong to any society working for the abolition of the death sentence'.[41]

Doubts about guilt and shaky evidence were also expressed in letters on behalf of Louisa Merrifield (on her case, see Chapter Three). A correspondent worried that Merrifield was 'not getting fair justice' as it seemed possible that Sarah Ann Ricketts could have died from natural causes.[42] This possibility was highlighted by others, along with alternative explanations that Mrs Ricketts could have poisoned herself[43] or died of liver disease.[44] Amateur sleuthing from some letter writers indicated that they were readers of 'golden age' detective fiction.[45] Alternative suggestions for the presence of phosphorous in Rickett's blood included 'eating mussels'[46] and ingesting it 'from the head of a match'.[47] Doubts about the certainty of Merrifield's conviction were also related to the perception that her trial had not been fair. In addition to 'unsafe evidence', there had been a 'prejudiced judge'.[48] In stronger terms, a woman from London stated 'the trial reminded me and many of my friends of a mediaeval witch trial', with the judge clearly being against Merrifield.[49]

Louisa Merrifield's case took place after fears had emerged about Timothy Evans' innocence and after the troubling execution of Derek Bentley, and

36 Letter signed by eleven people, Bridgnorth, undated, HO45/24497.
37 Letter, gender unknown, Keighley, 30 December 1949, HO45/24497.
38 Letter, retired major, Folkestone, undated, HO45/24497.
39 Letter, gender unknown, Hampstead, undated, HO45/24497.
40 Letter, gender unknown, Stamford Hill, 28 December 1949, HO45/24497.
41 Letter, married couple, Wokingham, 21 December 1949, HO45/24497.
42 Letter, gender unknown, Perthshire, 15 September 1953, HO291/229.
43 Letter, female author, Canonbie, 5 September 1953, HO291/229.
44 Letter, gender unknown, unaddressed, undated, HO291/229.
45 D'Cruze argues that these novels were a popular way for crime and law to be talked through, S. D'Cruze, '"Dad's Back": Mapping Masculinities, Moralities and the Law in the Novels of Margery Allingham', *Cultural and Social History*, 2004, 1(3): 256–79.
46 Letter, gender unknown, Birmingham, 4 September 1953, HO291/229.
47 Letter, male author, Wirral, 31 August 1953, HO291/229.
48 Letter, male author, Newquay, 5 September 1953, HO291/229.
49 Letter, female author, London, 11 September 1953, HO291/229.

anxiety about these cases echoed in letters about her. A woman from Banwell argued that '[a]fter the case of "Timothy Evans" circumstantial evidence should not be sufficient for such a terrible decision'.[50] An author from Eastbourne pointed out that '[i]t is well known that innocent people have been hanged' and stated that 'Bentley, Evans and Christie' should not have been executed.[51] There was the danger of a 'tragic injustice'[52] and two women writing on behalf of St Helens Women's Co-operative Guild urged the Home Secretary to avert a 'miscarriage of justice'.[53]

By the mid-1950s, the cumulative effects of high-profile cases in which there was doubt over the guilt of the condemned or the soundness of the legal process was reflected in letters sent to the Home Office.[54] In January 1956, three men were granted free pardons and compensated for wrongful conviction and imprisonment. They had been sentenced two years previously for the grievous bodily harm of a police officer during a raid on a post office in Buckinghamshire. Two other prisoners confessed to the crime and a campaign for the release of Leonard Emery, Arthur Thompson and James Powers was pursued by their families, MPs and the Council for Civil Liberties.[55] If the police officer had died from his injuries, it was possible that the men would have been executed as they would have been found guilty of murder. Along with the Evans/Christie case, this appeared to be further evidence of the criminal justice system's fallibility. A letter writer from Northern Ireland asked '[i]s it possible that an innocent person could be hanged in error? The recent case of three men compensated for wrongful imprisonment answers yes'.[56] A man from Winchester wrote that 'after presumably a fair trial three men were wrongfully convicted of shooting a policeman', highlighting the legal system's inadequacy.[57] Referring to this wrongful conviction as an example, a correspondent from Rugby argued that only with abolition could the system be 'free from the danger of making mistakes that put us beyond any form of restoration'.[58]

Such concerns weighed on respondents to Mass Observation's Capital Punishment survey 1955/6. As discussed, due to the significance of contentious

50 Letter, female author, Banwell, 16 August 1953, HO291/229.
51 Letter, gender unknown, Eastbourne, 14 September 1953, HO291/229.
52 Letter signed 'Harassed Tory', Malvern, 11 September 1953, HO291/229.
53 Letter from two women for St Helens Women's Co-operative Guild, St Helens, undated, HO291/229.
54 This has parallels with the situation in the United States post-2000, whereby recognition that the possibility for wrongful conviction is not 'vanishingly rare' has deepened unease about the death penalty, L. C. Marshall, 'The Innocence Revolution and the Death Penalty', *Ohio State Journal of Criminal Law*, 2004, 2: 573–84, p. 577. See also M. A. Godsey and T. Pulley, 'The Innocence Revolution and our "Evolving Standards of Decency" in Death Penalty Jurisprudence', *University of Dayton Law Review*, 2004, 29(2): 265–87.
55 See 'Pardon Granted to Three Men', *The Times*, 14 January 1956 and 'MP to Ask About Freed Men', *The Times*, 16 January 1956.
56 Letter, gender unknown, County Antrim, 13 February 1956, HO291/92.
57 Letter, male author, Winchester, 13 February 1956, HO291/92.
58 Letter, gender unknown, Rugby, 10 February 1956, HO291/92.

high-profile cases, the 1950s' survey contained a question that asked respondents if there was anything they had 'seen or heard' that had influenced their views on the death penalty. Answers such as 'there is always the possibility of hanging an innocent person',[59] '[s]ometimes an innocent man has been hanged'[60] and 'if a mistake is made, there is no going back'[61] illustrated the damage that perceived miscarriages of justice had done to the death penalty's credibility. Responses showed the importance of Timothy Evans and Derek Bentley in creating doubt about capital punishment. A retired shipwright from North Shields stated that 'Christie was the murderer and Evans should have got off'[62] and a female receptionist from Oldham mentioned Bentley and Evans as 'two people who didn't do the murder'.[63] Some respondents specifically articulated how these cases had changed their thinking. For a female typist from Sunderland, the 'Bentley case made me feel uncertain'[64] and an engine driver from Nottingham explained 'the case of Evans being unjustly hung was the turning point in my opinion'.[65] A housewife from Prestonpans reasoned that with abolition '[a]t least an innocent man would never lose his life then, and if a mistake had been made, we could give restitution'.[66]

Mitigation

The failure to recognise mitigating circumstances was a strong and recurrent theme in letters to the Home Office. Implicitly, the stress on mitigating factors was always connected to perceptions of justice as responses questioned the soundness of capital punishment in cases where these factors had not been adequately taken into consideration. Some letter writers also explicitly linked the failure to take account of mitigating circumstances to the symbol of justice and to concerns that the legal system was not working properly. As explained, Daniel Raven's defence was twofold – that he had not carried out the murders of the Goodmans and that, due to epilepsy, he should be found guilty but insane if the jury concluded that he had killed them. This dual argument was also made in some of the letters to the Home Office. A correspondent from Kilburn, signing herself 'old lady of 74', questioned whether Raven was guilty and also contended '[i]f he did commit the crime he must have had a brain storm'.[67] A woman from Birmingham pointed out that there was 'no

59 Female County Welfare Officer, 40, Rothbury, Capital Punishment Survey 1955–56, MOA/72–73-A.
60 Male Chief Petty Naval Office, 40, East Lothian, 72–73-A.
61 Male Shoe Repairer, 53, Coatbridge, 72–73-A.
62 Male retired Shipwright, 70, North Shields, 72–73-C.
63 Female Receptionist, 28, Oldham, 72–73-D.
64 Female Typist, 30, Sunderland, 72–74-B.
65 Male Engine Driver, 44, Nottingham, 72–74-B.
66 Housewife, 61, Prestonpans, 72–75-E.
67 Letter, female author, Kilburn, 4 January 1950, TNA/HO45/24497.

certainty' that Raven committed the murder, but if he had 'it must have been done under great emotional stress'.[68]

Others accepted that Raven had killed his parents-in-law but argued execution would be a miscarriage of justice as he had been suffering from a 'brainstorm' at the time.[69] He was 'morally innocent, but insane'.[70] The combination of epilepsy and youth as mitigating factors was articulated by a male author from Swindon, who explained that epilepsy could cause 'feelings and conditions of mind, with which a *young* man, unmatured in the experience of grappling with the difficulties of the world, could not cope', meaning execution 'would be a grave miscarriage of justice'.[71]

Derek Bentley's case, as discussed below, was perceived to be unjust because he did not carry out the murder but mitigating factors were also a theme in correspondence to the Home Office. A married couple from Birmingham pointed out that he was unable to read or write, commenting that there was 'something cockeyed' with justice in Britain.[72] Chapter Two explored how Bentley's youth added to the contentiousness of his execution, and concern about 'hang[ing] a child'[73] and a young man who had not 'grown up' was articulated by letter writers.[74] In addition to his youth, Bentley was perceived as having been 'led astray' by Christopher Craig.[75] The failure to reprieve 'an acknowledged halfwit' who had been recommended to mercy was challenged by a male correspondent from Essex.[76] A female author from London felt that the government and judiciary were 'headstrong' in their desire for 'harsher measures' which 'tends seriously to prevent consideration being given to the circumstances of particular cases'.[77] Historically, petitioning for mercy had established a strong tradition of highlighting mitigating factors as a reason to grant clemency. By the 1950s there was also emphasis from letter writers on failure to recognise such factors as an injustice, which cast doubt on the integrity of the legal system and the Home Secretary's decision-making, rather than being simply an element of supplication.

Arbitrariness

Like doubt, perceived arbitrariness in clemency or capital sentencing found the 'tragic limit' of common meanings of the death penalty, and revealed the

68 Letter, female author, Birmingham, 4 January 1950, HO45/24497.
69 Record of telephone call to Home Office from male caller from Edmonton, 5 January 1950, HO45/24497.
70 Letter, male author to the King, Bournemouth, 4 January 1950, HO45/24497.
71 Letter, male author, Nr Swindon, 4 January 1950, HO45/24497.
72 Letter, married couple, Birmingham, 22 January 1953, HO291/225.
73 Letter, male author, Plymouth, 13 January 1953, HO291/225.
74 Letter, female author, Berkshire, 11 January 1953, HO291/225.
75 Letter, five members of one family, London, 13 January 1953, HO291/225.
76 Letter, male author, Essex, 14 February 1953, HO291/225.
77 Letter, female author, London, 26 January 1953, HO291/225.

law's violence. Letter writers questioned the failure to reprieve Daniel Raven when child killers had received mercy. A family from Wimbledon protested that 'Mrs Tierney, who killed a baby, was reprieved'[78] and a 'Mother of Four Children' asked 'Why not hang Mrs Tierney and also the WRAC woman'.[79] A man from Bexleyheath challenged the Home Secretary for being 'inconsistent' with clemency, explaining 'I am activated only by an underlying passion for fair play'.[80]

Anxieties about arbitrariness haunted responses to the hanging of Margaret Allen in 1949. She was a single woman who frequently wore men's clothes and went by the name 'Bill'. Her crime was to have beaten to death her elderly neighbour, Nancy Chadwick, with a hammer.[81] Letter writers argued that other violent murderers had escaped the gallows after committing worse crimes. A correspondent from Middlesex stated 'other murderers are getting away with the same dastardly act day after day'[82] and a man from Leicester queried why Allen was to be hanged and not other 'arch villains'.[83] Many were explicit about which cases they thought more deserving of the death penalty. Referring to the example of Donald Thomas, who was reprieved for the murder of a police officer, a letter writer scorned '[d]o you call that justice. Well I don't'.[84] A male author from Liverpool cited the 'equally heinous crimes' of the rape and murder of an actress and killing of a policeman that had resulted in reprieve in order to question whether it was 'right or fair' to hang Allen.[85] Cassandra's column in the *Daily Mirror* made the same point that Allen's case was 'utterly different' from one like the murder of a policeman.[86]

Similar concerns were raised in relation to Ruth Ellis, especially due to the compelling mitigating circumstances that surrounded her case. A woman from Jersey pointed out that 'there are men, who have violated and killed little

78 Letter from a family, Wimbledon, 5 January 1950, HO45/24497. Nora Tierney was found guilty of murdering a three-year-old girl, the daughter of a neighbour, by beating her to death with a hammer. She was certified insane and sent to Broadmoor, which was different from receiving a reprieve. See 'Murdered Child: Woman Sentenced to Death', *The Times*, 19 October 1949 and 'Mrs Tierney Ordered to Broadmoor', *The Times*, 22 November 1949.

79 Letter, female author, Bilston, 4 January 1950, HO45/24497. The 'WRAC woman' was Margaret Williams, 21, a private in the WRAC, who stabbed to death her 35 year old husband, Sergeant Major Montague Williams, in barracks in Austria. See 'W.R.A.C. Sentenced to Death', *The Times*, 20 September 1949 and 'Woman Reprieved', *The Times*, 1 October 1949.

80 Letter, male author, Bexleyheath, 5 January 1950, HO45/24497.

81 On Margaret Allen's case, see A. Ballinger, *Dead Woman Walking*, Aldershot: Ashgate, 2000, pp. 145–57 and A. Oram, *Her Husband was a Woman!: Women's Gender-Crossing in Popular Culture*, London: Routledge, 2007, pp. 143–5.

82 Letter, gender unknown, Middlesex, 10 January 1949, HO45/23935.

83 Letter, male author, Leicester, 9 January 1949, HO45/23935.

84 Letter, 'a friend', undated, unaddressed, HO45/23935.

85 Letter, male author, Liverpool, 9 January 1949, HO45/23935. The 'rape and murder of an actress' is likely to refer to Gay Gibson, murdered by James Camb, and mentioned below. See 'Camb Guilty of Liner Murder', *Manchester Guardian*, 23 March 1948.

86 Cassandra, 'Without a Hitch', *Daily Mirror*, 14 January 1949.

girls, who were put in prison, and are now free', whereas Ellis had 'killed under grave provocation'.[87] Similarly, a man from London argued that sex murderers should be executed, but hanging should not be the penalty for a crime like Ellis'.[88] The case of Donald Thomas recurred in letters on behalf of Ellis. A 'firm believer' in capital punishment argued that if Thomas could be reprieved for shooting a police officer, then Ellis should receive clemency too.[89] Letters about Allen and Ellis referred to the murder of Gay Gibson, who was pushed through a porthole into the sea by James Camb, as a worse crime for which the culprit was reprieved.[90] In relation to Ellis, there was also protest that mercy had been shown to 'young thugs',[91] 'hooligans'[92] and 'teddy boys'[93] who posed a danger to society, whereas her crime was committed under 'provocation and an intense emotional impulse'.[94] Respondents to the Mass Observation Capital Punishment Survey made similar points. A house-wife from Warrington said, 'when you see these others getting reprieved who've done murders worse than hers [Ellis']'[95] was something which had affected her views on the death penalty and a housewife from County Durham answered '[w]hy should Ruth Ellis have had to hang and other murderers get off'.[96] An editorial in the *Yorkshire Post* compared Ellis' case with that of Frederick Emmett-Dunne, who murdered a fellow sergeant, Reginald Watters, at their barracks in Duisberg and seven months later married Watters' widow.[97] His sentence was commuted as the death penalty had been abolished in Federal Germany. The editorial acknowledged that execution could not be carried out in Germany but argued '[t]he inconsistency in the respective fates of these two murderers may well cause a public revulsion against capital punishment'.[98]

These comparisons were particularly acute when there were different sen-tencing outcomes for the same crime. A letter writer on behalf of Derek Bentley explained that he would not 'lift a finger' to help Christopher Craig, but that Bentley had simply uttered the words of 'a young cinema-fed fool'.[99] A cor-respondent from Birmingham was 'in complete agreement with principles of

87 Letter, female author, Jersey, 23 June 1955, HO291/235.
88 Letter, male author, London, 30 June 1955, HO291/235.
89 Letter, gender unknown, London, 27 June 1955, HO291/235.
90 Letter about Margaret Allen, gender unknown, address illegible, undated, HO45/23935 and Letter about Ruth Ellis, gender unknown, London, 30 June 1955, HO291/235. Cassandra also mentioned this case in his column about Margaret Allen, 'Without a Hitch'.
91 Letter, gender unknown, Westcliff on Sea, 1 July 1955, HO291/235.
92 Letter, male author, London, 2 July 1955, HO291/235.
93 Letter, gender unknown, Surrey, 29 July 1955 and Letter, gender unknown, Amersham, 30 June 1955, HO291/235.
94 Letter, male author, London, 30 June 1955, HO291/235.
95 Housewife, 55, Warrington, Capital Punishment Survey 1955–56, MOA/72–76-A.
96 Housewife, 65, County Durham, 72–73-B.
97 'Emmett-Dunne Found Guilty', *Manchester Guardian*, 8 July 1955.
98 'The Fates of Two Murderers', *Yorkshire Post*, 21 July 1955.
99 Letter, male author, address illegible, 17 January 1953, TNA/HO291/225.

capital punishment' but was '[p]rompted by a sense of fair play' to write as the guilt was not equally shared between Bentley and Craig. Craig deserved the death penalty, Bentley life imprisonment.[100] An author from Sidcup was 'perturbed' at Bentley's death sentence, 'when the boy who did the shooting won't hang'.[101] Many letter writers echoed the view of a woman from Wirral that for Bentley to die 'for a murder he did not do' was 'unfair justice'.[102] A man from Gravesend pointed out that 'a life for a life' could not apply to Bentley because he had not committed the crime.[103] Justice was a strong symbol – a correspondent from Cardiff asked of the government 'have they no sense of justice?'.[104]

Louisa Merrifield stood trial along with her husband, Alfred, although he was acquitted. This struck many correspondents as unfair even though in this case the issue was not differential sentencing. A letter writer from Truro stated that Alfred was 'having the time of his life' and asked '[w]hy was he left to go free when his wife was hung?', arguing this was not 'fair justice'.[105] A married couple from London protested that it was not right to execute Louisa if Alfred had bought the poison and helped to administer it[106] and a man from Derby simply asked '[w]hy isn't her husband being executed?'.[107] Some authors referred back to the Derek Bentley case in order to highlight the recurrence of perceived arbitrariness in the parallel with Louisa facing execution and Alfred escaping.[108] Arbitrariness as a failure of justice also exercised letter writers who felt that reprieve would fail to recompense the crime. Derek Bentley was a reference point for authors questioning the reprieve of Michael Davis in 1954 (see Chapter Two). A correspondent pointed out that the Home Secretary had 'let Bentley hang' and asked 'what is it between the two cases?'.[109] A man from Shoreham complained that Davis' reprieve was 'a great shock' and Bentley had hanged 'yet he never fired a shot'.[110]

Inequity

Concerns about inequity in the application of the death penalty were different from objections to arbitrariness, as these responses alleged that due to social identity, certain condemned were more likely to be reprieved or executed than others. The inequity objection emerged particularly in relation to women,

---

100 Letter, gender unknown, Birmingham, 21 January 1953, HO291/225.
101 Letter, gender unknown, Sidcup, 13 January 1953, HO291/225.
102 Letter, female author, Wirral, 14 January 1953, HO291/225.
103 Letter, male author, Gravesend, 16 January 1953, HO291/225.
104 Letter, gender unknown, Cardiff, undated, HO291/225.
105 Letter, gender unknown, Truro, 10 October 1953, HO291/229.
106 Letter, male and female, London, 11 September 1953, HO291/229.
107 Letter, male author, Derby, 5 September 1953, HO291/229.
108 Letter, gender unknown, Norton-on-Tees, 17 September 1953, HO291/229.
109 Letter, gender unknown, Epsom, 25 January 1954, HO291/231.
110 Letter, male author, Shoreham, received 27 January 1954, HO291/231.

with letter writers fearing that women were likely to receive prejudicial treatment. Letter writers on behalf of Margaret Allen suspected that she failed to win a reprieve because she was a woman. A woman from London argued 'its [sic] definitely "look after the male sex and do nothing for the female sex"'[111] and a woman from Dorset sardonically noted 'a woman's eye for a woman's eye – and a woman's tooth for a woman's tooth – but rarely a man's eye for a woman's eye, a man's tooth for a woman's tooth'.[112] A correspondent from Cardiff was a supporter of capital punishment but felt 'nausea and revulsion' at the thought of hanging Allen as male murderers had been reprieved for 'callous crimes'.[113] Allen's poverty was also highlighted as a factor making it hard for her to win clemency. An author from Hove argued that if Allen had been wealthy 'there can be no doubt that a psychiatrist would have been employed, and not much doubt that reprieve would have been attained on the grounds of mental irresponsibility'.[114] That Allen had a background of 'poverty and squalor'[115] and 'had no decent home life'[116] was mentioned in the press, although more as a point in mitigation than to explicitly allege unequal treatment.

Allen's unconventionality was also identified as making reprieve unlikely. Cassandra and the *Manchester Guardian* described her as a 'misfit',[117] and for the *Daily Express* she was 'unnatural' and 'warped'.[118] Again, these points about her eccentricity were advanced as mitigation but to some correspondents to the Home Office, Allen's 'misfit' status made her subject to unequal treatment. A letter from 'A Single Woman' contended that '[i]f she had been a married woman, with somebody to speak for her, she would have been reprieved'[119] and an author from Scarborough angrily criticised the prison doctors for pronouncing Allen a 'perfectly normal woman', commenting '[b]ut she is ugly, not young and a spinster'.[120] Another letter writer succinctly asked '[a]re you sure this woman is being hanged for murder or is it because she was a Transvestite?'[121]

Letter writers detected unfairness on the basis of sex in Ruth Ellis' case. A woman from Barnet argued that male judges did not understand the reactions of women and that Ellis' treatment was symptomatic of 'spiteful hatred of men against women'.[122] Another female author proclaimed man-made

111 Letter, female author, London, 13 January 1949, HO45/23935.
112 Letter, female author, Dorset, 9 January 1949, HO45/23935.
113 Letter, gender unknown, Cardiff, 9 January 1949, HO45/23935.
114 Letter, gender unknown, Hove, 8 January 1949, HO45/23935.
115 Cassandra, 'Without a Hitch'.
116 'A Case for Reprieve', *Manchester Guardian*, 10 January 1949.
117 Ibid. and Cassandra 'Without'.
118 'Against It', *Daily Express*, 5 January 1949.
119 Letter, 'A Single Woman', unaddressed, 14 January 1949, HO45/23935.
120 Letter, anonymous, Scarborough, 5 January 1949, HO45/23935.
121 Letter, gender unknown, address illegible, undated, HO45/23935.
122 Letter, female author, Barnet, 29 June 1955, HO291/235.

laws 'stupid' and argued that 'it is time women had a say in things'.[123] For a woman from Altrincham, 'the law and weight of circumstances' were heavily against women, meaning that they needed 'a helping hand'.[124] A woman from Harrogate raised the potential significance of Ellis' perceived 'immorality', stating 'I cannot help feeling that her somewhat dubious moral record may have helped to influence and alienate the sympathies of the jury'.[125] That Ellis died 'at least partly, because she is what most people are content to call an immoral woman' was also a point made in the *New Statesman and Nation*, and quoted in the *Yorkshire Post*.[126]

The role of structural sexism[127] and socio-economic inequality in making it harder for some condemned prisoners to win reprieve than others was articulated in letters sent on behalf of Mary Wilson, the last woman to be reprieved from the death penalty in England and Wales.[128] Wilson's poverty and advanced years (she was 66) were understood to be to her disadvantage. A woman from Edgware, in a letter to the Queen, asserted capital punishment should either be abolished or retained, 'we want no favourites on the grounds of sex, or of class'.[129] A female author from Bolton referred to men who killed women and children, contending '[t]here appears to be one law for these men but not for this poor misguided woman who probably never had enough money and did not have nice holidays or smart garment'.[130] If 'vile men' who raped and brutalised 'little children and decent women' could be reprieved, then there were 'laws for the rich and laws for the poor; fines for one and prison for the other; laws for women and laws for men'.[131] These letter writers were motivated by what they perceived as injustice and inequity in the application of capital punishment, not necessarily by abolitionism or pleas for leniency. An anonymous letter pointed out that Wilson was 'an ugly old woman with no-one to fight for her' and stated 'I am all for hanging criminals, so many of the Public are, but if you are going to let men off, then you must be consistent for all, that's all we ask'.[132]

Mary Wilson's case is particularly interesting because it took place after the Homicide Act 1957. The defence of diminished responsibility, introduced by the Act, was successfully employed in appeals against convictions for the sexual murders of children and young people committed by men. Letter

---

123 Letter, female author, London, 7 July 1955, HO291/236.
124 Letter, female author, Altrincham, 2 July 1955, HO291/235.
125 Letter, female author, Harrogate, 1 July 1955, HO291/235.
126 'Ruth Ellis: Was Hanging the Only Way?', *Yorkshire Post*, 16 July 1955.
127 This is not a phrase from the time, but my analysis of this position.
128 Mary Wilson was found guilty of poisoning two of her husbands with phosphorous. As these killings were committed on separate occasions, she was convicted of capital murder. See L. Seal, *Women, Murder and Femininity: Gender Representations of Women who Kill*, Basingstoke: Palgrave MacMillan, 2010, pp. 160–1.
129 Letter, female author, Edgware, received 27 May 1958, HO291/242.
130 Letter, female author, Bolton, 22 May 1958, HO291/242.
131 Letter, gender unknown, Northwood, 22 May 1958, HO291/242.
132 Letter, anonymous, unaddressed, undated, HO291/242.

writers' reference to 'men who have murdered innocent children' can be placed within this context.[133] These men had not actually been reprieved, their convictions had been reduced to manslaughter, but they were high-profile cases that seemed more heinous than Mary Wilson's.[134] Lay perceptions of justice centred on the gravity of the crime and what people saw as the level of culpability of the convicted, in ways that often diverged from legal definitions.

Retributive

'Justice' was also a strong symbol for people who discerned excessive leniency or were concerned that the death penalty might be abolished. This was described in a letter to *The Times* from novelist Howard Wyce as the 'deep, emotional (but not necessarily therefore illogical) conviction: that justice demands the death of a killer'.[135] A correspondent on Louisa Merrifield stated simply 'if she is not hung there is no Justice in England'.[136] Letter writers who believed justice demanded retribution articulated emotions of indignation and outrage. A 'Lover of Justice' was 'greatly shocked to read in the Press that you have reprieved and set free two cruel cold blooded murderers'. One of these was John Armstrong, who had poisoned his baby son, and 'should have had petrol poured over him and set light to'.[137] For a correspondent in relation to John Christie, it made 'my blood curdle to read all this tripe about Christie and other murderers asking and getting sympathy and leniency', especially when 'all murderers after a fair trial by their own countrymen should hang'.[138]

Underpinning this outrage was the belief that victims and their relatives could not receive justice without capital punishment.[139] Objecting to reprieves being given to the murderers of women and girls, one letter writer commented '[i]t makes my blood boil to think how callous you men are, you don't think about a Brokenhearted [sic] Mother and Father'.[140] Protesting against the

---

133 Letter, female author, Shropshire, 30 March 1958, HO291/242.
134 In January 1958, Albert Matheson was convicted of murdering a 15-year-old boy (whom he had also raped). He also stole £35 from him, making the crime a capital offence under the Homicide Act. His murder conviction was overturned on appeal as three doctors had given evidence of his 'psychopathic personality' and so the jury should have been directed to find him guilty of manslaughter due to diminished responsibility, which is what his conviction was reduced to, L. Blom-Cooper and T. Morris, *With Malice Aforethought: A Study of the Crime and Punishment for Homicide*, Oxford: Hart, 2004, p. 69.
135 H. Wyce, 'Capital Punishment', Letter to the Editor, *The Times*, 22 February 1955.
136 Letter, gender unknown, Truro, 8 August 1953, HO291/229.
137 Letter, 'Lover of Justice', unaddressed, 6 February 1957, HO291/97.
138 Letter, gender unknown, London, 1 July 1953, HO291/227.
139 Lynch's analysis of American pro-death penalty discourse on the internet found that capital punishment was constructed as essential for the fulfilment of justice, 'Capital Punishment as Moral Imperative', p. 227. Gross and Ellsworth argue that in the United States, retribution remains as the predominant reason to favour the death penalty, as 'fair punishment' or necessary for justice, 'Second Thoughts', p. 31.
140 Letter, gender unknown, Westcliff on Sea, received 30 January 1956, HO291/92.

prospect of abolition, a man from Merthyr Tydfil argued that 'no sane father or mother would consider justice done by imprisonment for ten years for the murder of their children'.[141] The murder of children was a particular source of retributive emotion. A respondent to the Mass Observation survey stated that 'a reprieve for having killed a five-month-old boy and a little girl' had influenced her views on the death penalty.[142]

Where the symbol of justice was linked to retribution, the 'tragic limit' of shared meaning was still related to the acts of interpretation that needed to take place to grant or withhold reprieve, but was employed to register disapproval at failure to use the legitimate violence of the death penalty. Some letter writers expressed affirmation for hangings carried out. In response to the case of George Riley, hanged in 1961 (see Chapter Six), a retired Justice of the Peace congratulated Rab Butler with 'Sir, I proudly thank you for your justice', shoring up a perceived shared meaning.[143] Similarly, a female respondent to the Mass Observation survey commented on Ruth Ellis 'I think justice was done there. She asked for trouble but it didn't give her the right to kill'.[144]

Conclusion

Fears that justice had been compromised in the administration of capital punishment could be related to abolitionist concerns, but were not necessarily. Responses in the form of letters from the public were primarily occupied with questions of justice and failure to uphold it. This distinction is important because analysis of letter and survey responses reveals unease over doubts about the safety of certain convictions, or concern that the death penalty was not applied fairly, which illustrated its deepening contentiousness in a way that simply asking people whether they favoured its abolition or retention did not. The growing number of letters that the Home Office received in relation to certain capital cases in the late 1940s showed both its growing cultural, as well as political, salience. In particular, cases such as Daniel Raven and Margaret Allen demonstrated that while 'Evans, Bentley, Ellis' were significant to enhancing anxiety over capital punishment, concerns over the safety of conviction and unfairness in its application were already attached to mid-twentieth-century cases before this well-known triumvirate. In the context of the contemporary United States, Gross and Ellsworth argue that the wrongful conviction argument has been associated with specific people, but concrete cases are not always influential. They suggest '[i]t may be that a memorable story only makes a claim of injustice more powerful if the

141 Letter, male author, Merthyr Tydfil, 7 June 1948, HO45/25084.
142 Housewife, 25, Monkseaton, Capital Punishment Survey 1955–56, MOA/72–74-B. The five-month-old boy is likely to refer to the Armstrong case.
143 Letter, male author, Cricklewood, received 13 February 1961, TNA/HO291/250.
144 Housewife, 26, Nuneaton, MOA/72–74-A.

injustice claimed is one the audience cares about in the first place'.[145] There-fore, attention to particular cases could be a symptom of ambivalence about capital punishment, not its cause.

Dispute with meanings of justice created by the legal system highlighted the 'tragic limit' of these meanings, where the death penalty as an act of inter-pretation was called into question. As Garton contends, notions of mercy and clemency are a 'safety valve to maintain the legitimacy of the legal system and a means of displaying the power of the law to safeguard justice'.[146] Increasingly in Britain from the late 1940s, this valve was perceived to have blown, which led to questioning of the system's legitimacy. Postwar transfor-mations in British citizenship towards greater inclusivity and equality (at the level of discourse at least)[147] meant that the shadow of the law's violence needed greater and surer justification. These transformations did not mean that conceptions of citizenship were not riven by class, gender and ethnic differences, but that the status of working-class Britons had been elevated.[148] Against this context, the secrecy of the reasons for the exercise of the royal prerogative of mercy had become rather anachronistic, recalling as it did sovereign power. In a more democratic and (in theory at least) equal society, the lack of con-sultation and public deliberation involved in granting or withholding a reprieve was increasingly unacceptable in high-profile cases that caught the press and public imagination.[149] This held true in relation to concerns about excessive leniency as it did in fears of wrongful execution. Garland points out that the death penalty as a tool of penal policy was out of place in the humanist culture of Western European Welfare States.[150] In itself, death as a punishment did not necessarily trouble the public in mid-twentieth-century Britain but, in certain cases, inconsistencies and high-handedness in its application did.

The symbol of justice was a crucial one for articulating anxieties about the operation of the death penalty in mid-twentieth-century Britain. Parallels can be drawn with the United States. In the 1950s, concerns about arbitrariness and racial bias in relation to capital punishment were mobilised as part of the wider burgeoning civil rights movement. Weisberg argues that the Supreme Court's decision to suspend the death penalty in *Furman v Georgia* in 1972

---

145 Gross and Ellsworth, 'Second Thoughts', p. 38.
146 Garton, 'Managing Mercy', p. 685.
147 For a review of scholarship on postwar social citizenship in Britain (albeit one that stresses this may have been conceived in more limited terms than has been understood), see M. Powell, 'The Hidden History of Social Citizenship', *Citizenship Studies*, 2002, 6(3): 229–44.
148 S. O. Rose, *Which People's War: National Identity and Citizenship in Britain, 1939–1945*, Oxford: Oxford University Press, 2004.
149 The secrecy of the royal prerogative had been questioned at other times – in 1923 the *Daily Mail* asked 'should not the grounds for a reprieve be made known to the public?', 'Reprieves', 2 November 1923.
150 D. Garland, 'Modes of Capital Punishment', D. Garland, R. McGowen and M. Meranze (eds), *America's Death Penalty: Between Past and Present*, New York: New York University Press, 2011, p. 59.

was 'an act of apology and pardon' for the moral failure of its operation in the United States.[151] Its arbitrary and capricious nature was the reason for finding capital punishment unconstitutional.[152] The post-2000 'new abolitionism' stresses the unfairness and inaccuracy of the death penalty, issues which have the power to resonate beyond those opposed in principle to death as punishment. Where the application of the American death penalty is concerned, the 'aura of infallibility has been shattered',[153] leading to greater support for a national moratorium on a system that falls short of justice.[154]

Archival collections

Mass Observation (MOA)
The National Archives, Home Office (HO)

Newspapers and Magazines

Daily Express
Daily Mirror
Manchester Guardian
The Times
Yorkshire Post

Bibliography

Ballinger, A., *Dead Woman Walking: Executed Women in England and Wales, 1900–55*, Aldershot: Ashgate, 2000.
Baumgartner, F. R., De Boef S. L. and Boydstun, A. E., *The Decline of the Death Penalty and the Discovery of Innocence*, Cambridge: Cambridge University Press, 2008.
Beattie, J. M., 'The Royal Pardon and Criminal Procedure in Early Modern England', *Historical Papers*, 1987, 22(1): 9–22.
Block, B. P. and Hostettler, J., *Hanging in the Balance: A History of the Abolition of Capital Punishment in Britain*, Winchester: Waterside Press, 1997.
Blom-Cooper, L. and Morris, T., *With Malice Aforethought: A Study of the Crime and Punishment for Homicide*, Oxford: Hart, 2004
Bruckweh, K., 'Fantasies of Violence: German Citizens Expressing their Concepts of Violence and Ideas about Democracy in Letters to Referring to the Case of the Serial Killer Jurgen Bartsch (1966–71)', *Crime, History and Societies*, 2006, 10(2): 53–82.
Burnett, C., 'Justice: Myth and Symbol', *Legal Studies Forum*, 1987, 11(1): 79–94.
Cover, R., 'Violence and the Word', *Yale Law Journal*, 1986, 95(8): 1601–29.

151 R Weisberg, 'Apology, Legislation, and Mercy', *North Carolina Law Review*, 2004, 82, 4, 1415–40, p. 1427. *Furman v Georgia* 408 US 238 (1972).
152 R G Hood and C Hoyle, *The Death Penalty Worldwide*, Oxford, Oxford University Press, 2008, p. 287.
153 C Haney, 'Exoneration and Wrongful Condemnations: Expanding the Zone of Perceived Injustice in Death Penalty Cases', *Golden Gate Law Review*, 2006, 37, 1, 131–74, p. 131.
154 Gross and Ellsworth, 'Second Thoughts', p. 29.

Cross, M. and Bland, C., 'Gender Politics: Breathing New Life into Old Letters', C. Bland and M. Cross (eds), *Gender and Politics in the Age of Letter Writing, 1750–2000*, Aldershot: Ashgate, 2004, 3–14.

Curtis, D. E. and Reswick, J., 'Images of Justice', *Yale Law Journal*, 1987, 96(8): 1727–72.

D'Cruze, S., '"Dad's Back": Mapping Masculinities, Moralities and the Law in the Novels of Margery Allingham', *Cultural and Social History*, 2004, 1(3): 256–79.

England, L. R., 'Capital Punishment and Open-End Questions', *Public Opinion Quarterly*, 1948, 12(3): 412–16

Erskine, H., 'Capital Punishment: The Polls', *Public Opinion Quarterly*, 1970, 34(2): 290–307.

Furman v Georgia 408 US 238 (1972).

Garland, D., 'Modes of Capital Punishment', D. Garland, R. McGowen and M. Meranze (eds), *America's Death Penalty: Between Past and Present*, New York: New York University Press, 2011, 30–71.

Garton, S., 'Managing Mercy: African Americans, Parole and Paternalism in the Georgia Prison System 1919–45', *Journal of Social History*, 2003, 36(3): 675–99.

Gatrell, V. A. C., *The Hanging Tree*, Oxford: Oxford University Press, 1996.

Godsey, M. A. and Pulley, T., 'The Innocence Revolution and our "Evolving Standards of Decency" in Death Penalty Jurisprudence', *University of Dayton Law Review*, 2004, 29(2): 265–87.

Gregory, J., *Victorians Against the Gallows*, London: I. B. Tauris, 2012.

Gross, S. R., 'American Public Opinion on the Death Penalty – It's Getting Personal', *Cornell Law Review*, 1998, 83(6): 1448–74.

Gross, S. R., and Ellsworth, P., 'Second Thoughts: Americans' Views on the Death Penalty at the Turn of the Century', Public Law and Legal Theory Research Paper 00.05, University of Michigan, 2001: http://conium.org/~maccoun/LP_Gross%20Ellsworth2003.pdf.

Haney, C., 'Exoneration and Wrongful Condemnations: Expanding the Zone of Perceived Injustice in Death Penalty Cases', *Golden Gate Law Review*, 2006, 37(1): 131–74.

Hay, D., 'Property, Authority and the Criminal Law', D. Hay, P. Linebaugh, J. G. Rule, E. P. Thompson and C. Winslow (eds), *Albion's Fatal Tree*, London: Allen Lane, 1975, 17–63.

Hood, R. G. and Hoyle, C., *The Death Penalty Worldwide*, Oxford: Oxford University Press, 2008.

King, P., 'Decision-Makers and Decision-Making in the English Criminal Law, 1750–1800', *The Historical Journal*, 1984, 27(1): 25–58.

Kirchmeier, J. L., 'Another Place Beyond Here: The Death Penalty Moratorium Movement in the United States', *University of Colorado Law Review*, 2002, 73(1): 1–116.

Langhamer, C., '"The Live Dynamic Whole of Feeling and Behaviour": Capital Punishment and the Politics of Emotion, 1945–57', *Journal of British Studies*, 2012, 51(2): 416–41.

Lee, T., *Mobilizing Public Opinion: Black Insurgency and Racial Attitudes in the Civil Rights Era*, Chicago, IL: University of Chicago Press, 2002.

Lynch, M., 'Capital Punishment as Moral Imperative: Pro Death Penalty Discourse on the Internet', *Punishment and Society*, 2002, 4(2): 213–36.

Marshall, L. C., 'The Innocence Revolution and the Death Penalty', *Ohio State Journal of Criminal Law*, 2004, 2: 573–84.

Oram, A., *Her Husband Was a Woman!: Women's Gender-Crossing in Popular Culture*, London: Routledge, 2007.

Potter, H., *Hanging in Judgment: Religion and the Death Penalty in England*, London: SCM Press Ltd, 1993.

Powell, M., 'The Hidden History of Social Citizenship', *Citizenship Studies*, 2002, 6(3): 229–44.

Radelet, M. L., and Borg, M. J., 'The Changing Nature of Death Penalty Debates', *Annual Review of Sociology*, 2000, 26: 43–61.

Rose, S. O., *Which People's War: National Identity and Citizenship in Britain, 1939–1945*, Oxford: Oxford University Press, 2004.

Seal, L., 'Public Reactions to the Case of Mary Wilson, the Last Woman to be Sentenced to Death in England and Wales', *Papers from the British Criminology Conference*, 2008, 8: 65–84.

——*Women, Murder and Femininity: Gender Representations of Women who Kill*, Basingstoke: Palgrave MacMillan, 2010.

——'Ruth Ellis and Public Contestation of the Death Penalty', *The Howard Journal*, 2011, 50(5): 492–504.

Unnever, J. D. and Cullen, F. T., 'The Social Sources of Americans' Punitiveness: A Test of Three Competing Models', *Criminology*, 2010, 48(1): 99–129.

Weisberg, R., 'Apology, Legislation, and Mercy', *North Carolina Law Review*, 2004, 82(4): 1415–40.

Wiener, M. J., 'The Sad Story of George Hall: Adultery, Murder and the Politics of Mercy in Mid Victorian England', *Social History*, 1999, 24(2): 174–95.

Wood, J. C., *The Most Remarkable Women in England*, Manchester: Manchester University Press, 2012.

6   Haunted by the ghosts

Edith Thompson and Timothy Evans

Certain high-profile cases, understood as miscarriages of justice, resonate in discussions and representations of capital punishment beyond their own place and time. The reappearance of such cases can raise doubts and anxieties about the operation of the death penalty, and is particularly useful to abolitionist arguments about the inequities of capital punishment and the dangers of executing the innocent. This chapter examines the cultural, political and legal re-emergence of two high-profile twentieth-century cases, those of Edith Thompson and Timothy Evans, in the years following their executions. In different ways, their stories were represented as emblematic of the failures and horrors of the death penalty. Edith Thompson, a woman carried nearly unconscious to the gallows, signified the inerasable bodily horror of hanging. The long process to gain a pardon for Timothy Evans and the symbolism of his execution as an archetypal miscarriage of justice was employed as a reproach to capital punishment, both before and after it had been abolished.

The stories of Edith Thompson and Timothy Evans did not end with their executions – the hanging of Evans was only the beginning of the long shadow he would cast over the question of capital punishment in Britain. Gordon's concept of haunting is employed in this chapter to analyse how the 'seething presence' of the ghosts of Thompson and Evans returned after their deaths.[1] Gordon argues that ghosts 'appear when the trouble they represent and symptomize is no longer being contained or repressed or blocked from view'.[2] Their haunting is a 'reminder of lingering trouble' and, as such, signals that something needs to be done.[3] In this sense, the ghost reckons with the present in which it appears and is a social figure. It 'is always coming from the future even if it is from the past'.[4] Gordon compares the effect of the ghost's haunting to Barthes' concept of the punctum, the wound or prick caused by

1 A. Gordon, *Ghostly Matters: Haunting the Sociological Imagination*, Minneapolis: University of Minnesota Press, 2008, 2nd edition, p. 8.
2 Ibid., p. xvi.
3 Ibid., p. xix.
4 J. Gunn, 'Mourning Humanism, or, the Idiom of Haunting', *Quarterly Journal of Speech*, 2006, 92(1): 77–102, p. 82.

'an affectively moving episode'.[5] Contact with the ghost frequently involves encountering 'what the state has tried to repress'.[6]

Ghostliness and haunting signal traumatic events and the need to come to terms with a horrible occurrence.[7] The executions of Edith Thompson and Timothy Evans can both be understood as traumatic, Evans' only subsequently so in 1953 when John Christie was revealed as a mass murderer. In advancing this argument, there is no intention to suggest that these cases were *universally* perceived as traumas or horrible events. Rather, it is important to examine the points at which the ghosts of Thompson and Evans appeared, and why. Both were metaphorically constructed as haunting the debate on capital punishment in Britain, indicating how the notion of botched or unfair execution as unresolved trauma was rhetorically deployed in abolitionist arguments. Whilst this could be rejected or ignored by many, it contributed to the ambivalent position that capital punishment held in the second half of the twentieth-century. Thompson and Evans were not the only 'haunting' cases. Others, such as Derek Bentley, Ruth Ellis and James Hanratty, can also be seen through this lens. However, close attention to Thompson and Evans enables analysis of themes of gender, horror, error and injustice.

Edith Thompson

Chapter Three explored how the trial and executions of Thompson and Bywaters were sensations, provoking high culture anxieties about the demeaning effects of execution as entertainment. To briefly recount the details of the case, Thompson, a businesswoman of 28 and Bywaters, a sailor of 20 conducted an affair, during which they exchanged passionate love letters. Bywaters stabbed and killed Thompson's husband, Percy, when she and Percy returned home to Ilford from an evening at the theatre in London. Although both Thompson and Bywaters insisted that she knew nothing of his murderous intentions, the letters which she had written to him[8] were used as evidence that she had incited him to kill.[9] These were read out in court and reported verbatim in newspaper articles. Both were found guilty in December 1922 and hanged in January 1923, despite a huge petition of 900,000 signatures collected on behalf of Bywaters by the *Daily Sketch* and efforts to support a reprieve for Thompson by the *Daily Express* and the Howard League.[10] Thompson did not generate the same degree of public sympathy as Bywaters – during the trial,

5 Gordon, *Ghostly*, p. 106.
6 Ibid., p. 127.
7 Gunn, 'Mourning', p. 91.
8 Thompson had destroyed the letters that Bywaters sent to her.
9 Rene Weis, *Criminal Justice: The True Story of Edith Thompson*, London: Penguin, 1988, p. 247. On Edith's letters as an expression of modern selfhood, see M. Houlbrook, '"A Pin to See the Peep Show": Culture, Fiction and Selfhood in Edith Thompson's Letters, 1920–22', *Past & Present*, 2010, 207(1): 215–49.
10 Weis, *Criminal*, pp. 255, 290.

she had been portrayed as both immoral and dominating, attributes which painted her as a deviant woman.[11] There were concerns, as articulated by her defence barrister, Henry Curtis-Bennett, that she was punished for her immorality, rather than on the basis of firm evidence that she had incited the murder.[12]

Rumours and reports about the horrific nature of Edith Thompson's execution began immediately in the days following it. There were conflicting reports 'by reason of the unfortunate fact that no representatives of the Press were allowed to be present to describe to the public what took place'.[13] Central News had revealed that Thompson was 'prostrate all night'.[14] She 'was in a state of torpor, and was only partially conscious when the hour arrived, so that she had to be carried to the scaffold'.[15] The *Daily Express* revealed details 'that … accentuate the horror inseparable from the execution of a neurotic woman of ill-balanced mind and character'. As she was unable to walk, 'two warders then made a chair of their forearms, raised her on it, and carried her to the scaffold'.[16] Conservative MP, Sir Robert Newman, asked in the House of Commons whether Thompson 'was in a state of collapse, had to be medically treated for several hours before the time fixed', and whether she was carried to the scaffold 'in an almost unconscious condition'.[17] Also circulating from the evening of Thompson's execution on 9 January were murkier rumours that her 'insides' had fallen out when she was hanged, possibly because she had been pregnant.[18]

These rumours about the execution were an example of the how the experience of great distress at the scaffold and evisceration after the drop turned state-controlled killing into a 'spectacle of horror'.[19] Instead of a modern, civilised procedure, in this case hanging induced primal terror and caused bodily disfigurement. As Sarat *et al.* argue, concern about botched execution points to ambivalence 'about whether or not the government can ever properly control the violence inherent in the death penalty'.[20] In terms of newspaper reporting, the emphasis was on Thompson's intense distress, resulting in her inability to walk to the gallows. Paradoxically, the extreme degradation of being carried to

11 R. Kennedy, 'The Media and the Death Penalty: The Limits of Sentimentality, the Power of Abjection', *Pain and Death: Politics, Aesthetics, Legalities*, 2007, 14(2): 29–48, pp. 38–9 and L. Bland, 'The Trials and Tribulations of Edith Thompson: The Capital Crime of Sexual Incitement in 1920s England', *Journal of British Studies*, 2008, 47(3): 624–48, p. 645.

12 A. Logan, *Feminism and Criminal Justice: A Historical Perspective*, Basingstoke: Palgrave Macmillan, 2008, p. 134.

13 'Mrs Thompson and Bywaters Hanged', *Chelmsford Chronicle*, 12 January 1923.

14 Ibid.

15 'Edith Thompson Carried to the Scaffold', *Evening Telegraph*, 9 January 1923.

16 'Mrs Thompson: How She Was Carried to the Scaffold', *Daily Express*, 11 January 1923.

17 'Edith Thompson: Was She "Practically Carried to the Scaffold"', *Evening Telegraph*, 21 February 1923.

18 Weis, *Criminal*, p. 304.

19 A. Sarat *et al.*, 'Gruesome Spectacles: The Cultural Reception of Botched Executions in America, 1890–1920', *British Journal of American Legal Studies*, 2012, 1(1): 1–30, p. 9.

20 Ibid., p. 1.

the scaffold subverted hanging as degradation ceremony.[21] If the condemned seems 'to have been wronged, to be weak, frail or deeply repentant, the punishment of death appears to be barbaric and repressive rather than just, righteous or moral'.[22] Traumatic accounts of Thompson's execution made capital punishment profane. This modern woman had died in an anti-modern way.[23]

Edith Thompson was the first woman to be hanged on the British mainland since Rhoda Willis in 1907.[24] She was also undeniably feminine, a fashionable woman who knew how to dress and, from the details that emerged during her trial, embraced her sexuality. Like Ruth Ellis thirty years later, this counted against her – she was immoral – but Thompson's spectacular femininity highlighted the inescapably corporeal aspect of hanging.[25] Her body, which had been a focus of attention during her trial, was destroyed. In relation to Ruth Ellis, Rose argues that:

> the thinness of the boundary between criminal and legal murder, the uncomfortable proximity between them, presents itself too starkly when it is a woman who is executed. It seems also that the spectacle of execution – 'seen or imagined' (The Lancet) – is too powerful when it is a woman[26]

Women's executions, which were rare in twentieth-century Britain, attracted attention and provoked debate about capital punishment. Certain women's cases caused a greater response than others and the performance of spectacular femininity by the condemned was significant to this.

The horror of Thompson's execution, and the suspicion that it was gorier and more terrible than the authorities had been willing to admit, haunted subsequent discussions of capital punishment. The toll that such a trauma exacted on those involved became an established narrative about Thompson's hanging. Eighteen months after she was executed, her hangman, John Ellis attempted suicide by shooting himself.[27] The *Hull Daily Mail* reported that his friends 'say he has been nervous, depressed, and troubled with insomnia' since her execution. The newspaper reminded readers that the Home Secretary had given an 'evasive' reply in Parliament to Sir Robert Newman's question about the hanging and 'the careful way in which it was worded made it

21 P. Smith, 'Executing Executions: Aesthetics, Identity, and the Problematic Narratives of Capital Punishment', *Theory and Society*, 25(2): 235–61, p. 241.

22 Ibid., p. 242.

23 Bland explores how in the 1920s Thompson was an archetypally modern woman, who was fashionable, worked in London and consumed leisure in the West End, 'The Trials', p. 628.

24 This was a 'baby farming' case, and Willis, hanged in Cardiff, was the only woman to be executed in Wales in the twentieth century, see A. Ballinger, *Dead Woman Walking*, Aldershot: Ashgate, 2000, pp. 89–103.

25 Bland describes Edith as a 'sexual spectacle', 'The Trials', p. 633.

26 J. Rose, 'Margaret Thatcher and Ruth Ellis', *New Formations*, 1988, 6: 3–29, p. 15.

27 See Chapter Three on John Ellis.

obvious that the account could not be denied'.[28] In 1932, John Ellis committed suicide by cutting his own throat. The *Daily Express* sutured this tragedy to Thompson's hanging, with the headline 'Ellis the Hangman Commits Suicide: Haunted by the Memory of Mrs Thompson's Execution', and quoted his son as stating: 'He was haunted. We all knew what prevented him from sleeping. I don't think it was the memory of the 200 executions he had taken part in, but the recollection of the hanging of two women that drove him to suicide'.[29] Similarly, the *Daily Mail* ran the headline 'Fate of Ellis, Ex-Hangman Found Dead: Executed Mrs Thompson', and reported that 'his nerves had been upset by having to hang Mrs Edith Thompson'.[30] An editorial in the *Western Times* on the occasion of Ethel Major's execution in 1934[31] stated that 'Mrs Edith Thompson was carried swooning to the scaffold, an execution in circumstances which afterwards drove the hangman out of his mind' and reflected that '[t]here is something revolting about hanging a woman'.[32]

In reporting John Ellis' suicide, the *Daily Express* explicitly employed the metaphor of haunting. The figure of the haunted, suicidal hangman replayed the rumoured gothic horror of the Thompson execution without the need for specifics. Terrible, unknowable horror was implied by the experience of John Ellis' tortured decade of life after hanging her. Grant argues that in 'gothicized cases' the myth of 'reasoned and just law is exposed as a screen'.[33] She continues '[h]orror arises as the edges between things collapse and their contents flow out and mingle, threatening defilement of both the mythical rule of modern law and the rational public sphere of civilized conduct and dialogue'.[34] Unlike the live woman who embodied suburban modernity, the ghost of Edith Thompson insinuated the bloody violence of anti-modern punishment.

The Thompson/Bywaters case inspired a variety of fictional retellings. In particular, Thompson's letters were the inspiration for Dorothy L. Sayers' *The Documents in the Case*, which is composed of letters and statements, including a suburban housewife's letters to her young lover.[35] Glugg and Issy in James Joyce's *Finnegans Wake* 'speak in language that originates almost entirely in Bywaters and Thompson's intimate letters',[36] which were published in Filson

28 'Ex-Hangman Found Shot', *Hull Daily Mail*, 26 August 1924.
29 'Ellis the Hangman Commits Suicide: Haunted by the Memory of Mrs Thompson's Execution', *Daily Express*, 21 September 1932. The other woman was Susan Newell, also executed in 1923.
30 'Fate of Ellis, Ex-Hangman Found Dead: Executed Mrs Thompson', *Daily Mail*, 21 September 1932.
31 Ethel Major was hanged at Hull Prison for the murder of her husband, see Ballinger, *Dead*, pp. 257–77.
32 'Capital Punishment', *The Western Times*, 21 December 1934.
33 C. Grant, *Crime and Punishment in Contemporary Culture*, Abingdon: Routledge, 2004, p. 123.
34 Ibid.
35 D. L. Sayers and R. Eustace, *The Documents in the Case*, London: Victor Gollancz, 1930. The role of Margaret, the Thompson figure, is ambiguous as it is not clear from her letters whether she intended to drive her lover to poison her husband. She is not prosecuted and only her lover, Harwood, hangs.
36 D. Rando, *Modernist Fiction and the News*, New York: Palgrave, 2011, p. 69.

Young's account for the notable trials series. F Tennyson Jesse's *A Pin to See the Peepshow* remains the most well-known fictionalisation of Edith Thompson's story and was intended to portray her story as a miscarriage of justice.[37] It is written from the perspective of main character, Julia Starling, a lower middle-class woman with a rich, imaginative inner life, who chafes at the restraints imposed by her life in Chiswick, firstly with her parents and then with her older husband, Herbert. Jesse perceived Thompson as a victim of the jury's sexual prejudice. Her biographer explains that 'the story and the woman haunted her mind, and only by re-creating them in fiction form could she rid herself of the uncanny knowledge of the affair that seemed to possess her'.[38] The novel was subsequently adapted as a stage play and, in the 1970s, a successful television series.

Hilda Lewis' *Because I Must* vaguely echoes Thompson/Bywaters. Narrator Nellie Woodward's mother stabbed to death Nellie's father after she had an affair with a lodger. Lewis strongly employs tropes of horror and haunting, with Nellie's mother appearing to her as an apparition 'with a rope around her neck ... and her head swinging to one side'.[39] She describes herself as a child 'haunted by hangings and a dead woman ... till my nights and days was [sic] a burden and a horror'.[40]

The horror of Thompson's execution reappeared in the House of Commons in debates on the Criminal Justice Bill 1948 – specifically in relation to whether to abolish capital punishment. Conservative MP Beverley Baxter, who had been editor of the *Daily Express* when Thompson was hanged, made a statement recounting a visit from two warders from Holloway to the *Express* offices the day after her execution. In evocative, horror-inflected language, Baxter related how '[t]heir faces were not human. They were like something out of another world. For, somehow, they had to get Edith Thompson to the gallows after she had disintegrated as a human creature'.[41] He also suggested that Thompson had suffered a prolapsed womb after being hanged and that, subsequently, female condemned had to be sewn into leather knickers to prevent this from happening. In a follow up article for the *Evening Standard*, Baxter explained 'I confirmed the horrors of Mrs Thompson's death and gave it as my opinion that she was hanged not for murder but for adultery'. He described how 'suddenly and unexpectedly, the ghost of Mrs Thompson appeared' and that it seemed 'a woman's ghost' had played a part in the vote for a moratorium on hanging.[42] This metaphor of haunting was also deployed in an article on murder in the *Picture Post*, which captioned a large

37 J. Stobbs, 'Tracing the Female Triptych of Space', T. Gomez Reus and A. Usandizaga (eds), *Inside Out*, Amsterdam: Rodopi, 2008, p. 142.

38 J. Colenbrander, *A Portrait of Fryn: A Biography of F Tennyson Jesse*, London: A Deutsch, 1984, p. 134 quoted in Stoobs, p. 142.

39 H. Lewis, *Because I Must*, Cheltenham: Cheltenham Press Ltd, 1946, p. 38.

40 Ibid., p. 24.

41 'Anderson Says – Was Mrs Thompson Guilty? Of course', *Daily Express*, 15 April 1948.

42 B. Baxter, 'The Ghost of Mrs Thompson', *Evening Standard*, 15 April 1948.

photograph of Thompson and Bywaters, 'Ghost behind the House of Commons debate on capital punishment was the case of Bywaters and Mrs Thompson … The story of the case, and particularly the hanging of Mrs Thompson, has haunted the public conscience ever since'.[43]

Thompson's ghost was a persistent presence in discussions of the death penalty in the late 1940s and the 1950s, and exposed ambivalence about the inescapable violence of capital punishment. Ernest Gowers, chairman of the Royal Commission on Capital Punishment, read out a passage to five prison governors, which suggested Thompson's hanging was such a terrible event that the executioner had later killed himself, another warder had gone mad and every other prison officer involved had left the service. The governors denied that the execution was especially traumatic, or that John Ellis' suicide had been connected with it.[44] However, in 1950, Margery Fry, Vice-President of the Howard League, informed the Commission that the Holloway prison chaplain, Reverend Glanville Murray, had told her 'the impulse to rush in and save [Edith Thompson] by force was almost too strong for me' and that Fry had never 'seen a person look so changed in appearance by mental suffering as the governor appeared to be'.[45]

The alleged trauma experienced by those involved in Thompson's hanging illustrated the development of an emotional public sphere around the issue of capital punishment. Criticisms that it was barbaric or uncivilised were not restricted to lofty theoretical abstractions but could be connected to the awful toll exacted on those who carried out the violence of the law. Suffering, trauma and torment were portrayed as capital punishment's legacy through abolitionist discourse. It is important to acknowledge that this form of abolitionist argument mobilised the 'powers of horror' of execution, rather than simply contrasting cool abolitionist logic with bloodthirsty retentionist fervour.

The publication of Lewis Broad's *The Innocence of Mrs Thompson* in 1952, and its partial serialisation in the *Sunday Dispatch,* meant that Thompson's 'tragic story' continued to haunt the culture of the death penalty. The first *Sunday Dispatch* article established her as an 'innocent woman who suffered the shameful death of hanging'.[46] The final one described how Thompson spent her final days 'in a state of collapse. Her hair turned grey. She had to be carried to the scaffold. She was hanged, practically unconscious, on January 9, 1923'. Broad also argued that outraged morality had been a 'factor in sending an innocent woman to the gallows'.[47] He recreated the sense of gothic horror

43 H. Rhodes, 'Is there a Cure for Murder?', *Picture Post,* 8 May 1948.
44 'Scaffold Scene Denied', *Dundee Courier,* 7 October 1949 and 'Prison Governors and Chaplains Say "Retain Hanging"', *Western Morning News,* 7 October 1949.
45 'Royal Commission Told: Mrs Thompson's Execution was Shock to Prison Staff', *Dundee Courier,* 3 February 1950.
46 L. Broad, 'The Innocence of Edith Thompson', *Sunday Dispatch,* 26 October 1952.
47 L. Broad, 'They Carried an Innocent Woman to the Scaffold', *Sunday Dispatch,* 30 November 1952.

that permeated reconstructions of the execution, as well as continuing the narrative of her case as a miscarriage of justice.[48] In the book, he emphasised weaknesses in the evidence against Thompson. Her letters, in which 'criminal passages in the letters were as scarce as raisins in an austerity pudding' had been treated very selectively by the prosecution.[49] According to the *Daily Mirror*, in 1952, the argument about Edith's guilt 'still runs fiercely'.[50]

These two aspects of the Edith Thompson case – the miscarriage of justice and the horror the execution – were important in debates about abolition in the mid-1950s. In 1955, *The Spectator*, a conservative leaning magazine, published an abolitionist editorial under the title 'Judicial Barbarism'. This discussed the Timothy Evans case but also asserted that the executions of Norman Thorne and Edith Thompson meant it was 'rash' of Maxwell Fyfe to claim in 1948 that there had been no wrongful hangings in Britain.[51] In response, a letter writer was 'very interested to read you agreed that Mrs Thompson was wrongly hanged' and, as a result of a recent trial, the correspondent had been 'forced to the conclusion that no woman past her first youth who admits in Court to having a lover would ever get a fair trial'.[52]

The writer Arthur Koestler, who was active in Victor Gollancz's National Campaign for the Abolition of Capital Punishment, offered to write an anti-death penalty book to aid the campaign. This would 'arouse the reader's emotions … by painting a vivid picture of its injustices and the suffering of its victims'.[53] He was supported in this by David Astor, editor of *The Observer*, who agreed to serialise the book in his newspaper and to provide staff for research assistance.[54] One of these serialisations, 'Behind the Bulletins', recounted how in 1948 Beverley Baxter had 'mentioned the case of a sick woman of twenty-eight whose insides fell out before she vanished through the trap' and how two warders had told him Edith Thompson had 'disintegrated as a human creature'.[55] Koestler also quoted Reverend Glanville Murray, who wanted to 'rush in and save her by force'. He began the article by citing confidential Home Office instructions to Prison Governors, which directed them to make an official statement after all hangings to the effect that they had been 'carried out expeditiously and without a hitch', and contrasted this

48 L. Broad, *The Innocence of Edith Thompson*, London: Hutchinson, 1952, p. 219 – Broad explicitly described the case as a miscarriage of justice.

49 Ibid., p. 195.

50 D. Howell, 'The Deadly Dream that Led to the Gallows', *Daily Mirror*, 13 November 1952.

51 'Judicial Barbarism', *The Spectator*, 11 February 1955. Norman Thorne was hanged in 1925 for the murder of his fiancé. His defence was that she had committed suicide as she was known to be 'neurotic', see J. J. Eddleston, *Blind Justice: Miscarriages of Justice in Twentieth-Century Britain?* Santa Barbara, CA: ABC-CLIO, 2000, pp. 143–50.

52 C. Whitehead, 'Judicial Barbarism', Letter to the Editor, *The Spectator*, 18 February 1955.

53 M. Scammell, *Koestler: The Indispensable Intellectual*, London: Faber and Faber, 2010, p. 445.

54 Ibid., p. 444.

55 A. Koestler, 'Behind the Bulletins', *The Observer*, 4 March 1956.

with Thompson's horrific experience. In seeking to engage the readers' emotions, he described 'the horror of the operation' exemplified by:

> the brisk, business-like opening of that door, the pinioning of the hands behind the back and the walking or dragging of him [sic] in solemn procession to the execution shed and on to the white chalk mark on the trap.[56]

By highlighting the secrecy and possible mendacity of official descriptions of executions, Koestler also emphasised their anti-democratic nature.[57]

Lord Mancroft, Under Secretary of State for the Home Department, stated in the House that Koestler's article had given a 'misleading impression' about the instructions given to Prison Governors as the full instructions directed them to disclose that something had gone wrong if the execution was not 'without a hitch'. He also rejected the allegations about Edith Thompson as untrue. When asked by Lord Templewood, former Home Secretary turned abolitionist, why the government had not scotched the rumours about Thompson's hanging in 1948 when they were repeated by Beverley Baxter, Mancroft replied that 'it has now become necessary because this legend has recurred' and that as Koestler was planning to publish a book, the claims would appear in a more permanent format.[58] Koestler responded strongly in *The Observer* that he had quoted instructions to prison governors exactly as they had been published in previous books.[59] Like Templewood, he argued that rumours about Thompson could have been disclaimed in 1948, but were not. Baxter had been contacted by Sir John Anderson in 1948 on behalf of one of the men who hanged Thompson and 'took exception' to Baxter's description of it. However, this refutation did not become public knowledge. Koestler pointed out that Baxter was not the only source he had drawn on, but also evidence given to the Royal Commission on Capital Punishment. He referred Mancroft to a letter published in *The Lancet* in 1955, which 'describes a certain measure, taken before the execution of women, which represents the total degradation of a human being'.[60] He explained that he had 'hesitated a long time whether or not to include the terrible Thompson case in *The Observer*' but concluded 'if such things are done in the nation's name, the nation had a right to know'.[61]

---

56 Ibid.
57 One of Koestler's main objections to capital punishment was its role as a 'symbol of terror' in 'modern totalitarianism'. A. Koestler, 'The Lure of the Gallows', *Picture Post*, 12 May 1956.
58 '"Misleading Impression" in Article on Capital Punishment', *Manchester Guardian*, 9 March 1956.
59 A. Koestler, 'Lord Mancroft's "Omissions"', *The Observer*, 11 March 1956.
60 Ibid. The letter to which Koestler referred described as one of the 'gruesome technicalities of hanging' the fact that condemned women had to be changed into canvas underwear on the morning of their execution, I. H. Milner, 'The Death Penalty', *The Lancet*, Letter to the Editor, 20 August 1955.
61 Koestler, 'Lord Mancroft's "Omissions"'.

Lord Mancroft conceded that Koestler could not have known that the instructions to the prison governors were not the most up-to-date version and made what the *Daily Mirror*'s Cassandra described as a 'bristling apology' to Koestler, who had 'implicated the Home Office deeper in their secrecy as to what goes on in hanging'.[62] Cassandra argued that such denials indicated there was 'little doubt' that 'hideous scenes took place' at Thompson's hanging and called for the Home Office files to be made available to MPs.[63] Koestler had reawakened the ghost of Edith Thompson and, as well as being a miscarriage of justice and a horror story, the secrecy surrounding her execution indicated the government's failure to keep track with contemporary shifts in citizenship towards greater equality and openness.

Abolitionist MPs Reginald Paget (Labour), Robert Boothby (Conservative) and Fenner Brockway (Labour) asked for the full details of Thompson's execution to be made public and for the text of the prison governors' instructions to be published. In a written reply, the Home Secretary, Lloyd George, explained that Thompson had been sedated prior to being hanged so the governor of Holloway 'had her carried and she was supported on the scaffold. Apart from this nothing unusual occurred'.[64] She could have walked with assistance, but the governor decided that having her carried was 'more humane'.[65] Lloyd George insisted that she did not scream, have to be held down, 'disintegrate as a human creature' and that her insides did not fall out.[66] Brockway asked whether there should be an inquiry in the light of the admission that Thompson had to be carried and supported, but Lloyd George responded that all the facts about the case were known. In the midst of the controversy over Koestler's article, Sydney Silverman won a second reading for his Death Penalty Abolition Bill, which was passed on a free vote of 286 to 262. *The Times*' Parliamentary Correspondent complained that the 'newspaper controversy' about Thompson's execution 'detracted' from the main issue.[67]

Edith Thompson's case was by no means the only one mentioned during the debates but the fact that questions about her execution could form a controversy more than thirty years after it took place testified to its power to haunt the issue of capital punishment. Suspicion that her execution had been horribly botched and covered up was an example of encountering what the state had tried to repress. The dark stories about Thompson's hanging challenged the dominant official representation of the modern death penalty as methodical and civilised. Her femininity was particularly important to this. The 'powers of horror' in Thompson's case derived from the unbounded

62 Cassandra, 'The Suspect Mourners', *Daily Mirror*, 19 March 1956.
63 Ibid.
64 'More Questions on Hanging', *The Observer*, 1 April 1956.
65 'Why Murderess was Carried to Gallows', *Daily Mirror*, 28 March 1956.
66 'More Questions on Hanging' and 'Why Murderess was Carried to Gallows'.
67 'Vote to End Hanging', *The Times*, 13 March 1956.

nature of the female body, which could expel its insides after falling through the trapdoor, making the hanging of a woman inherently more troublesome and less civilised than the hanging of a man.[68] Discussion of women needing leather or canvas underwear to prevent this from happening underlined a collision between the horror of the female child-bearing body and the horror of execution. The official description of the hanging that Lloyd George provided was inadequate to allay the horror story. He acknowledged that Thompson had to be sedated, which suggested that she was in extreme distress, and also confirmed that she was carried to the scaffold.[69] In his 1988 account of Thompson's life (and death), Weis notes that the details of her internal examination have not been completed on the post-mortem report, which he interprets as indicating that there is truth in the rumours about her insides falling out.[70]

The narrative of Edith Thompson's execution as a miscarriage of justice that demonstrated the sexism encoded into the criminal justice system has predominated in academic and cultural representations of the case. She has remained a compelling figure able to 'exercise imaginations and consciences',[71] at least partly because she can be perceived as a woman out of time. Thompson's desire for fulfilment through love and sex, and her frustration experienced in a marriage that did not provide it, can be understood as consistent with recent ideals of heteronormativity,[72] whereby sexuality and desire are central to women's self-fulfilment.[73] Jill Dawson's novel, *Fred & Edie*, explores Edie's developing sexual selfhood through her memories of her unfolding relationship with Freddie.[74] Reviewing the book for *The Times*, Koning praised Edie's 'hauntingly authentic voice', which gave 'contemporary resonance to her story'.[75] A feature on Edith Thompson in the *Sunday*

---

68 Film scholar, Barbara Creed, draws on Julia Kristeva's work on abjection to theorise the representation of the female body as monstrous in horror films. Certain 'abominations' are forms of abjection – these include sexual immorality and perversion, decay and death, murder, the corpse, bodily wastes and the feminine body, B. Creed, *The Monstrous-Feminine: Film, Feminism and Psychoanalysis*, London: Routledge, 1993, p. 9. From this list, the especial potential for horror in relation to female executions is apparent. The rumours about Thompson's 'insides' and possible pregnancy enhanced the horror of her execution. According to Creed, the monstrous-feminine is particularly related to 'woman's reproductive and mothering functions', p. 14.

69 'More Questions on Hanging'.

70 Weis, *Criminal*, p. 304.

71 R. Weis, 'Not Innocent, Not Guilty', *The Guardian*, 10 November 1993.

72 S. Jackson, 'Interchanges: Gender, Sexuality and Heteronormativity', *Feminist Theory*, 2006, 7(1): 105–21. Jackson defines heteronormativity as 'not only a normative sexual practice but a normal way of life', p. 107.

73 See R. Gill, 'Mediating Intimacy and Postfeminism: A Discourse Analytic Examination of Sex and Relationships Advice in a Women's Magazine', *Discourse and Communication*, 2009, 3(4): 345–69.

74 J. Dawson, *Fred & Edie*, London: Sceptre, 2000. A film about the Thompson/Bywaters case, *Another Life*, was released in 2001, P. Goodhew [Motion Picture], Alibi Pictures, UK.

75 C. Koning, 'Sex, Violence and Poetry', *The Times*, 26 August 2000.

Express explained that Dawson was 'struck by how modern Edith's voice sounded' in her letters and quoted Dawson as stating that 'Edie's story has all the components of the ways in which women's lives have changed over the past century'.[76]

Timothy Evans

In the second half of the twentieth century, the name of Timothy Evans became a byword for wrongful execution. There had been previous capital cases that were argued to be miscarriages of justice, as the foregoing discussion of Edith Thompson demonstrated. In 1928, Oscar Slater had his 1919 murder conviction (for which the death sentence was commuted) quashed by the Edinburgh Appeal Court on the grounds that the jury had been misdirected. Efforts to overturn the verdict had been pursued for many years, most notably by Arthur Conan Doyle. Walter Rowland was hanged for the murder of Olive Balchin in 1947 despite the fact that someone else confessed to the crime while he was awaiting execution. This confession was withdrawn but in 1951, John Ware, the man who had made it, was convicted of the attempted murder of a woman carried out in exactly the same way – by hitting her over the head. Neither of these cases had the same haunting power as Timothy Evans, however. Oscar Slater could at least be released and compensated. Walter Rowland had previously been reprieved for the murder of his son and so was not an especially sympathetic figure.

Little notice was taken when Evans was hanged for the murder of his baby daughter in 1950.[77] He was an illiterate, 25-year-old van driver who lived with his wife, Beryl, and daughter, Geraldine, in a flat in 10 Rillington Place, Notting Hill. Also living in the house was John Christie, a middle-aged civil servant, who had been a special police constable during the war. In November 1949, Evans went to stay with an aunt in Merthyr Tydfil, unaccompanied by Beryl or Geraldine. On the 30th of that month, he walked into the local police station in Merthyr and told them that he had put Beryl's body down a drain in the backyard of 10 Rillington Place. Dismayed to find herself pregnant again when they could least afford another child, he claimed that Beryl had died as a result of taking abortifacient pills.

It took three police officers to remove the cover from the drain, which Evans claimed to have moved unassisted, and there was no body. Further searches revealed the bodies of Beryl and Geraldine hidden in the backyard's washhouse. When confronted with this information (and possibly after being told that they had both been strangled), Evans confessed to strangling Beryl

---

76 C. Stonehouse, 'The Forbidden Passion that Led a Liberated Woman to the Gallows', *Sunday Express*, 23 July 2000.

77 Jesse notes it was the 'torso case' – of a murder victim whose torso was dropped into some marshes from a hired plane – that captured the public imagination at this time, F. T. Jesse, *Trials of Evans and Christie*, London: Hodge and Co. Ltd, 1957, p. xxvii.

with some rope and Geraldine with a tie. However, on the same evening he changed his account and stated that his neighbour, John Christie, had performed an abortion on Beryl, which had gone wrong. Evans had seen her dead body but Christie had offered to dispose of it and to find people to take care of Geraldine.

Evans' defence at his trial was that he had initially confessed to killing his wife and child because he feared the police but that Christie was the real murderer. Christie, who despite having past criminal convictions, appeared to be more respectable than the average resident of Notting Hill[78] and was a witness for the prosecution. Evans' rather outlandish sounding explanations failed to convince the jury and he was found guilty of murder and hanged. Three years' later, a new occupant of 10 Rillington Place found the corpse of a woman in a plastered over alcove in the kitchen of what had been the Christie's ground floor flat. The police discovered two more bodies in the alcove and a further three buried under the house and yard. Once he had been apprehended, Christie confessed to murdering the six women whose bodies had been discovered at Rillington Place, as well as Beryl Evans. He denied killing Geraldine.

The discovery of Christie's crimes presented the very real possibility that an innocent man had been hanged. After Christie had been found guilty, there were calls from MPs and the Howard League for an inquiry into Evans' conviction.[79] In his closing speech at Christie's trial, defence barrister, Dennis Curtis-Bennett had stated '[o]ne wonders about the possibilities of two stranglers living in the same premises at Notting Hill'.[80] Christie's conviction raised the issue of abolition. Sydney Silverman attempted to introduce a bill to suspend capital punishment as there were grounds for believing that a miscarriage of justice had been perpetrated against Evans.[81] This was defeated, although not without Silverman asking Home Secretary, Maxwell Fyfe, if he stood by his claim in the 1948 debate on capital punishment that 'it was virtually impossible that anyone should be hanged by mistake for murder'.[82] In *The People*, 'a doctor', commenting on expert appraisals of Christie's sanity, argued 'if further inquiry does sustain the view that Evans did not commit murder, there will be an unanswerable case for abolishing capital punishment'.[83] The voices of Timothy Evans' relatives appeared in the press. The *Daily Sketch* reported that Evans' mother, Agnes Probert, intended to fight to prove his innocence and the *Daily Mirror* quoted her as saying '[a]

78 Notting Hill was notorious as a poor area in which many Jamaican immigrants lived, whereas John Christie was white and 'presented a public face of respectability', see F. Mort, *Capital Affairs: London and the Making of the Permissive Society*, New Haven, CT: Yale University Press, 2010, p. 110.

79 'The Evans Case', *Manchester Guardian*, 26 June 1953 and 'MPs to Ask for Evans Inquiry', *The Times*, 27 June 1953.

80 'Christie Guilty of Murder', *Daily Mail*, 26 June 1953.

81 '5 Year Ban on Hanging Sought', *Manchester Guardian*, 27 June 1953.

82 'Bill to Suspend Death Penalty Rejected', *Manchester Guardian*, 2 July 1953.

83 'The Doctors and Christie' by a Doctor, *The People*, 28 June 1953.

mother always knows her son and I believe Tim'.[84] Evans' sister, Eleanor Ashby, told *Empire News* that if Christie's 'past and his habits had been more thoroughly investigated' her brother would not have hanged.[85]

A private inquiry, headed by John Scott Henderson, QC, was carried out hastily over the course of the week before Christie was executed. Abolitionist Labour MP, Reginald Paget, criticised the secrecy of the inquiry in an article for *Reynolds News* and highlighted the improbability of the 'coincidence that two stranglers were working independently and unknown to each other in Rillington Place'.[86] Some Labour MPs attempted to have Christie's execution postponed as he was an important witness in relation to Evans,[87] and George Rogers attempted unsuccessfully to force a debate on the Evans report before Christie was hanged.[88] Scott Henderson published his report on 14 July and concluded that the case against Evans was 'overwhelming'.[89] The prison chaplain at Pentonville had given evidence that Christie had subsequently denied killing Beryl Evans and had only confessed to this murder in support of his insanity defence.[90]

Scott Henderson's report was greeted with a largely positive reception from the press. An editorial in *The Times* argued 'Mr Scott Henderson has disposed of any shadow of suspicion that justice might have miscarried when Timothy John Evans was hanged'.[91] The *Liverpool Daily Post* confidently asserted that 'Henderson destroys ground for argument that capital punishment should be abolished because of the execution of an innocent man'.[92] The report was conducted 'painstakingly, scrupulously and with great ability' according to the *News Chronicle* and,[93] for the *Glasgow Herald*, meant no-one 'can be left in any doubt of Evans's guilt'.[94] It had, stated the *Yorkshire Post*, 'stilled controversy' and assuaged public discussion of capital punishment until the Royal Commission on Capital Punishment published its report.[95] At this point in time, the haunting metaphor was employed in order to dispel it. *The Times* reassured readers '[i]t is now possible to face the great question of capital punishment unhaunted by the dreadful suspicion that an innocent man has lately been hanged'.[96] For *The Star*, the report had 'banished' the

---

84 F. Pynn, 'Fight to Clear Evans' Name', *Daily Sketch*, 26 June 1953 and 'His Grim Confession Brings Comfort to a Mother', *Daily Mirror*, 26 June 1953.

85 'Sister Tells of Evans' Death Cell Vow', *Empire News*, 5 July 1953.

86 R. T. Paget, 'Justice – Take the Bandage off her Eyes', *Reynolds News*, 12 July 1953.

87 'MPs' Bid to Stop Christie Execution', *Daily Worker*, 14 July 1953.

88 'Christie: Execution Eve Drama', *Daily Mail*, 14 July 1953.

89 'Case Against Evans Overwhelming', *The Times*, 15 July 1953.

90 Ibid.

91 'Misgivings Relieved', *The Times*, 15 July 1953.

92 'The Evans Report', *Liverpool Daily Post*, 15 July 1953.

93 'The Evans Inquiry', *News Chronicle*, 15 July 1953.

94 'Evans and Christie', *Glasgow Herald*, 15 July 1953.

95 'Royal Commission', *Yorkshire Post*, 16 July 1953.

96 'Misgivings Relieved'.

'spectre' that a wrongful execution had taken place.[97] The Scott Henderson report had apparently exorcised the ghost of Timothy Evans that had arisen with the discovery of Christie's crimes.

There were criticisms of the inquiry's secrecy. *The Star* concluded that doubts remained 'about some aspects of this last-minute investigation, most of all the insistence on holding it in private', noting that justice must be seen to be done.[98] This sentiment was echoed by the *Daily Herald*.[99] The *Daily Mirror* lamented that the privacy of the investigation was 'all the more regrettable because of the nature of the findings, which exonerate the State completely of any error'.[100] The clash between the establishment assumption that authority knew best and postwar dissatisfaction with paternalistic secrecy would resurface in relation to the Evans case. Whilst the editorial line of the major national and local papers was supportive of the Scott Henderson report's finding that there had been no miscarriage of justice, the disbelief propounded by abolitionist Labour MPs was kept in the public domain. There were demands for a new inquiry and articles by figures such as Michael Foot and Reginald Paget that highlighted doubts related to the 'astronomical coincidences involved in the assumption of Evans' guilt'.[101] Paget and Silverman collaborated to publish *Hanged – and Innocent* (which included an epilogue by abolitionist Conservative MP, Christopher Hollis) later the same year. This included chapters on Walter Rowland and Derek Bentley, as well as Evans. It highlighted problems with the Evans case, such as doubt over how much information about the killings the police revealed to him in their questioning and argued that 'a case that appears absolutely clear may yet be a false case'.[102]

As the salience of capital punishment continued to increase, Evans haunted the issue. When the House of Commons voted against suspending capital punishment in February 1955, former Labour Home Secretary, James Chuter Ede, stated that he would 'have given a different decision on the exercise of the prerogative of mercy' if he had known about the other bodies hidden in 10 Rillington Place.[103] Ede did not go as far, at this point, as proclaiming Evans' factual innocence but this was a stunning admission nevertheless. As another former Home Secretary (and current president of the Howard League), Lord Templewood, commented 'never before, so far as I know, has a probable error of this kind been publicly admitted by a Home Secretary'.[104] Ede's admission, made with 'deep emotion',[105]

97 ' ... Seen to be Done', *The Star*, 15 July 1953.

98 Ibid.

99 'Evans was Guilty', *Daily Herald*, 15 July 1953.

100 'The Evans Document', *Daily Mirror*, 15 July 1953.

101 See I. Trethowan, '17 MPs Want New Evans Inquiry', *Yorkshire Post*, 15 July 1953, M Foot, 'Evans: A Blow to British Justice', *Daily Herald*, 17 July 1953 and R. T. Paget, 'Evans or Christie? Doubts Remain', *Reynolds News*, 19 July 1953.

102 R. T. Paget and S. S. Silverman, *Hanged – and Innocent?*, London: Victor Gollancz, 1953, p. 179.

103 Lord Templewood, 'Hanging: 30 Other States Prove Us Wrong', *The Star*, 16 February 1955.

104 Ibid.

105 W. L. A., 'Problems of Crime and Punishment', *Yorkshire Post*, 15 February 1955.

was sympathetically received and fitted into the emotional public sphere that had developed around the death penalty in the 1950s. His statement 'I hope no future Home Secretary will ever have to feel that, although he did his best, in fact he sent a man who was not guilty as charged, to the gallows'[106] underlined the importance of 'feeling', as did his description of his unease as a 'personal matter'.[107] The *Daily Mail* described him as '[b]reaking the silence of five nightmare years'[108] and Alan Brinton in the *News Chronicle* stated that '[r]arely has the Commons known such painful minutes'.[109] The debate had been one in which, according to the *Daily Express*, '[p]ersonal opinions and emotions were much mixed up' and Ede's 'words fell with shattering emphasis on MPs' ears'.[110]

Responding to Ede's hope about future Home Secretaries, the same paper editorialised that '[i]t is intolerable that one man must bear the harrowing burden of this supreme decision. Better for it to be taken by a majority judgment'.[111] That capital punishment was an emotional burden on the sensitive was not a new theme and, as the quote from the *Daily Express* editorial made clear, could be offered as a reason for reform rather than abolition. However, the mid-twentieth-century emotional public sphere around the death penalty, as contributed to by the popular press, was not elitist and included the relatives of the condemned. Under the headline 'Evans' Mother – I Forgive Chuter Ede', the *Daily Sketch* quoted Agnes Probert as stating 'I feel for Mr Ede. My heart nearly broke when I heard what he'd done', as well as reporting her call for another inquiry.[112] Here, a working-class woman was granted the authority to forgive a former Home Secretary – and to identify with him sufficiently to feel heartbroken on his behalf. In an article calling for a fresh inquiry, Michael Foot opined that Ede was 'still haunted by the dreadful suspicion' that Timothy Evans was innocent.[113]

From the mid-1950s, the ghost of Timothy Evans accompanied public discussion of the death penalty, which was intensifying. In the wake of the shock of Ruth Ellis' execution in July 1955, the National Campaign for the Abolition of Capital Punishment was launched by publisher, Victor Gollancz, and received newspaper coverage of their suggestion to 'close … shops and stay … away from places of entertainment on the eve of execution'.[114] In September, Eddowes' *The Man on Your Conscience* was published, which argued that Evans had been framed by Christie. When executed, Evans had 'passed from sight and memory'[115] but after the revelations about Christie, 'public confidence in

106 M. Pentreath, 'Death Penalty to Stay', *Yorkshire Post*, 11 February 1955.
107 A. Brinton, 'Hanging Stays by 31 Votes', *News Chronicle*, 11 February 1955.
108 'Ede Admits Hanged Man Error', *Daily Mail*, 11 February 1955.
109 Brinton, 'Hanging Stays'.
110 'Should Evans Have Hanged?', *Daily Express*, 11 February 1955.
111 'The Final Decision', *Daily Express*, 15 February 1955.
112 'Evans' Mother – I Forgive Chuter Ede', *Daily Sketch*, 12 February 1955.
113 M. Foot, 'The Evans Case Must be Heard Again', *Daily Herald*, 18 February 1955.
114 'Justify it or End it', *Yorkshire Observer*, 27 August 1955.
115 M. Eddowes, *The Man on Your Conscience*, London: Cassell and Co. Ltd, 1955, p. 93.

English law and justice has been shaken'.[116] With the title of his book, Eddowes explicitly made Evans' execution a matter for the 'public conscience'[117] and established what became a recurrent trope of the Evans case – that it was a reproach to the system of capital punishment.

In a letter to *The Times*, Linton Andrews, editor of the *Yorkshire Post*, Ian Gilmour, editor of the *Spectator* and John Grigg, editor of the *National and English Review*, argued that a further inquiry was needed to 'restore the good name of the police'.[118] They made this assertion on the basis of a recently published book on Scotland Yard by Harold Scott, which stated that the police knew a human skull in the Rillington Place area had been dug up by a dog. This turned out to be from one of Christie's victims, but was not mentioned during Evans' trial as the police assumed the skull had been transferred from a bomb site. Their letter provoked some refutations from senior police officers[119] and the controversy was covered in other newspapers apart from *The Times* – an editorial in the *Daily Herald* stated that there was now an 'overwhelming' case for a new inquiry into the Evans case.[120] Andrews, Gilmour and Grigg also pursued the cause behind the scenes, requesting to meet with the Home Secretary. In a letter to the Home Office, Grigg referred to *The Times* letter and explained that it was 'important to show that the desire for such an inquiry was not just a Left-Wing fad, but was shared by at least three Right-Wing editors'.[121]

In February 1956, the Commons voted in favour of the abolition or suspension of the death penalty. Reflecting on this in an article for *The Observer*, Arthur Koestler agreed with retentionists that 'emotionalism' surrounded the issue but argued this could be found 'in both camps'. This illustrated the 'depths of moral passion that were stirred up' and showed how 'the silence of a Timothy Evans drowns out even the voice of a Nikita Kruschev'. Miscarriage of justice had been 'anxiously and gravely debated' and this, Koestler suggested, was because 'the ghost of Timothy Evans seemed to have taken possession of the collective subconscious of the House'.[122] F. Tennyson Jesse, for the

116 Ibid., p. 92.
117 'Crime and the Public Conscience', *Times Literary Supplement*, 23 September 1955.
118 L. Andrews, I. Gilmour and J. Grigg, 'Evans and Christie Trials', Letter to the Editor, *The Times*, 16 September 1955.
119 For example, Police Chief, Sir John Nott Bower responded that the police had no reason to think that the skull was from Christie's garden at the time of Evans' arrest and trial, see P. Hoskins, 'Police Chief Hits Back', *Daily Express*, 17 September 1955.
120 'Christie and Evans', *Daily Herald*, 19 September 1955.
121 Letter from John Grigg to G. Lloyd George, London, 23 September 1955, TNA/HO45/25654: Grigg also stated that anyone who had read *The Man on Your Conscience* 'cannot fail to feel most unhappy about the whole business'. Grigg, Gilmour and Linton, as well as David Astor of *The Observer*, met with the Home Secretary, Lloyd George and senior civil servant, Frank Newsam, in October 1955. They were disappointed with the Home Office reaction. See 'Deputation to the Home Secretary about the Case of Timothy Evans', 26 October 1955 and Letter from John Grigg, London, 27 October 1955.
122 A. Koestler, 'The "Honourable" Paradox', *The Observer*, 19 February 1956.

Notable British Trials series, described Evans as 'not an attractive or pleasant ghost, but still the ghost of a man who was not a murderer'.[123]

The haunting metaphor was especially prominent in press coverage of the publication of Lord Altrincham (John Grigg) and Ian Gilmour's pamphlet on the case in April 1956. This charged that Evans' rights had been violated 'through the wickedness and incompetence of others' and described the argument that Rillington Place had coincidentally housed two murderers, both stranglers, as 'moving in the realm of fantasy'.[124] An article in the *Daily Mirror* commended the pamphlet, and stated '[t]here's a ghost that won't lie down and it is haunting the Home Office. It is the wraith of Timothy John Evans'.[125] In the *Daily Herald*, Allen Andrews claimed of Evans that 'his memory has not ceased to haunt the thoughts of lawyers and politicians and men in public life'. There was 'an insistent note of doubt – WAS HE INNOCENT?'. If this turned out to be the case then 'NO SPACE OF TIME COULD WIPE OUT A STAIN ON BRITISH JUSTICE'.[126] Andrews captured the essential point about the Evans case (and wrongful executions in general), which was that it could never be fully rectified. In *Reflections on Hanging*, published in 1956, Koestler contended that the only way to avoid execution of the innocent was to abolish the death penalty.[127]

Pressure for a new inquiry was sustained into the early 1960s.[128] Ludovic Kennedy's *10 Rillington Place* began with an open letter to the Home Secretary calling for just this. He demanded whether Butler could 'put your hand on your heart and say with Mr Scott Henderson that there can be no doubt that Evans murdered his wife and child. I am asking this question of you personally.'[129] Kennedy highlighted problems with Evans' confession, which included vocabulary that he was unlikely to have used. In violation of the Judge's Rules of evidence, it had not been recorded and Evans' mother claimed that he had been kept awake until 5am by the police.[130] Kennedy described this as 'the Communist pattern of interrogation' and argued that it was equivalent to brainwashing.[131]

In February 1961, the case of George Riley, 21, also became a focus for anxieties about the safety of capital convictions that were largely secured on

123 Jesse, *Trials*, 1957, p. xcii.

124 'Reopen the Evans Case, Says Peer', *News Chronicle*, 12 April 1956. Lord Altrincham and I. Gilmour, *The Case of Timothy Evans: An Appeal to Reason*, London: The Spectator Ltd, 1956, p. 25.

125 'Ghost that Won't Lie Down', *Daily Mirror*, 12 April 1956.

126 A. Andrews, 'Evans: The Name Still Haunts the Country', *Daily Herald*, 12 April 1956. Altrincham and Gilmour warned that the Evans case would 'become a permanent and corrosive stain', *The Case*, p. 26.

127 A. Koestler, *Reflections on Hanging*, London: Victor Gollancz, 1956, p. 109.

128 'Pressure on Mr Butler', *The Guardian*, 27 January 1961.

129 L. Kennedy, *10 Rillington Place*, London: Victor Gollancz, 1961, p. 18.

130 Ibid., pp. 105–6.

131 Ibid., pp. 124–5.

the basis of confession. Riley was found guilty of murdering Adeline Smith, a 62-year-old neighbour of his in Shrewsbury. He confessed to having broken into her house in order to steal money and beating her to death. Although no money had been stolen, his stated motive made the crime capital murder under the Homicide Act 1957. He later withdrew his confession. Riley was described in the press as 'Another Evans Case' and 'Evans No. 2'.[132] *The Guardian* claimed that, as 'Mr Ludovic Kennedy's recent book *Ten Rillington Place* has reminded us', Riley's situation was 'not unlike that of Evans' who 'confessed under police examination ... and later withdrew his confession'.[133] A solicitor's clerk from Shrewsbury wrote a report comparing the Riley case with Evans and sent it to Kennedy.[134] Newspapers such as the *Daily Herald* and the *Daily Sketch* supported the efforts of Riley's family and Labour MP Victor Yates to secure a reprieve.[135] The *Sketch* pointed out that, due to the vagaries of the Homicide Act, Riley would hang 'on the strength of five words "I only wanted some money"'.[136] Support for Riley as 'another Evans' was not universal. The *Daily Express* argued that in comparing Riley with Evans 'propagandists have attempted to exploit the Evans case in order to work up public emotion'.[137] Attempts to secure reprieve were unsuccessful and Riley was hanged on 9 February, which further connected his case with that of Evans. An editorial in the *Yorkshire Post* stated that '[t]he Timothy Evans case, and the case of George Riley ... have troubled many people who hitherto based their belief in capital punishment on the assumption that British justice could not err'.[138]

The identification of Riley as 'another Evans' also appeared in letters to the Home Office on the case, especially in response to a 5 February article in *The Observer*. A woman from Bristol enclosed the article with her letter, which asked 'at whose conscience will the murder of George Riley gnaw?' and pointed out that no amount of 'anguish and remorse' could bring the 'legally murdered' Evans back to life.[139] A male correspondent from Islington stated that the *Observer*'s summary of the case had made him think of Timothy Evans and Ronald Marwood and that 'immediate consideration of police methods' employed in taking statements was needed.[140] A married couple

132 'Another Evans Case?', *The Observer*, 5 February 1961, 'Bid to Save "Another Timothy Evans"', *Daily Herald*, 6 February 1961, 'Evans No. 2: 1000 Join to Fight to Save Boy who Confessed to Murder', *Daily Mail*, 6 February 1961, '3 Days to Live – Death Cell Plea', *Daily Mirror*, 6 February 1961 and G. Eden, 'An Innocent Man Might Die ... ', *Daily Sketch*, 6 February 1961.
133 'George Riley's Case', *The Guardian*, 6 February 1961.
134 'Butler Gets New Facts on Murder Trial', *Daily Herald*, 7 February 1961.
135 'Bid to Save "Another Timothy Evans"' and 'Two Days to Go: Must this Boy Hang?', *Daily Sketch*, 7 February 1961.
136 'Two Days to Go'.
137 'Let Him Die in Peace', *Daily Express*, 7 February 1961.
138 'Justice and Mercy', *Yorkshire Post*, 17 February 1961.
139 Letter from female author to the Home Office, Bristol, 6 February 1961, TNA/HO291/250.
140 Letter, Male author, Islington, 6 February 1961, HO291/250.

from Leeds expressed their doubts about the evidence in the Riley case, having read the *Observer* article. They had also heard Ede say on the radio that he received no requests for Evans' reprieve so they felt it important to write on behalf of Riley.[141] Timothy Evans' ghost haunted George Riley's case, raising doubts about the reliability of the police and the soundness of British justice. It is striking that, eight years after the Scott Henderson Report supposedly allayed fears of a miscarriage of justice, the public discussion of Evans in relation to Riley assumed Evans' innocence and his case was understood as symbolic of wrongful execution. Later that year, Rab Butler agreed that Evans would not have been hanged if all the facts had been known,[142] but declined to open a new inquiry on the basis that there were no 'significant new facts' and no precedent for granting a posthumous free pardon.[143]

In 1965, the campaign to pardon Timothy Evans was rejuvenated when it caught the attention of Harold Evans, editor of the *Northern Echo*. The paper called for a new inquiry and ran regular stories on the case that were flagged with a 'Man on Our Conscience' logotype, appropriating Eddowes' reproachful title.[144] With Ludovic Kennedy, Harold Evans formed the Timothy Evans Committee, which after four months gained the signatures of 109 MPs in support of a new inquiry. Harold Evans maintained a media profile on the case, giving television and radio interviews.[145] Eventually, Labour Home Secretary, Frank Soskice, agreed to order a new inquiry headed by Justice Sir Daniel Brabin. Eric Clark in *The Observer* related how the combination of a public campaign and personal approaches to Soskice from MPs, including Ede, had yielded results.[146] Under the subheading 'Haunted for 12 Years', he stated '[t]he ghost of Evans has haunted people in Britain'.[147] Following the Death Penalty (Abolition) Act's suspension of capital punishment for five years, John Grigg noted in *The Guardian* that a legacy 'that still looms reproachfully is the case of Timothy John Evans'.[148]

The findings of the Brabin Report, published in October 1966, were a somewhat implausible interpretation of the events. The report stated that it was 'probable' that Evans had killed his wife, for which he had not been tried, but not his baby, for which he had been hanged.[149] It was greeted with 'a chorus of scepticism',[150] according to *The Guardian,* but the report finally made possible a free pardon, issued by Roy Jenkins, who wanted to bring some

141 Letter, Married couple, Leeds, 5 February 1961, HO291/250.
142 '"This Man Would Not Have Hanged": But MPs are Told "No Free Pardon"', *Daily Mirror*, 16 June 1961.
143 'No New Inquiry into Timothy Evans Case', *The Guardian*, 16 June 1961.
144 H. Evans, *My Paper Chase*, London: Little Brown, 2009, p. 258.
145 Ibid., p. 260.
146 E. Clark, 'Why Soskice Decided to Probe Evans Case', *The Observer*, 22 August 1965.
147 Ibid.
148 J. Grigg, 'Legacy of Shame', *The Guardian*, 11 November 1965.
149 '"Probable" that Evans Killed Wife but not Baby', *The Guardian*, 13 October 1966.
150 'A Sceptical Reception for the Judge's Conclusions', *The Guardian*, 13 October 1966.

relief to Evans' family.[151] The Brabin Report obviated the need for contrition on the part of the state, as Evans was still labelled a 'probable' murderer. However, it also made it possible to acknowledge that an error of justice had taken place in 1950, at a time when the suspension of the death penalty preceding abolition made such an admission less incendiary than it would previously have been. An editorial in *The Times* concluded 'capital punishment was always hated by those who feared the risk of a miscarriage of justice, and this case came close to it. That risk now has, properly, gone with the Abolition Act'.[152]

Evans' ghost had still not 'laid down' however. The *Daily Mirror* reported that despite the Brabin Report his mother, Agnes Probert, would 'always feel bitter' because '[n]othing will bring my son back'.[153] This ongoing grief on the part of his family could not be assuaged. Cultural portrayals of the Evans case emphasised the horror of his story. Folk singer Ewan Maccoll's *The Ballad of Timothy Evans* branded the judge and jury in the case 'murderers' for executing Evans for Christie's crime.[154] Reviewing *The Dreams of Timothy Evans* in 1970, the first episode in a series of ITV dramas recreating sensational murder cases, Henry Raynor acknowledged that 'the involvement of Evans in the story [of 10 Rillington Place] is an irritating sore on our consciences'.[155] The Richard Fleischer directed *10 Rillington Place* remains the most well-known portrayal of the Evans/Christie story.[156] Released in 1971, the film developed an anti-capital punishment message through John Hurt's depiction of Timothy Evans as a naïve and bewildered young man tricked and manipulated by Richard Attenborough's quietly menacing John Christie. The death penalty for murder had been fully and finally abolished in 1969, and the last executions carried out in 1964, but Timothy Evans still stood as a reproach to an imperfect system. Interviewed by *The Times*, Attenborough summed up the film's 'devastating' argument against the death penalty as '[y]ou can argue about the moral issues, you can argue about statistics but you cannot argue about the fact that a mistake was made'.[157]

After abolition, there were periodic calls to reinstate capital punishment in Britain and Timothy Evans' ghost could be invoked as a reproach to these calls – or was at least a presence that those in favour of capital punishment had to reckon with. A campaign for restoration of the death penalty in February 1973, which started in response to the murder of a milkman in Surrey, was given fresh impetus by the explosion of two bombs in London on 8 March of

---

151 G. R. Rubin, 'Posthumous Pardons, the Home Office and the Timothy Evans Case', *Criminal Law Review*, 2007, 41–59, p. 45. A pardon was not the same as an acquittal, which could only be granted by judges.
152 '10 Rillington Place', *The Times*, 13 October 1966.
153 P. Jones, 'I Will Always Feel Bitter, Says the Mother of Timothy Evans', *Daily Mirror*, 19 October 1966.
154 E. Maccoll, 'The Ballad of Timothy Evans', [Song] *Distant Shore*, 1968.
155 H. Raynor, 'Repulsion', *The Times*, 19 September 1970.
156 R. Fleischer, *10 Rillington Place* [Motion Picture] Filmways Pictures, UK, 1971.
157 'Christie's Ghost Returns', *The Times*, 18 May 1970.

that year and Richard Nixon's call for reinstatement in the United States. The campaign was led by Colonel Carol Mather, Conservative MP for Esher, who supported capital punishment for murder by explosives, of police officers and of prison wardens. His answer to the Timothy Evans problem was that the death penalty would be used only sparingly, reducing the chances of a mistake.[158]

Margaret Thatcher's Conservative Party was elected in 1979 on the first manifesto in a British general election to forefront 'respect for the rule of law' and the 'fight against crime'.[159] It promised a free vote on the issue of capital punishment, although votes in 1979, 1982 and 1983 were heavily defeated in the House of Commons. Timothy Evans remained part of the discussion. In 1979, Conservative MP, George Gardiner, squarely faced down this lingering ghost, arguing that 'those innocently executed must be placed in the scale alongside other lives of innocent victims of killers'.[160] However, Evans' case continued to be mobilised as a reproach to attempts to bring back hanging. In 1983, a *Daily Mirror* editorial warned '[t]he name of Timothy Evans ought to make every pro-hanger shudder'[161] and Colin Brown in *The Guardian* activated the haunting metaphor, contending '[t]he ghost of Timothy Evans will loom large in the Commons debate on hanging'.[162]

By the twenty-first century, Timothy Evans was no longer as well remembered, although his name could still be deployed as a cautionary warning in relation to capital punishment. Commenting on the ascension of pro-death penalty Iain Duncan Smith to the leadership of the Conservative Party in 2001, Richard Ingrams reflected that it had been forty years since the publication of Kennedy's *10 Rillington Place*, which 'was responsible for the eventual abolition of capital punishment in this country'.[163] In 2000, Evans' sister and half-sister were awarded compensation in recognition of the 'profound effect of [his] wrongful conviction and execution'.[164] An assessment of the amount paid carried out by Lord Brennan concluded that the findings of both the Scott Henderson and Brabin reports should be rejected and that Evans' conviction and execution for the murder of his child was a miscarriage of justice. The Criminal Cases Review Commission decided in 2004 not to refer the case back to the Court of Appeal, on the grounds that quashing the conviction was not in the public interest as Evans had already been publicly exonerated and his relatives had been compensated.[165] Following judicial review, the decision was upheld as rightly

158 T. Devlin, 'Colonel in Search of an Ultimate Deterrent', *The Times*, 31 March 1973.
159 1979 Conservative Party General Election Manifesto, www.conservative-party.net/manifestos/ 1979/1979-conservative-manifesto.shtml. See also R. Reiner, *Law and Order: An Honest Citizen's Guide to Crime and Control*, Cambridge: Polity Press, 2007, p. 120.
160 C. Brown, 'Death Penalty Move Heavily Defeated', *The Guardian*, 20 July 1979.
161 'Hanging; Is this a Risk we Dare to Take?', *Daily Mirror*, 12 July 1983.
162 C. Brown, 'In-House Briefing', *The Guardian*, 8 July 1983.
163 R. Ingrams, 'Tory Hopeful Would Have Let Them Swing', *The Observer*, 19 August 2001.
164 *Westlake v CCRC* [2004] EWHC 2779.
165 F. Gibb, 'Rillington Place Case Reopened', *The Times*, 15 November 2004 and Westlake v CCRC [2004] EWHC 2779.

being at the CCRC's discretion. Both judges who carried out the review agreed that Evans was 'wrongly convicted and that there was a serious miscarriage of justice'.[166]

Conclusion

Edith Thompson and Timothy Evans were both 'seething presences' in the story of the death penalty in twentieth-century Britain. Constructed as miscarriages of justice, their cases starkly demonstrated capital punishment's flaws and made it possible for the death penalty to be understood as a form of social violence. The cases were qualitatively different; Evans was a purer example of miscarriage of justice in relation to actual innocence, but Thompson highlighted other death penalty hauntings. In addition to doubt over her culpability, the gendered body horror of Thompson's execution brought what were supposed to be the hidden blood and guts of the process into view – and the suffering female body was particularly shocking. The mistake of Evans' wrongful conviction and execution was repressed by the state but his ghost – his metaphorical haunting – could not be exorcised. Both figures were presences in mid-twentieth-century political debates about capital punishment, but also in public discourse on the death penalty. Gordon argues that ghosts signal that something needs to be done and the traumatic echoes of the Thompson and Evans cases were deployed by abolitionists to demonstrate the need to remove the death penalty in order to come to terms with its tragedies and, in relation to Evans, to highlight the foolishness of restoring it. Edith Thompson and Timothy Evans were two ghosts with the haunting power to prick the certainty of the operation of capital punishment in Britain. They underlined the inescapable ambivalence of an imperfect system and its potential to cause trauma.

Archival collections

The National Archives, Home Office (HO)

Newspapers and magazines

Chelmsford Chronicle
Daily Express
Daily Herald
Daily Mail
Daily Mirror
Daily Sketch

---

166 Ibid. The Evans/Christie story has recently been fictionalised in Laura Wilson's *A Capital Crime*, which pairs the haunting power of Evans' wrongful execution (depicted as the character, John Davies) with the ever-present grief of main character, Inspector Stratton, who is haunted by the trauma of his wife's murder, see L. Wilson, *A Capital Crime*, London: Quercus, 2011.

Daily Worker
Dundee Courier
Empire News
Evening Standard
Evening Telegraph
Glasgow Herald
Hull Daily Mail
Liverpool Daily Post
Manchester Guardian
News Chronicle
Picture Post
Reynolds News
Sunday Dispatch
Sunday Express
The Guardian
The Lancet
The Observer
The People
The Spectator
The Star
The Times
The Western Times
Times Literary Supplement
Western Morning News
Yorkshire Observer
Yorkshire Post

Bibliography

Altrincham, Lord and Gilmour, I., *The Case of Timothy Evans: An Appeal to Reason*, London: The Spectator Ltd, 1956.

Ballinger, A., *Dead Woman Walking: Executed Women in England and Wales, 1900–55*, Aldershot: Ashgate, 2000.

Bland, L., 'The Trials and Tribulations of Edith Thompson: The Capital Crime of Sexual Incitement in 1920s England', *Journal of British Studies*, 47(3): 624–48.

Broad, L., *The Innocence of Edith Thompson*, London: Hutchinson, 1952.

Colenbrander, J., *A Portrait of Fryn: A Biography of F Tennyson Jesse*, London: A Deutsch, 1984.

Conservative Party General Election Manifesto, www.conservative-party.net/manifestos/1979/1979-conservative-manifesto.shtml, 1979.

Creed, B., *The Monstrous-Feminine: Film, Feminism and Psychoanalysis*, London: Routledge, 1993.

Dawson, J., *Fred & Edie*, London: Sceptre, 2000.

Eddleston, J. J., *Blind Justice: Miscarriages of Justice in Twentieth-Century Britain?* Santa Barbara: ABC-CLIO, 2000, pp. 143–50.

Eddowes, M., *The Man on Your Conscience*, London: Cassell and Co. Ltd, 1955.

Evans, H., *My Paper Chase*, London: Little Brown, 2009.

Fleischer, R., *10 Rillington Place* [Motion Picture] Filmways Pictures, UK, 1971.

Gill, R., 'Mediating Intimacy and Postfeminism: A Discourse Analytic Examination of Sex and Relationships Advice in a Women's Magazine', *Discourse and Communication*, 2009, 3(4): 345–69.

Goodhew, P., *Another Life* [Motion Picture], Alibi Pictures, UK, 2001.

Gordon, A., *Ghostly Matters: Haunting the Sociological Imagination*, Minneapolis, University of Minnesota Press, 2008, 2nd edition.

Grant, C., *Crime and Punishment in Contemporary Culture*, Abingdon: Routledge, 2004.

Gunn, J., 'Mourning Humanism, or, the Idiom of Haunting', *Quarterly Journal of Speech*, 2006, 92(1): 77–102.

Houlbrook, M., '"A Pin to See the Peep Show": Culture, Fiction and Selfhood in Edith Thompson's Letters', *Past & Present*, 2010, 207(1): 215–49.

Jackson, S., 'Interchanges: Gender, Sexuality and Heteronormativity', *Feminist Theory*, 2006, 7(1): 105–21.

Jesse, F. T., *A Pin to See the Peepshow*, London: Heinemann, 1934.

——*Trials of Evans and Christie*, London: Hodge and Co. Ltd, 1957.

Joyce, J., *Finnegans Wake*, London: Faber and Faber, 1939.

Kennedy, L., *10 Rillington Place*, London: Victor Gollancz, 1961.

Kennedy, R., 'The Media and the Death Penalty: The Limits of Sentimentality, the Power of Abjection', *Pain and Death: Politics, Aesthetics, Legalities*, 2007, 14(2): 29–48.

Koestler, A., *Reflections on Hanging*, London: Victor Gollancz, 1956.

Lewis, H., *Because I Must*, Cheltenham: Cheltenham Press Ltd, 1946.

Logan, A., *Feminism and Criminal Justice: A Historical Perspective*, Basingstoke: Palgrave MacMillan, 2008.

Maccoll, E., 'The Ballad of Timothy Evans', [Song] *Distant Shore*, 1968.

Mort, F., *Capital Affairs: London and the Making of the Permissive Society*, New Haven, CT: Yale University Press, 2010.

Paget, R. T. and Silverman, S. S., *Hanged – and Innocent?* London: Victor Gollancz, 1953.

Rando, D., *Modernist Fiction and the News*, New York: Palgrave MacMillan, 2011.

Reiner, R., *Law and Order: An Honest Citizen's Guide to Crime and Control*, Cambridge: Polity Press, 2007.

Rose, J., 'Margaret Thatcher and Ruth Ellis', *New Formations*, 1988, 6: 3–29.

Rubin, G. R., 'Posthumous Pardons, the Home Office and the Timothy Evans Case', *Criminal Law Review*, 2007, 41–59.

Sarat, A. *et al.*, 'Gruesome Spectacles: The Cultural Reception of Botched Executions in America, 1890–1920', *British Journal of American Legal Studies*, 2012, 1(1): 1–30.

Sayers, D. L. and Eustace, R., *The Documents in the Case*, London: Victor Gollancz, 1930.

Scammell, M., *Koestler: The Indispensable Intellectual*, London: Faber and Faber, 2010.

Smith, P., 'Executing Executions: Aesthetics, Identity, and the Problematic Narratives of Capital Punishment', *Theory and Society*, 25(2): 235–61.

Stoobs, J., 'Tracing the Female Triptych of Space', T. Gomez Reus and A. Usandizaga (eds), *Inside Out*, Amsterdam: Rodopi, 2008, 125–48.

Weis, R., *Criminal Justice: The True Story of Edith Thompson*, London: Hamish Hamilton, 1988.

Westlake v CCRC [2004] EWHC 2779.

Wilson, L., *A Capital Crime*, London: Quercus, 2011.

7 Penal currents in the post-abolition era

The abolition of capital punishment in 1965 did not mean that it disappeared from the wider culture or political attention. Inevitably, the fact of abolition was significant to cultural reactions to the death penalty. Anxieties that contributed to ending the use of hanging lost their urgency and pro-death penalty sentiment could no longer be assuaged with actual executions. Grant argues that 'British penality has been haunted by the shadow of the death penalty' and points out that this has garnered little criminological attention.[1] This chapter examines capital punishment's lingering place in British culture in the decades after abolition and traces some of its meanings. It does not offer a comprehensive overview of execution's cultural legacy but rather discusses competing currents of perception and understanding of capital punishment in Britain since abolition. Three significant strands of the post-abolition era are addressed – ongoing support for capital punishment, with particular attention to terrorism, the Moors murders and a 'culture of punitiveness' – the shadow of miscarriages of justice and the alternative imaginary of the American death penalty.

Ongoing support for capital punishment

A truism about the abolition of the death penalty in Britain is that it was enacted in the face of majority support for retention. A Gallup poll from July 1964 found 67 per cent were against abolishing capital punishment altogether and another from January 1965 found 77 per cent in favour of retention (with 58 per cent agreeing there could be extenuating circumstances where it should not apply).[2] As previous chapters have explored, a more nuanced picture of responses to capital punishment can be gained through attention to the ambivalence produced by certain high-profile cases, especially in relation to concerns about justice. However, opinion polls, which largely measure views

---

1 C. Grant, *Crime and Punishment in Contemporary Culture*, Abingdon: Routledge, 2004, p. 125.
2 H. Erskine, 'The Polls: Capital Punishment', *Public Opinion Quarterly*, 1970, 34(2): 290–307, pp. 299–300.

in the abstract, showed majority support for capital punishment across the second half of the twentieth century.[3]

Conservative MP, Duncan Sandys, launched a campaign in 1966 for the restoration of capital punishment for the murder of police and prison officers. This followed the murder in Shepherd's Bush of three policemen by prisoners escaping from Wormwood Scrubs prison. His campaign was supported by the Police Federation and the Prison Officers' Association.[4] Certain types of murder, and certain types of murderers, have continuously been more likely to arouse pro-death penalty and retributive sentiment than others. These include the sexual murders of children, 'serial killings' (known as 'mass killings' in the mid-twentieth century) and terrorist killings. Cases such as these, which were frequently high-profile, sparked calls for the reintroduction of the death penalty and the expression of retributive attitudes.

In the 1970s, Irish nationalist terrorist bombings of England, particularly those in Guildford and Birmingham in 1974, stirred pro-death penalty sentiment. Capital punishment for terrorist murders was discussed in the House of Commons after bombs exploded in London in June 1974, killing two people and injuring others. Some MPs explained that such incidents had led them to revise their previously abolitionist views because 'society needed to take steps to protect itself' and that terror bombing represented a 'new crime' by perpetrators who did not know how many victims they would create.[5] Labour MP, Arthur Lewis, was formerly against capital punishment but stated '[o]n this issue, I have no doubts whatsoever. They [terrorists] should be shot'.[6] A female letter writer to the *Daily Mail* commented that it was 'a pity' that the 'deep-seated repugnance' for the death penalty felt by Home Secretary, Roy Jenkins, 'has not been overwhelmed by an even greater repugnance of the deaths of innocent victims'.[7]

Bombs planted in two pubs in Guildford in October of the same year killed five people and injured fifty. Conservative Shadow Home Secretary, Keith Joseph, stated that the reintroduction of capital punishment for terrorists would be considered, although party leader, Edward Heath, joined the Prime Minister and Liberal Party leader in describing the death penalty as a matter of conscience, rather than party policy.[8] Joseph made clear his opposition to

---

3 Ipsos Mori findings were as follows: Agreeing that the death penalty was sometimes justified: 1978 = 77 per cent, 1981 = 78 per cent and 1995 = 76 per cent, Ipsos Mori, 'Attitudes Towards Capital Punishment', 1995, www.ipsos-mori.com/researchpublications/researcharchive/2243/Attitudes-Towards-Capital-Punishment.aspx.
4 N. Twitchell, *The Politics of the Rope*, Bury St Edmunds: Arena, 2012, pp. 92–4. Sandys' attempt to introduce a Bill was defeated by a majority of 122, 'Death Penalty Refused for Police Murders', *The Times*, 24 November 1966.
5 'MPs Admit Changing Views on Punishment', *The Times*, 26 July 1974. The first quote was from Scottish Nationalist, Donald Stewart and the second, Conservative Michael Ancram.
6 'Shoot the Bombers, Says MP', *Daily Mail*, 19 July 1974.
7 V. McLoughlin, 'Repugnance', Letter to the Editor, *Daily Mail*, 25 July 1974.
8 'Party Leaders Resist Demands to Reintroduce the Death Penalty for Acts of Terrorism', *The Times*, 8 October 1974.

capital punishment in ordinary murder cases, which were usually not pre-meditated, but argued that it could be a deterrent against acts of terrorism, which were planned.[9]

In the political domain, debate centred on whether hanging could be an effective deterrent against terrorism and whether execution risked making martyrs out of terrorists. In a letter to *The Times*, Conservative MP, Julian Critchley, expressed the need for retribution in the form of the death penalty, arguing that the public should be 'permitted catharsis, an act of revenge'.[10] After the Birmingham pub bombings in November, a *Times* editorial made the case for using capital punishment for terrorist murders as a special cate-gory, on the grounds that the IRA was committing acts of war. Breaking with earlier *Times* tradition, the editorial stated that an 'emotional response' was the 'soundest one' and 'healthier' than attempting to rationalise events like the Birmingham bombings.[11] A letter writer to the paper in December 1974 contended that utilitarian concerns should not be the only factor in weighing the death penalty for terrorism because 'we have to take note of the view that some crimes are so evil that those who commit them should be executed'.[12] A similar view was expressed in a letter to *The Guardian* by a friend of Professor Gordon Hamilton Fairley, who was murdered with a terrorist bomb in 1975. The correspondent argued for the deterrent effect of capital punishment, but also for the 'public's desire for revenge for such outrageous acts' as ultimately being a more important justification.[13]

According to Peter Jenkins in *The Guardian*, the debate on capital punish-ment had 'changed fundamentally' because of terrorism, losing its 'moral simplicity'. There was a 'powerful public clamour for the restoration of a death penalty' (which he believed should be resisted).[14] As leader of the opposition, Margaret Thatcher gave her personal view that capital punish-ment should apply to terrorists.[15] However, motions for the reintroduction of the death penalty for terrorism were defeated in 1974 and 1975,[16] showing how far it had receded from being politically viable.

---

9 'Death Penalty Would Demonstrate Will to Win', *The Times*, 12 December 1974.

10 J. Critchley, 'Why I Now Believe in Hanging', Letter to the Editor, *The Times*, 15 October 1974.

11 'This *Is* an Act of War', *The Times*, 23 November 1974. A year later, a more equivocal *Times* editorial argued that there was no moral case against executing terrorists but that it would be tactically disadvantageous, making it more difficult for the police to catch them, 'Would the Death Penalty Help?', 10 December 1975.

12 S. F. Cumberland, 'Punishment for Terrorists', Letter to the Editor, *The Times*, 4 December 1974.

13 D. Cadisch, 'Bomb Victim: Life for a Death', Letter to the Editor, *The Guardian*, 27 October 1975.

14 P. Jenkins, 'Hanging Fire', *The Guardian*, 4 December 1975.

15 'Terrorists Forfeit Right to Life – Mrs Thatcher', *The Times*, 29 November 1974.

16 'MPs Reject Motion to Restore Hanging but Majority is Down', *The Times*, 12 December 1975. The 1975 vote gained a smaller majority against, described by Simon Hoggart as a 'marginal swing towards the rope', 'Small Swing to the Rope', *The Guardian*, 12 December 1975.

Myra Hindley and Ian Brady

If the terrorist bombings of the mid-1970s were a key impetus to retributive feeling and discussion of restoration of the death penalty, the imprisonment of Myra Hindley and Ian Brady in 1966 for the 'Moors murders' provided an enduring symbol for unslaked retributivism. The crimes of which they were convicted were of the kind that provoked widespread outrage – the abduction, torture and murder of children and young people.[17] Ian Brady was largely perceived as the instigator of the crimes but the involvement of a young woman, Myra Hindley, made them especially shocking. There is a well-developed feminist literature on legal and cultural portrayals of Myra Hindley as an abject, monstrous woman, who has been perceived both as Brady's dupe and as the mastermind behind the crimes.[18] From being charged with murder in 1965 until her death in prison in 2002 she remained a focus for media attention and a culturally resonant gendered icon of evil.[19]

An important aspect of the persistence of Myra Hindley and Ian Brady in the penal imagination is that they 'cheated death by a year' and instead of being hanged received sentences of life imprisonment.[20] They were charged with their crimes eleven days after the Murder (Abolition of the Death Penalty) Act had received royal assent in 1965. In the 1966 general election, which preceded the trial, Patrick Downey, the uncle of one of the victims, stood for Parliament in Sydney Silverman's constituency of Nelson and Colne as a 'pro hanging' independent.[21] He lost his deposit and Silverman was returned with an increased majority. However, the perceived failure to achieve adequate retribution for the Moors murders without the death penalty became an enduring theme. In an article on his impressions of Hindley and Brady for *The Guardian*, Maurice Richardson commented that '[a] big murder trial when capital punishment has been abolished is like a Portuguese bullfight'.[22] A self-proclaimed abolitionist, he 'couldn't help wondering how differently those two would behave if they were facing the death penalty'.[23] The ending

---

17 Ian Brady was found guilty of three murders – Pauline Reade, 16, Edward Evans, 17 and Lesley Ann Downey, 10. Photographs and a tape-recording of Lesley Ann Downey were found by the police, and the recording of her begging for her life was played in court. Myra Hindley was found guilty of two murders and of harbouring and providing comfort to Ian Brady in relation to the third. In 1986, she confessed to having been involved with Brady in killing a further two victims. See L. Seal, *Women Murder and Femininity: Gender Representations of Women Who Kill*, Basingstoke: Palgrave MacMillan, 2010, pp. 41–2.
18 See ibid. for a discussion of some of this literature.
19 Grant, *Crime*, p. 135.
20 G. Tynedale, 'Time for the Gallows to Return ... and the Critics Can Go Hang', *Sunday Mercury*, 23 September 2012.
21 'Sydney Silverman Has a Stroke', *Daily Mirror*, 30 April 1966.
22 M. Richardson, 'What is One to Make of the Moors Murders?', *The Guardian*, 8 May 1966.
23 Ibid.

of capital punishment had reduced the retributive frisson of the murder trial. Execution could no longer act as 'a symbolic scapegoat ceremony'.[24]

Post abolition, the mandatory sentence of life imprisonment was the most severe punishment that could be meted out for murder. This, Grant argues, allowed capital punishment to live on in the 'public spectacle of the scaffold' that was encoded into life imprisonment.[25] Rather than being a more lenient approach than the death penalty, the life sentence enabled the continuation of penal severity through 'death in life' for those like Myra Hindley and Ian Brady who languished in prison.[26] Shifts within the penal culture have been argued to be significant to Myra Hindley's punishment. The trial judge interpreted Brady's influence as significant to her involvement in the crimes and had envisioned her eventual release.[27] In 1990, a whole-life tariff was imposed on Mrya Hindley by the Home Secretary without her knowledge and was upheld as legal by the House of Lords in 2000.[28] Lord Steyn stated in his ruling that the Moors murders had been 'uniquely evil'[29] and that Hindley's role within them had been 'pivotal'.[30] Explicitly invoking the shadow of the scaffold, he also observed that before 1965, 'persons convicted of heinous murders were sentenced to death and executed'.[31]

The whole-life sentence in Hindley's case was therefore given a retributive equivalence with the death penalty. Gurnham attributes the decision to uphold as lawful Hindley's whole-life tariff to 'a larger apparent resurgence of retributive ideology in recent years',[32] and Murphy and Whitty note that judicial attitudes seemed to 'harden over time' in relation to Hindley.[33] The Law Lords' decision may well have indicated this hardening of attitudes but the issue of whether Myra Hindley should ever be released had previously been considered in relation to retribution. In 1977, BBC2 discussion show, *Brass Tacks*, debated whether Hindley should be paroled as she became eligible to be considered for a formal review of the possibility for parole in 1978.[34] Penal campaigner and supporter of Hindley, Lord Longford, was one of those arguing for her release. He asserted that she was remorseful for her crimes, understood their gravity and was not a danger to society.

24 Ibid.
25 Grant, *Crime*, p. 129.
26 Ibid., p. 131.
27 T. Murphy and N. Whitty, 'The Question of Evil and Feminist Legal Scholarship', *Feminist Legal Studies*, 2006, 14(1): 1–26, p. 9.
28 C. Appleton and B. Grover, 'The Pros and Cons of Life Without Parole', *British Journal of Criminology*, 2007, 47(4): 597–615, p. 602.
29 D. Gurnham, 'The Moral Narrative of Criminal Responsibility and the Principled Justification of Tariffs for Murder: Myra Hindley and Thompson and Venables', *Legal Studies*, 2003, 23(4): 605–22, quoted p. 617.
30 Murphy and Whitty, 'The Question', p. 9.
31 Ibid., p. 10.
32 Gurnham, 'The Moral', p. 607.
33 Murphy and Whitty, 'The Question', p. 9.
34 W. S. Gilbert, 'The Week in View', *The Observer*, 3 July 1977.

Taking up the issue of Hindley's release in *The Times*, Bernard Levin pointed out that 'political reasons' would make the Home Secretary reluctant to free her from prison. The 'inevitable fury' that this would cause was 'based on the theory of punishment that was supposed to have no place in our system, to wit the retributive'.[35] A letter writer in response to Levin's article asserted that it was 'fortunate' that in practice the law allowed an element of retribution as there were times when this was 'salutary, necessary and right'.[36] Sympathising with Levin, another correspondent asked 'what Home Secretary of whatever party would dare to rubber stamp the normal release of Hindley?'[37]

Ann West, mother of Lesley Ann Downey, wrote to *The Times* in response to a letter it had published by Lord Longford that defended his views on Hindley. She argued that for 'Hindley and Brady, in fact all murderers, the punishment should be a definite life sentence or death by hanging' and criticised Longford for attacking the role of public opinion, asking '[d]o we live in a democratic society where the majority decision overrides the minority?'[38] West's letter was reported in the *Daily Mirror*, which described her as a 'tragic' and 'tortured' mother.[39] The *Daily Mail* explained that '[t]ime has done nothing to diminish the torment of Mrs West, who looks ill and is still easily moved to tears when she recalls Lesley Ann'.[40] The emotional public sphere that developed in the 1950s around capital punishment, and in particular around the relatives of the condemned, was paralleled in the late 1970s in the emotional public sphere that developed around crime victims. A letter writer to the *Mirror* made the retributive argument in relation to Hindley of 'an eye for an eye and a tooth for a tooth' and called for the reintroduction of the death penalty.[41]

The prospect of whole-life terms for Hindley and Brady added another element to the discussion, which was that such a sentence was possibly worse than hanging. One correspondent to *The Times* argued that, in the wake of abolition, murderers like them must be readmitted to society 'or we are condemning them to a fate far more horrible than the rope's end. We are insisting that they endure living death'.[42] These various themes of retribution, the emotions and wishes of the victims' relatives and whether 'living death' was worse than execution remained the constituent parts of the public discussion of the fate of the Moors murderers.

---

35 B. Levin, 'Is There Any Chance of Myra Hindley Ever Being Freed?', *The Times*, 21 December 1977.
36 P. D. R. Talbot Willcox, 'Future of the Moors Murderers', Letter to the Editor, *The Times*, 23 December 1977.
37 Matthew D. Oliver, 'The Moors Murderers', Letter to the Editor, *The Times*, 31 December 1977.
38 A. West, 'Future of the Moors Murderers', Letter to the Editor, *The Times*, 3 January 1978.
39 'Angry Plea of a Tortured Mother: Don't Free Hindley', *Daily Mirror*, 3 January 1978.
40 F. Thompson, 'Visit Hindley in Jail? I'd Kill Her!', *Daily Mail*, 18 January 1978.
41 A. Turner, 'Killers Must Stay Caged', Dear Jo Letters Page, *Daily Mirror*, 3 January 1978.
42 B. Stewart, 'The Moors Murderers', Letter to the Editor, *The Times*, 6 January 1978.

In the years during which Myra Hindley attempted to win the right to have her whole-life tariff reviewed, she made public statements, via interviews with journalists, that it would have been better if she had been hanged in 1966.[43] Her death in prison in 2002 raised the issue of the death penalty as she was a high-profile murderer who had served a whole-life tariff. In *Scotland on Sunday*, Gerald Warner reflected that 'Myra Hindley became a damning icon of that inversion of the justice system effected in 1965'.[44] Execution, argued George Tyndale in the *Sunday Mercury*, would have allowed Hindley and Brady to be long forgotten 'as they so thoroughly deserved'.[45] Retributive sentiment was expressed. Journalist and writer, Tony Parsons, compared Myra Hindley in the *Mirror* to her 'hero', Nazi prison camp guard, Irma Grese, but noted that Grese was executed and 'Hindley lived a soft, long life'. Nothing could appease Hindley's crimes – even if she had 'forfeited her life, it would never have been enough'.[46] The *South Wales Echo* quoted the uncle of a murder victim (not one of Hindley and Brady's) as stating Hindley 'should have swung at the end of a rope' and reported that he was to deliver an 11,000 word petition to Downing Street calling for the restoration of capital punishment for child murder.[47]

Myra Hindley died three months after the very high-profile murder of two ten-year-old girls in Soham, Cambridgeshire by Ian Huntley, the caretaker at their school. This case had provoked discussion of the death penalty, with Lynda Lee Potter claiming in the *Daily Mail* that capital punishment should be used for such murders because '[p]aedophiles never change'.[48] Conservative MP, Ann Widdecombe, argued for the deterrent effect of execution.[49] The arrest of Huntley's girlfriend, Maxine Carr, led to comparisons between the Soham and Moors murders as it seemed to be another case of a couple killing children. This was incorrect – Carr did not participate in the murders but provided Huntley with a false alibi, which delayed his arrest.[50] However, this serves to demonstrate that Myra Hindley died at a

---

43 See 'Hindley: I Should Have Been Hung', *Daily Mirror*, 19 December 1994; R. Allison, 'Killer Hindley Wishes She Had Been Hanged', *Birmingham Post*, 1 March 2000 and 'Hindley Yearned for the Noose', *The Herald*, 1 March 2000.

44 G. Warner, 'Capital Punishment Splits Society Again as Myra Hindley Dies 37 Years Too Late', *Scotland on Sunday*, 24 November 2002.

45 G. Tyndale, 'Twist of Fate that Let Hindley Live for so Long', *Sunday Mercury*, 24 November 2002.

46 T. Parsons, 'She Was No Better than Nazi Sadist', *Daily Mirror*, 18 November 2002.

47 S. Tucker, 'She Should Have Swung at the End of a Rope', *South Wales Echo*, 16 November 2002.

48 L. L. Potter, 'Only One Penalty for Such Evil', *Daily Mail*, 21 August 2002.

49 P. Benn, 'Soham, Widdecombe and the Death Penalty', *Think*, 2003, 1 (3): 83–6.

50 Press coverage of the trial in 2003 drew comparisons between Maxine Carr and Myra Hindley. Many newspaper stories portrayed Carr as Huntley's accomplice and referenced Hindley in order to represent Carr as a 'monstrous' woman, see P. J. Jones and C. Wardle, 'Hindley's Ghost: The Visual Construction of Maxine Carr', K. J. Hayward and M. Presdee (eds), *Framing Crime: Cultural Criminology and the Image*, London: Routledge, 2010, p. 59.

time when retributive feeling was high and when the Moors murders had recently been evoked.

Myra Hindley's death and Ian Brady's ongoing attempts to be permitted to starve himself to death in prison focused discussion on whether whole-life sentences were more punitive than the death penalty. Advocating the reintroduction of capital punishment, journalist George Tyndale asked in the *Sunday Mercury* 'can we really believe that caging a human being for 36 years is actually more humane or even more morally acceptable than depriving them of their lives'.[51] Since 1999, Ian Brady has been on partial hunger strike in an attempt to kill himself and has undergone force feeding. He has attempted to apply to be transferred to a Scottish prison, where he would be allowed to die.[52] In the *Daily Mail*, Simon Heffer argued Brady's 'baleful presence' showed 'there has been no satisfactory solution for a society' in dealing with the 'wicked and depraved'. Execution, he argued, would have been better for Brady, as well as society.[53] An article in the *Yorkshire Post* contended that public opinion in Britain was in favour of the death penalty, but 'supposedly democratic governments have resisted the will of the people for almost 50 years'. The whole-life alternative meant that Hindley had an 'unimaginably bleak existence' and Brady lived on only through force feeding.[54] The lingering presence of Myra Hindley and Ian Brady into the twenty-first century was a condensing symbol for discussion of capital punishment.

Culture of punitiveness

Criminologists have identified a 'decisive shift' in British politics in the early 1990s, when both of the main parties adopted a 'tough' stance on crime.[55] Conservative Home Secretary, Michael Howard, famously stated in 1993 that 'prison works' and Labour leader, Tony Blair, claimed to be 'tough on crime and tough on the causes of crime'.[56] When the Labour government came to power in 1997, it implemented Howard's policy of automatic life sentences for repeat serious offenders and introduced legislation on 'anti-social behaviour'.

51 Tyndale, 'Twist of Fate'.
52 H. Carter, 'Moors Murderer Ian Brady Spends Second Night in Hospital', *The Guardian*, 4 July 2012.
53 S. Heffer, 'Brady's Victims Weren't Allowed to Choose if they Lived or Died. Neither Should He', *Daily Mail*, 5 July 2012. Ian Brady lost his attempt to be transferred from a secure psychiatric hospital to a prison in June 2013, 'Moors Murderer Ian Brady Loses Prison Move Bid', *BBC News UK*, 28 June 2013: www.bbc.co.uk/news/uk-23099582.
54 B. Carmichael, 'When Life is a Cruel Penalty', *Yorkshire Post*, 6 July 2012.
55 T. Newburn, '"Tough on Crime": Penal Policy in England and Wales', *Crime and Justice*, 2007, 36(1): 425–70, p. 426. See also I. Brownlee, 'New Labour – New Penology? Punitive Rhetoric and the Limits of Managerialism in Criminal Justice Policy', *Journal of Law and Society*, 1998, 25(3): 313–35.
56 T. Newburn and T. Jones, 'Symbolic Politics and Penal Populism: The Long Shadow of Willie Horton', *Crime, Media, Culture*, 2005, 1(1): 72–87, p. 84.

This was despite the fact that recorded crime fell after 1995.[57] The United States also underwent a more deeply entrenched punitive shift in the 1990s, with rising prison rates and increased use of the death penalty[58] (which declined again after 2000). However, in Britain the punitive climate did not put capital punishment back on the political agenda. In 1994, a Commons majority of 43 per cent voted against the reintroduction of the death penalty, up from 20 per cent in 1979. This increased majority was due to changed voting patterns amongst Conservative MPs as no Labour MP had voted in favour of capital punishment since 1983.[59] In 1998, the Labour government abolished the death penalty completely by removing it from statute for piracy and treason.

In addition to punitive rhetoric and policy-making, criminologists have argued that the public in the 1980s and 1990s often viewed the criminal justice system as too lenient and perceived crime as always rising even when this was not the case.[60] Research into public attitudes to crime and justice has, however, complicated assumptions about 'populist punitiveness', finding that harsher attitudes 'at a general or abstract level ... co-exist with more rehabilitative or restorative views at the level of particular cases'.[61] Matthews asks whether criminological concerns about increased punitiveness are overstated. He argues that populism is not intrinsically punitive or 'backward', but rather is a constituent part of democracy, and cites the reaction against the failure to prosecute Stephen Lawrence's killers in the 1990s as an example of populist currents 'confronting injustice'.[62] Crucially, Matthews contends that punitive and emotive strategies are an historically recurrent feature of criminal justice policies, rather than only characterising the late twentieth and early twenty-first centuries.[63]

---

57 Newburn, "Tough", p. 448.
58 D. Garland, *The Culture of Control*, Oxford: Oxford University Press, 2001, p. 135 and J. Pratt, D. Brown, M. Brown, S. Hallsworth and W. Morrison, 'Introduction', J. Pratt, D. Brown, M. Brown, S. Hallsworth and W. Morrison (eds), *The New Punitiveness: Trends, Theories, Perspectives*, Cullompton: Willan, 2005, p. xii.
59 P. Cowley and M. Stuart, 'Sodomy, Slaughter, Sunday Shopping and Seatbelts', *Party Politics*, 1997, 3(1): 119–30, p. 125.
60 M. Hough and J. V. Roberts, 'Sentencing Trends in Britain: Public Knowledge and Public Opinion', *Punishment and Society*, 1999, 1(1): 11–26, p. 12 and J. V. Roberts, L. J. Stalans, D. Indermauer and M. Hough, *Penal Populism and Public Opinion: Lessons from Five Countries*, Oxford: Oxford University Press, 2002, pp. 21–2.
61 N. Hutton, 'Beyond Populist Punitiveness?', *Punishment and Society*, 2005, 7(3): 243–58, p. 250. Hough and Roberts found that when people were asked to make sentencing decisions in relation to specific cases, the results did not suggest the British public was 'highly punitive, or ... consistently more punitive than sentencers', 'Sentencing', p. 22.
62 R. Matthews, 'The Myth of Punitiveness', *Theoretical Criminology*, 2005, 9(2): 175–201, p. 188–9. Stephen Lawrence was a black teenager stabbed to death in London in 1993 in a racist killing. It was not until 2012 that anyone was convicted of his murder, but the case became a pivotal one in terms of recognising 'institutional racism' in the Metropolitan Police Service.
63 Ibid., p. 195.

Matthews' point about historical continuities is important to consider in relation to perceptions of capital punishment in the post-abolition era. As the discussion of terrorism and the Moors murders demonstrates, retributivism has been a persistent aspect of calls for the reintroduction of the death penalty in relation to particular cases. The retributive and emotionally expressive pro-death penalty discourse that accompanied Myra Hindley's death and that was employed in relation to Ian Huntley and Maxine Carr could be interpreted in relation to the punitive penal culture of the early twenty-first century – but similar discourses could be found in the 1970s. The strong reactions to Violet van der Elst's appearance at Buck Ruxton's execution scene in 1936 also indicate continuities in twentieth-century retributive feeling towards especially violent or shocking murders, as does Chapter Five's analysis of the theme of retribution articulated in letters to the Home Office.

Miscarriages of justice

Anxiety about miscarriages of justice was another important current in cultural perceptions of capital punishment in the post-abolition era. The previous chapter explored the hauntings of Edith Thompson and Timothy Evans, and in particular the recurrence of Evans' case in the fifty years following his execution. The 1990s were especially significant in terms of legal and media acknowledgment of miscarriages of justice. Campaigns on behalf of the Guildford Four, the Birmingham Six and Judith Ward, all convicted of murder in relation to terrorist bombings in the 1970s, were pursued from the mid-1980s. Television documentaries highlighted problems with the forensic evidence and witness statements in the Birmingham Six case, and with the police methods of obtaining confessions in relation to the Guildford Four.[64] Journalist Chris Mullin campaigned assiduously for the Birmingham Six's convictions to be reviewed, publishing a book on the case in 1986.[65] In 1989, the convictions of the Guildford Four were quashed and the following year the related convictions against the Maguire Seven were ruled unsafe. After previously unsuccessful attempts, the Birmingham Six had their convictions overturned in 1991. Judith Ward, who was found guilty in 1974 of bombing a coach and killing twelve soldiers, was released from prison in 1992.[66]

These miscarriages of justice affected people who would, in all likelihood, have been executed if Britain had reintroduced capital punishment for terrorist murders.[67] Sarah Boseley noted in *The Guardian* that the Guildford Four

---

64 B. Woffinden, *Miscarriages of Justice*, London: Coronet, 1988, pp. 417–20.
65 Ibid., pp. 424–5; 432–7. C. Mullin, *Error in Judgment*, London: Chatto, 1986.
66 See G. Gudjonsson, 'Disputed Confessions and Miscarriages of Justice in Britain', *Manitoba Law Journal*, 2006, 31(3): 489–521.
67 R. Milne, S. Poyser, T. Williamson and S. P. Savage, 'Miscarriages of Justice: What Can we Learn?', J. R. Adler and J. M. Gray (eds), *Forensic Psychology: Concepts, Debates and Practice*, Abingdon: Willan, 2010, p. 32.

were told at their trial that they would have received the death sentence if it had been available.[68] The revelations of evidence fabricated by the police and allegations of the coercion of suspects demonstrated how it was possible for innocent people not only to be wrongfully convicted, but also to be framed. Convictions which had, in the 1970s, girded calls for the reinstatement of the gallows were by the 1990s a warning against their irreversibility. The 1993 film, *In the Name of the Father*, depicted the story of the Guildford Four and the Maguire Seven, and in particular the relationship between Gerry Conlon and his father, Guiseppe, who died in prison.[69] It also portrayed the use of police brutality in order to secure confessions and the failure of the prosecution to disclose a statement to the defence that supported Gerry Conlon's alibi.

The cases of the Birmingham Six led to a Royal Commission on Criminal Justice, which resulted in the Criminal Appeal Act 1995 that created the Criminal Cases Review Commission (CCRC).[70] The CCRC reviews possible miscarriages of justice in England, Wales and Northern Ireland and can refer cases to the appeal courts.[71] This has led to the quashing of capital cases from the 1950s, the most high-profile of which was the case of Derek Bentley.[72] His conviction was overturned in 1998. Highly emotional and contentious at the time, Bentley's execution still haunted British justice at the end of the twentieth century. A number of books examining the case had been published in the intervening decades and in 1990 a cross-party group of MPs launched a campaign for a posthumous pardon.[73] Bentley's sister, Iris, presented a case to the Home Office with new evidence casting doubt on whether he had said 'Let him have it' and forensic evidence that the bullet which killed PC Miles might not have come from Craig's gun.[74] A new book and a television programme highlighted doubts over the 'Let him have it' statement, and presented new testimony from a retired police officer who had been at scene of the crime.[75]

---

68 S. Boseley, 'Wrongs Which Cannot be Righted', *The Guardian*, 15 December 1990.

69 J. Sheridan, *In the Name of the Father* [Motion Picture], Hell's Kitchen Films, Ireland, 1993.

70 Gudjonsson, 'Disputed', p. 501 and Milne *et al. Miscarriages*, p. 27.

71 On the CCRC, see A. James, 'Miscarriages of Justice in the 21st Century', *Journal of Criminal Law*, 2002, 66(4): 326–37.

72 The conviction of Mahmood Massan Hussein, hanged in Cardiff in 1952, was also quashed by the CCRC in 1998, see J. Minkes and M. Vanstone, 'Gender, Race and the Death Penalty: Lessons from Three 1950s Murder Trials', *Howard Journal*, 2006, 45(4): 403–20, pp. 411–13. In 2003, the appeal court found the guilty verdict of George Kelly, executed at Walton jail in 1950, unsafe, see O. Bowcott, 'Man Hanged 53 Years Ago Was Innocent', *The Guardian*, 11 June 2003.

73 C. Moncrieff, '"Pardon" Campaign for Man Hanged After PC's Killing', *Press Association*, 25 July 1990.

74 B. Levin, 'Not Just a Few Rotten Apples, Enough to Taint the System', *The Times*, 30 July 1990.

75 S. Boseley, 'Evidence Casts Doubt on Guilt of Hanged Man', *The Guardian*, 11 September 1990. The book was M. J. Trow, *Let Him Have It, Chris*, London: Constable, 1990 and the programme was *Thames Reports*, screened on ITV on 11 September 1990.

In 1991, *Let Him Have It*, a film portraying the case was released, starring Christopher Eccleston as Derek Bentley.[76] In addition to his innocence, it emphasised the significance of Bentley's learning disabilities – his inability to fully understand his circumstances – to the miscarriage of justice perpetrated by his execution. The film helped to reignite interest in the case and was intended by its producer, Robert Warr, to be 'a massive campaigning tool', with the recent release of the Guildford Four and Maguire Seven making the time ripe for attention to miscarriages of justice.[77] In 1992, Home Secretary, Kenneth Baker, agreed to examine new evidence in the case. Reviewing the release of *Let Him Have It* on video, Shaun Usher in the *Daily Mail* argued that it was likely to increase 'public pressure for Bentley to be pardoned'.[78] Press attention to the dedicated campaigning efforts of Iris Bentley echoed the importance given to relatives of the condemned in the mid-twentieth-century emotional public sphere surrounding the death penalty.[79] Despite expectations, Bentley was not pardoned in 1992 on the basis that there was no compelling evidence of his innocence. According to the press, this left Iris Bentley 'tearful' and 'shattered'.[80] In *The Guardian*, Kenneth Allen, a journalist who in 1953 had been tasked by his editor with 'doorstepping' the Bentley's at their home, recalled how they welcomed him and how 'I was there when they returned each day – mum, dad, and 21 year old Iris – from visiting Derek in the condemned cell'.[81]

In 1993, Home Secretary, Michael Howard, granted Derek Bentley a posthumous pardon on the grounds that the decision to carry out the death penalty was 'clearly wrong'.[82] This time, Iris 'wept tears of joy' and was reported as having dreamt of Derek, which could have been a 'sign'.[83] His conviction was finally overturned in 1998, after the case was referred to the Court of Appeal by the Criminal Cases Review Commission.[84] The judgment found that the summing up of Lord Goddard was sufficiently flawed as to constitute an unfair trial for Bentley.[85] According to the *Birmingham Post*, his case 'had rested uneasily on the British conscience for almost half a century' and 'was a powerful argument against the reintroduction of the death penalty'.[86] Carol Sarler, a columnist for *The People*, agreed. She wrote that she had 'been

76 P. Medak, *Let Him Have It* [Motion Picture], British Screen Productions, UK, 1991.
77 S. Garfield, 'The Case of Derek Bentley Runs and Runs', *The Guardian*, 29 June 1991.
78 S. Usher, 'A Sister's Search for Justice', *Daily Mail*, 29 February 1992.
79 'Sister of Derek Bentley Asks for a Posthumous Pardon', *The Independent*, 29 January 1992.
80 S. Weale, 'Tears as Sister Condemns Pardon Refusal', *Press Association*, 1 October 1992 and H. Mills, 'Hanged Man's Sister Sees Hope Shattered', *The Independent*, 2 October 1992.
81 K. Allen, 'No Pardon for the Family Left Behind', *The Guardian*, 2 October 1992.
82 'Bentley's Sister Weeps Tears of Joy Over Pardon', *Evening Standard*, 30 July 1993.
83 Ibid.
84 *R v Derek William Bentley (Deceased)* [1998] EWCA Crim 2516.
85 'Bentley Trial Unfair Through Flawed Summing Up', *The Times*, 31 July 1998.
86 'Smoothing Out the Faults of Yesteryear's Rough Justice', *Birmingham Post*, 31 July 1998.

haunted all my life by the execution of Derek Bentley' and argued 'if we brought back the rope, we would use it to hang innocent people'.[87]

In addition to raising the issue of hanging in error, Bentley's full pardon was also linked in the press to other possible historical wrongful executions. Several news stories reported the intention of Ruth Ellis' sister, Muriel Jakubait, to have the Ellis verdict reconsidered, especially in the light of the Bentley case.[88] There was a long-running campaign to establish James Hanratty's innocence, which had received media attention in the 1990s. A documentary made by Bob Woffinden, shown on Channel 4 in 1992, called for DNA testing of the evidence and presented a new confession of guilt from the original suspect, Peter Alphon. It was screened again in 1994.[89] In 1997, after an 18-month police inquiry into the case, *The Independent* reported that Home Office officials had 'concluded that Hanratty was innocent' and 'the conviction [was] expected to be quashed'.[90] However, although the case was referred back to the Court of Appeal by the CCRC in March 1999, DNA testing of original exhibits seemed to confirm his guilt[91] and the appeal was dismissed in 2002. In relation to Ruth Ellis, the Court ruled in 2003 that a defence of diminished responsibility, which did not exist in England and Wales at the time of the trial, could not be retrospectively applied and that a defence of provocation had been rightly rejected in the original trial.[92] Although not officially accepted as miscarriages of justice, like Derek Bentley, these cases had been a lasting focus for unease about capital punishment.[93] Hanratty's

87 C. Sarler, 'The Only Thing to Drop Now is the Call to Bring Back Hanging', *The People*, 2 August 1998.
88 See 'Ruth Ellis's Family Inspired by Quashing of the Bentley Conviction', *Birmingham Post*, 13 August 1998 and 'Sister's Justice Bid for Hanged Killer Ruth', *Western Daily Press*, 13 August 1998.
89 P. Archer, 'Plea to Reopen Hanratty Murder Case', *Press Association*, 31 March 1992. The documentary was B Woffinden, *The Mystery of Deadman's Hill* [Documentary], Channel 4, UK, repeated 10 October 1994.
90 J. Bennetto, 'The Hanratty Case: I'm Dying Tomorrow, Please Clear my Name', *The Independent*, 27 January 1997.
91 'DNA Blow to Hanratty Case', *Mail on Sunday*, 6 June 1999.
92 On the Ruth Ellis appeal and the continued failure of the law to adequately recognise the social context of gender in relation to such killings by women, see A. Ballinger, 'A Muted Voice from the Past: The "Silent Silencing" of Ruth Ellis', *Social and Legal Studies*, 2012, 21(4): 445–67.
93 A film based on Ruth Ellis was released in 1987 and there have been a number of books about her and the case, including by her sister: M. Newell, *Dance with a Stranger* [Motion Picture], Goldcrest Films International, UK, 1985 and M. Jakubait with M. Weller, *Ruth Ellis: My Sister's Secret Life*, London: Robinson, 2005. The campaign for Hanratty's release dates from the 1960s and has been the subject of books, television documentaries and even a film by John Lennon and Yoko Ono (*Hanratty Film*, shown at St Martin-in-the-Fields Church, London, 17 February 1972). In 1966, an episode of the BBC current affairs programme, *Panorama*, reconstructed the murder to show flaws in the case, 'Dramatic Reconstruction of A6 Murder Case', *The Times*, 8 November 1966, and another man, Peter Alphon, confessed to the crime on a television interview in May 1967, *ITN Reporting 67*, www.itnsource.com/shotlist/BHC_ITN/1967/05/17/X17056701/?v=0. Calls for a public inquiry were rejected in 1967 and 1971.

family and supporters dispute the safety of the DNA evidence, arguing it could have been contaminated over the years and continue to ask for the case to be reviewed further,[94] although the DNA results have meant that for the most part the case is no longer regarded as a miscarriage of justice.[95]

Perceptions of the American death penalty

Evi Girling has analysed the increased significance of abolitionism to the imagined penal identity of the European Union. Since 1994, new states joining the Council of Europe have had to agree to place an immediate moratorium on the death penalty and to achieve abolition within one to three years.[96] She argues that for Europeans, the United States is a 'cognate other', largely embracing the same civilised values as Europe. However, its failure to end capital punishment makes it a 'Europe gone adrift'.[97] European political bodies have repeatedly called on the American government and state governors to abolish, or at least limit, the death penalty and European officials have made death row visits. There is also a well organised European anti-death penalty movement of campaigning organisations that opposes American executions.[98] The successful abolition of capital punishment in Europe is part of the European narrative of triumph over barbarity and the guarantee of a civilised future. American executions erupt as a 'global spectacle', challenging this future.[99] In particular, the spectres of 'error and failure of mercy' are significant to European abolitionist campaigning on the United States and to European media reporting of American capital cases.[100] Girling argues that the possibility of error in application of the death penalty haunts both American retentionism and European abolitionism.[101] The British penal imagination is not consonant with the 'European community of sentiment' explored by Girling but the haunting of miscarriage of justice, and fascination with the spectacle of American capital punishment, are both highly relevant to the place of the American death penalty within it.

In 1977, the United States resumed the death penalty with the execution by firing squad of Gary Gilmore in Utah. In the following decade, a majority of American states reinstated capital punishment and both public approval and

94 'Calls for James Hanratty Murder Case to be Reviewed', *Daily Telegraph*, 30 October 2010.
95 See, for example, L. McKinstry, 'He Was the Killer All Along', *The Express*, 31 March 2012.
96 E. Girling, 'European Identity and the Mission Against the Death Penalty in the United States', A. Sarat and C. Boulanger (eds), *The Cultural Lives of Capital Punishment*, Stanford, CA: Stanford University Press, 2005, p. 115.
97 J. L. Cebrian, 'The Media and European Identity', *New Perspectives Quarterly*, 1999, 16: 39–42, p. 41 quoted in Girling, p. 120.
98 Girling, p. 116.
99 Ibid., p. 118.
100 E. Girling, 'The Witnessing of Judgment', A. Sarat and J. Martschukat (eds), *Is the Death Penalty Dying?* Cambridge: Cambridge University Press, 2011, p. 111.
101 Ibid., p. 120.

execution rates climbed. This enthusiastic resumption of capital punishment was counter to the trend in the rest of the Western world towards abolition.[102] For British observers, the American death penalty presented an imagined alternative penal reality in which execution still took place. The Adverts' punk single, *Gary Gilmore's Eyes*, imagined a transplant patient who had received his eyes from the executed Gilmore.[103] An editorial in *The Times* concluded that '[i]t is not for us in Britain to pass judgement on the United States',[104] although the counterpoint to abolition that American capital punishment offered was a means to reflect on longstanding issues associated with the practice. *The Guardian* took up the theme of execution as a focus for spectacle and sensationalism, stating 'though America stages it on a bigger, exotic and often obscene scale, it shouldn't be supposed that more phlegmatic Britain is immune from the same sick fascination'.[105]

Spectacle remained an important theme in British press coverage of the American death penalty. Roderick Gilchrist in the *Daily Mail* commented that capital punishment had become 'showbusiness' with some condemned wanting their executions to be shown on primetime television.[106] In the same paper, several years later, Peter Sheridan noted the 'ghoulish carnival' of '[t]ourists and voyeurs, priests and protestors' that took place outside the gates of San Quentin prison in California when a stay of execution was granted to Robert Alton Harris.[107] His subsequent execution in the gas chamber in April 1992 was California's first since 1967. Anxieties about capital punishment as entertainment were reconfigured in the late twentieth century, with the possibility of televisation threatening cultural depravity.[108] Disapproval of the spectacular American death penalty echoed the theme of tension between modernity and civilisation that emerged in Britain in the earlier part of the century, whereby modern communications facilitated the vulgar spectacle. In post-abolition Britain this disapproval was now transferred to the 'cognate other' of the United States – although as *The Guardian* suggested, British observers could share 'sick fascination' with the death penalty.

102 See D. Garland, *Peculiar Institution: America's Death Penalty in an Age of Abolition*, Oxford: Oxford University Press, 2010, for an overview and analysis of the American death penalty after its resumption in the late 1970s.

103 The Adverts, *Gary Gilmore's Eyes* [Song], Anchor Records, 1977. This reached number 18 in the British charts and was performed on *Top of the Pops* in August 1977.

104 'The Execution of Mr Gilmore', *The Times*, 18 January 1977.

105 'The American Way of Death', *The Guardian*, 18 January 1977.

106 R. Gilchrist, 'Brutality Hogs the Limelight', *Daily Mail*, 15 January 1977.

107 P. Sheridan, 'Carnival of Ghouls as Killer Wins Time', *Daily Mail*, 20 April 1992.

108 On the legal attempt by a public television station to gain the right to film and televise Harris' execution and related cultural issues, see W. Lesser, *Pictures at an Execution: An Inquiry into the Subject of Murder*, Cambridge, MA: Harvard University Press, 1993. See also Sarat and Schuster's challenge to her argument against televising execution, A. Sarat and A. Schuster, 'To See or Not to See: Television, Capital Punishment, and the Law's Violence', *Yale Journal of Law and the Humanities*, 1995, 7(2): 397–432.

Historical yet still contentious cases such as Derek Bentley's were important to the formation of cultural memories of British capital punishment but, after Gary Gilmore, the imagined death penalty was frequently American, with its imagery of the electric chair and the gurney replacing that of the gallows.[109] American capital cases have regularly appeared in the British news media and television documentaries have explored various aspects of the American death penalty. In addition to entertainment media, the internet means that American capital punishment websites are internationally accessible.[110]

The international penetration of American entertainment media means that procedural crime dramas, which sometimes allude to the death penalty,[111] are screened on British television and Hollywood films on the issue are shown in cinemas and on TV. The most successful of these commercially and critically were *Dead Man Walking* and *The Green Mile*.[112] These films tackle different aspects of capital punishment. The condemned man in *Dead Man Walking*, Matthew Poncelot as played by Sean Penn, is guilty of a brutally violent murder but maintains his innocence. After bonding with prison visitor and nun, Sister Helen Prejean (Susan Sarandon), he finally admits guilt before he is executed by lethal injection. The portrayal of his execution is interspersed with the murder of the victims. Themes of retribution and redemption predominate.[113] British reviewers commented on the potential for films such as *Dead Man Walking* to open up the death penalty to public view as it portrayed Poncelot's last moments in 'minute detail'[114] and 'offered a closer view of an execution than any spectator had at Rainy Bethea's

109 See E. Carrabine, 'The Iconography of Punishment', *The Howard Journal*, 2011, 50(5): 452–64 on the visual imagery of punishment, including Warhol's Little Electric Chair paintings. See also P. Smith, *Punishment and Culture*, Chicago, IL: University of Chicago Press, 2008, pp. 162–6 on artistic representations of the electric chair.
110 On such websites, see M. Lynch, 'Capital Punishment as Moral Imperative: Pro-death Penalty Discourse on the Internet', *Punishment and Society*, 2002, 4(2): 213–36, although since Lynch's article the advent of social media websites such as Facebook and Twitter are likely to be highly significant to the expression of contemporary death penalty sentiment (pro and anti) and require analysis.
111 Examples include the *CSI* and *Law and Order* franchises.
112 T. Robbins, *Dead Man Walking* [Motion Picture], Polygram, USA, 1995 and F. Darabont, *The Green Mile* [Motion Picture], Castle Rock Entertainment, USA, 1999.
113 *Dead Man Walking* has been variously interpreted as effectively conveying the ambiguities of the death penalty debate – see R. M. Harding, 'Celluloid Death: Cinematic Depictions of Capital Punishment', *University of San Francisco Law Review*, 1996, 30(4): 1167–79, capturing both the humanity of the condemned and the fact of his horrific crime – see D. R. Dow, 'Fictional Documentaries and Truthful Fictions', *Constitutional Commentary*, 2000, 17(3): 511–54 and as favouring an individualised portrayal of criminal responsibility over 'a more structural account of crime' – see A. Sarat, *When the State Kills*, Princeton, NJ: Princeton University Press, 2001, p. 228. O'Sullivan argues that *Dead Man Walking* aimed to 'reopen a discussion which appeared to have been closed' by helping to raise the anti-death penalty view in a pro-death penalty era, S. O'Sullivan, 'Representing the "Killing State": The Death Penalty in Nineties Hollywood Cinema', *The Howard Journal*, 2003, 42(5): 485–503, p. 491.
114 Q. Curtis, 'Crimes and Misdemeanours', *The Independent*, 31 March 1996.

hanging'.[115] The preparation for lethal injection 'leaves one in no doubt that this "humane" means of execution was designed to make things more humane for the executioner'.[116]

The Green Mile is largely set in the 1930s and centres on the wrongful conviction and execution by electric chair of John Coffey, a gentle African American man with supernatural powers. The story begins as a flashback from 1999 by an elderly corrections officer who is burdened with the guilt of Coffey's execution.[117] The film was released just at the point when concerns about execution of the innocent were gathering speed in the United States – albeit it transposes these to an historical setting. The film depicts three executions by electric chair, in which the smoke comes off the head of the condemned, and pays 'close – some might say voyeuristic – attention … to the brutal mechanics of electrocuting someone to death'.[118]

The American death penalty figures in the British penal imagination in different ways. One is as a repository for retributive and punitive sentiment. This can also apply to wider perceptions of American punishment as generally being tougher than it is in Britain. Another is as a warning in relation to the flaws in the capital punishment system, which means that not only are the innocent put to death but also that poverty and race are deciding factors in the application of the death penalty. BBC documentary, *Fourteen Days in May*, exemplifies this portrayal.[119] It follows the looming execution of Edward Earle Johnson in Mississippi and the efforts of his young British lawyer, Clive Stafford-Smith, to gain a stay of execution or pardon. Johnson was a young African American man convicted of the murder of a white police officer. The documentary evokes themes of racial and socio-economic inequality, highlighting Earle's inadequate legal representation at his original trial. After he was executed by lethal injection, a new witness came to light who could have provided him with an alibi for the time of the murder. It ends with this revelation of his probable innocence. American documentary, *The Thin Blue Line*,[120] depicts the inadequacies and perversions of 'a Kafkaesque nightmare of Texan justice'[121] in Dallas County that led to the capital conviction of Randall Adams, like

---

115 I. Katz, 'Pictures at an Execution', *The Guardian*, 26 July 1996. Rainy Bethea was the last person to be publicly hanged in the United States in 1936.
116 A. Walker, 'Soul Sister's Quality of Mercy', *Evening Standard*, 28 March 1996.
117 As O'Sullivan highlights, *The Green Mile* can be read in a multitude of ways, 'Representing'. It has been criticised for its portrayal of a 'magical' African American male character whose purpose is to save white people – see H. J. Hicks 'Hoodoo Economics: White Men's Work and Black Men's Magic in Contemporary American Film', *Camera Obscura*, 2003, 18(2): 27–55 and C. L. Glenn and L. J. Cunningham, 'The Power of Black Magic: The Magical Negro and White Salvation in Film', *Journal of Black Studies*, 2009, 40(2): 135–52 – although as Smith suggests, it also raises the issue of race and justice, with the electric chair becoming a lynching machine, *Punishment*, p. 166.
118 M. Jaggi, 'Death Row. Just the Place for a Feelgood Movie, Right?', *The Scotsman*, 2 March 2000.
119 P. Hamann, *Fourteen Days in May* [Documentary], BBC, UK, 1987.
120 E. Morris, *The Thin Blue Line* [Documentary], American Playhouse, USA, 1988.
121 D. Robinson, 'Going for Broke', *The Times*, 16 March 1989.

Edward Earle Johnson, for the murder of a police officer. Unlike Johnson, Adams' death sentence was commuted but he remained in prison under a life sentence despite the fact that someone else had originally confessed to the murder. The film revealed that perjured witness testimony was given at Adams' trial and he was released from prison in 1989.

Conclusion

These three currents flowed into the British penal imagination at the end of the twentieth century and into the twenty-first, and demonstrate the significance of both pro-death penalty sentiment and the legacy of unease bequeathed by miscarriages of justice. Although the last executions in Britain took place in 1964, the resumption of capital punishment in the 'cognate other' of late twentieth-century America presented an alternate reality, in which execution still happened for good or ill.

Newspapers, magazines and news websites

BBC News UK
Birmingham Post
Daily Mail
Daily Mirror
Daily Telegraph
Evening Standard
ITN Source
Mail on Sunday
Press Association
Scotland on Sunday
South Wales Echo
Sunday Mercury
The Express
The Guardian
The Herald
The Independent
The Observer
The People
The Scotsman
The Times
Western Daily Press
Yorkshire Post

Bibliography

Adverts, The, *Gary Gilmore's Eyes* [Song], Anchor Records, 1977.
Appleton, C. and Grover, B., 'The Pros and Cons of Life Without Parole', *British Journal of Criminology*, 2007, 47(4): 597–615.

Ballinger, A., 'A Muted Voice from the Past: The "Silent Silencing" of Ruth Ellis', *Social and Legal Studies*, 2012, 21(4): 445–67.

Benn, P., 'Soham, Widdecombe and the Death Penalty', *Think*, 2003, 1(3): 83–6.

Brownlee, I., 'New Labour – New Penology? Punitive Rhetoric and the Limits of Managerialism in Criminal Justice Policy', *Journal of Law and Society*, 1998, 25(3): 313–35.

Carrabine, E., 'The Iconography of Punishment', *The Howard Journal*, 2011, 50(5): 452–64.

Cebrian, J. L., 'The Media and European Identity', *New Perspectives Quarterly*, 1999, 16: 39–42.

Cowley, P. and Stuart, M., 'Sodomy, Slaughter, Sunday Shopping and Seatbelts', *Party Politics*, 1997, 3(1): 119–30.

Darabont, F., *The Green Mile* [Motion Picture], Castle Rock Entertainment, USA, 1999.

Dow, D. R., 'Fictional Documentaries and Truthful Fictions', *Constitutional Commentary*, 2000, 17(3): 511–54.

Erskine, H., 'The Polls: Capital Punishment', *Public Opinion Quarterly*, 1970, 34(2): 290–307.

Garland, D., *The Culture of Control*, Oxford: Oxford University Press, 2001.

——*Peculiar Institution: America's Death Penalty in an Age of Abolition*, Oxford: Oxford University Press, 2010.

Girling, E., 'European Identity and the Mission Against the Death Penalty in the United States', A. Sarat and C. Boulanger (eds), *The Cultural Lives of Capital Punishment*, Stanford, CA: Stanford University Press, 2005, 112–28.

——'The Witnessing of Judgment', A. Sarat and J. Martschukat (eds), *Is the Death Penalty Dying?* Cambridge: Cambridge University Press, 2011, 109–25.

Glenn, C. R., and Cunningham, L. J., 'The Power of Black Magic: The Magical Negro and White Salvation in Film', *Journal of Black Studies*, 2009, 40(2): 135–52.

Grant, C., *Crime and Punishment in Contemporary Culture*, Abingdon: Routledge, 2004.

Gudjonsson, G., 'Disputed Confessions and Miscarriages of Justice in Britain', *Manitoba Law Journal*, 2006, 31(3): 489–521.

Gurnham, D., 'The Moral Narrative of Criminal Responsibility and the Principled Justification of Tariffs for Murder: Myra Hindley and Thompson and Venables', *Legal Studies*, 2003, 23(4): 605–22.

Hamann, P., *Fourteen Days in May* [Documentary], BBC, UK, 1987.

Harding, R. M., 'Celluloid Death: Cinematic Depictions of Capital Punishment', *University of San Francisco Law Review*, 1996, 30(4): 1167–79.

Hicks, H. J., 'Hoodoo Economics: White Men's Work and Black Men's Magic in Contemporary American Film', *Camera Obscura*, 2003, 18(2): 27–55.

Hough, M. and J. V. Roberts, 'Sentencing Trends in Britain: Public Knowledge and Public Opinion', *Punishment and Society*, 1999, 1(1): 11–26.

Hutton, N., 'Beyond Populist Punitiveness?', *Punishment and Society*, 2005, 7(3): 243–58.

Ipsos Mori, 'Attitudes Towards Capital Punishment', 1995, www.ipsos-mori.com/research publications/researcharchive/2243/Attitudes-Towards-Capital-Punishment.aspx.

Jakubait, M. with Weller, M., *Ruth Ellis: My Sister's Secret Life*, London: Robinson, 2005.

James, A., 'Miscarriages of Justice in the 21st Century', *Journal of Criminal Law*, 2002, 66(4): 326–37.

Jones, P. J., and Wardle, C., 'Hindley's Ghost: The Visual Construction of Maxine Carr', K. J. Hayward and M. Presdee (eds), *Framing Crime: Cultural Criminology and the Image*, London: Routledge, 2010, 53–67.

Lesser, W., *Pictures at an Execution: An Inquiry into the Subject of Murder*, Cambridge, MA: Harvard University Press, 1993.

Lynch, M., 'Capital Punishment as Moral Imperative: Pro-death Penalty Discourse on the Internet', *Punishment and Society*, 2002, 4(2): 213–36.

Matthews, R., 'The Myth of Punitiveness', *Theoretical Criminology*, 2005, 9(2): 175–201.

Medak, P., *Let Him Have It* [Motion Picture], British Screen Productions, UK, 1991.

Milne, R., Poyser, S., Williamson, T. and Savage, S. P., 'Miscarriages of Justice: What Can we Learn?', J. R. Adler and J. M. Gray (eds), *Forensic Psychology: Concepts, Debates and Practice*, Abingdon: Willan, 2010, 17–37.

Minkes, J. and Vanstone, M., 'Gender, Race and the Death Penalty: Lessons from Three 1950s Murder Trials', *Howard Journal*, 2006, 45(4): 403–20.

Morris, E., *The Thin Blue Line* [Documentary], American Playhouse, USA, 1988.

Mullin, C., *Error in Judgment*, London: Chatto, 1986.

Murphy, T., and Whitty, N., 'The Question of Evil and Feminist Legal Scholarship', *Feminist Legal Studies*, 2006, 14(1): 1–26.

Newburn, T., '"Tough on Crime": Penal Policy in England and Wales', *Crime and Justice*, 2007, 36(1): 425–70.

Newburn, T. and Jones, T., 'Symbolic Politics and Penal Populism: The Long Shadow of Willie Horton', *Crime, Media, Culture*, 2005, 1(1): 72–87.

Newell, M., *Dance with a Stranger* [Motion Picture], Goldcrest Films International, UK, 1985.

O'Sullivan, S., 'Representing the "Killing State": The Death Penalty in Nineties Hollywood Cinema', *The Howard Journal*, 2003, 42(5): 485–503.

Pratt, J., Brown, D., Brown, M., Hallsworth, S. and Morrison, W. 'Introduction', J. Pratt, D. Brown, M. Brown, S. Hallsworth and W. Morrison (eds), *The New Punitiveness: Trends, Theories, Perspectives*, Cullompton: Willan, 2005, xi–xxvi.

Robbins, T., *Dead Man Walking* [Motion Picture], Polygram, USA, 1995.

Roberts, J. V., Stalans, L. J., Indermauer, D. and Hough, M., *Penal Populism and Public Opinion: Lessons from Five Countries*, Oxford: Oxford University Press, 2002.

Sarat, A., *When the State Kills*, Princeton, NJ: Princeton University Press, 2001.

Sarat, A. and Schuster, A., 'To See or Not to See: Television, Capital Punishment, and the Law's Violence', *Yale Journal of Law and the Humanities*, 1995, 7(2): 397–432.

Seal, L., *Women Murder and Femininity: Gender Representations of Women Who Kill*, Basingstoke: Palgrave MacMillan, 2010.

Sheridan, J., *In the Name of the Father* [Motion Picture], Hell's Kitchen Films, Ireland, 1993.

Smith, P., *Punishment and Culture*, Chicago, IL: University of Chicago Press, 2008.

Trow, M. J., *Let Him Have It, Chris*, London: Constable, 1990.

Twitchell, N., *The Politics of the Rope*, Bury St. Edmunds: Arena, 2012.

Woffinden, B., *Miscarriages of Justice*, London: Coronet, 1988.

——*The Mystery of Deadman's Hill* [Documentary], Channel 4, UK, 1992.

8 Negotiating memories of capital punishment

This final chapter examines the negotiation of memories of capital punishment in oral history interviews from the late 1990s. These interviews were conducted for the BBC's 'A Century Speaks' radio series, which was broadcast on forty different local radio stations in 1999, and form the Millennium Memory Bank (MMB), held in the British Library Sound Archive. Oral history interviews are particularly good sources for unlocking how memory involves 'relationships between past and present, between memory and personal identity, and between individual and collective memory'.[1] Memories are socially and culturally produced, but are also mediated by individual experience. In making sense of the past, people draw on both individual experience and the wider social context. The past becomes part of the present as people use memory 'to interpret their lives and the world around them'.[2] Memories and their meanings evolve over time, reflecting how 'our relation to the past is conditioned by present circumstances'.[3] They are not fixed but get reshaped and reconfigured.[4] Therefore, rather than asking whether articulated memories are 'true' or not, it is important to interpret what they reveal about 'collective desires, needs, and self-definitions'.[5]

Like views on crime, views on punishment are expressed in relation to cultural themes and binaries,[6] such as order and disorder, right and wrong, safety and danger, and the appropriate role of the state. Concerns about social conditions and social values – and anxieties associated with these – affect individuals' support for different types of punishment.[7] Criminological research reveals that

---

1 A. Thomson, 'Four Paradigm Transformations in Oral History', *The Oral History Review*, 2007, 34(1): 49–70, p. 54.

2 M. Frisch, *A Shared Authority*, Albany: SUNY Press, 1990, p. 188 quoted in Thomson, p. 55.

3 S. Anderson, 'Loafing in the Garden of Knowledge: History TV and Popular Memory', *Film and History*, 2000, 30(1): 14–23, p. 15.

4 M. Sturken, *Tangled Memories*, London: University of California Press, 1997, p. 21.

5 Ibid., p. 2.

6 T. Sasson, *Crime Talk: How Citizens Construct a Social Problem*, New York: Aldine de Gruyter, 1997, p. 150.

7 T. R. Tyler and R. J. Boeckmann, 'Three Strikes and You're Out, but Why?', *Law and Society Review*, 1997, 31(2): 237–66, p. 238 and A. King and S. Maruna, 'Is a Conservative Just a Liberal Who has Been Mugged? Exploring the Origins of Punitive Views', *Punishment and Society*, 2009, 11(2): 147–69, pp. 160–1.

people's narratives of crime and punishment are frequently also narratives about social change.[8] The highly symbolic nature of the death penalty means that its place in articulated memories is especially ripe for cultural analysis. Loader and Mulcahy examine how 'policing is mobilized within competing memories and narratives of postwar social and political change'.[9] Policing institutions are the focus for fears and anxieties, hopes and fantasies, which are embedded in stories of social change. In relation to memory, they explore the features of postwar English policing that are perceived as significant and 'the manner in which they are reconstructed'.[10] A similar approach can be taken to memories and reconstructions of capital punishment. As a form of punishment no longer in use, memories of it are particularly likely to involve reflection on social change.

The oral history interviews in the MMB were collected in order to provide a 'snapshot' of Britain at the end of the twentieth century. The project was designed to be larger in scope than most oral histories both in terms of number of people interviewed and geographical reach. In all, 5429 interviews were carried out across every region of the country. Their aim was to encourage participants to reflect on change within their local community and covered six possible topics, one of which was crime and law. This involved asking interviewees how attitudes to and experience of crime had changed within their living memory, with the police, life in prison and the impact of law on everyday life being particular areas of interest. Interviews were conducted with people of a variety of ages, not just older people.[11] The inclusion of crime and law as a topic area meant that some participants discussed capital punishment. Due to the wide age range, the operation of the death penalty in Britain was not within living memory for all of them. However, interviewees could employ the past to make sense of the present whether capital punishment had existed in their lifetime or not.

Due to budgetary restrictions, not all of the interviews recorded for the MMB have been made accessible to the public.[12] Three hundred and ninety five are searchable via the British Library Sound Archive catalogue and can be requested for listening during a personal visit. Forty-five relevant interviews were identified through a keyword search of the catalogue, using search terms 'capital punishment', 'death penalty', 'execution' and 'hanging'. Two of these were inaccessible[13] meaning that in total the relevant sections of

8 K. T. Gaubatz, *Crime in the Public Mind*, Ann Arbor: University of Michigan Press, 1995, E. Girling, I. Loader and R. Sparks, *Crime and Social Change in Middle England*, London: Routledge, 2000 and A. King and S. Maruna, 'Moral Indignation in the East of England', S. Karstedt, I. Loader and H. Strang (eds), *Emotions, Crime and Justice*, Oxford: Hart Publishing, 2011, p. 138.

9 I. Loader and A. Mulcahy, *Policing and the Condition of England: Memory, Politics and Culture*, Oxford: Oxford University Press, 2003, p. 35.

10 Ibid., p. 56.

11 R. Perks, 'A Century Speaks: A Public History Partnership', *Oral History*, 2001, 29(2): 95–105.

12 Ibid., p. 100.

43 interviews were transcribed.[14] Of this 43, two interviews were with married couples so the voices of 45 individuals have been included. The catalogue records the name, year of birth, location and profession of the participants. For reasons of confidentiality, I have assigned interviewees with pseudonyms and have not included their location. Due to the nature of the topic, people connected with the criminal justice system, such as police officers, are over-represented in the sample of 45.[15] As Gallwey explains, the cataloguing of the MMB does have limitations for researchers. It contains summaries of interviews rather than full transcripts and these are variable in length and quality. There is very little information on the project's sampling strategies or the interview process.[16] However, the interviews have the advantage of recording participants' views on capital punishment as they were expressed during a more wide-ranging discussion of their memories. This reveals 'how penal questions actually figure in the everyday consciousness ... of people in the ordinary settings of their lives'.[17] As the analysis below explores, this captured the ambivalence of many of the interviewees towards the death penalty.

In a research project on families and food, Jackson *et al.* used three different oral history collections, one of which was the MMB. They argue for the need to contextualise secondary data, both in relation to the original context in which it was collected and also the context of its reuse.[18] The reuse of the interviews analysed below was made in order to gain qualitative views on capital punishment in the post-abolition era and also to assess how respondents employed negotiated memories in articulating these views. The fact that these interviews were carried out at the end of the twentieth century makes them particularly apposite for this book. When they were recorded, the official acknowledgement of high-profile miscarriages of justice such as the Birmingham Six and Guildford Four was still relatively recent. Derek Bentley's conviction had very recently been overturned and efforts to do the same for James Hanratty were in the news. The prominence of miscarriages of justice in the news media in the 1990s is reflected in the data. The previous chapter's

---

13 One had been recorded over with another interview, one was missing from the Soundserver.

14 This involved transcribing sections where capital punishment was discussed, but also other relevant aspects of the interview such as the participant's views on order in society, use of discipline in schools and so forth.

15 Ten participants either were, or had been, police officers at a variety of levels. The sample also included two prisoners, two retired prison officers, one former magistrate, one judge, one victim support volunteer, four solicitors/retired solicitors and one journalist who had covered crime.

16 A. Gallwey, *Lone Motherhood in England, 1945–1990: Economy, Agency and Identity*, Unpublished PhD Thesis, University of Warwick, 2011, p. 22.

17 M. Smith, R. Sparks and E. Girling, 'Educating Sensibilities: The Image of "The Lesson" in Children's Talk about Punishment', *Punishment and Society*, 2000, 2(4): 395–415, p. 396.

18 P. Jackson, G. Smith and S. Olive, 'Families Remembering Food: Reusing Secondary Data', Working Paper, University of Sheffield, undated: www.sheffield.ac.uk/polopoly_fs/1.1450761/file/FRF-resuse-paper-WP-pdf. Cited with permission of the authors. Accessed 7 February 2013.

exploration of relevant penal currents in the post-abolition era helps to further contextualise the interviewees' views and memories. Five main themes in relation to the death penalty were identified from analysis of the data. These were: memories of particular cases or events, the need for capital punishment (which included sub-themes of retribution and deterrence), the danger of miscarriage of justice, comparison with the United States, and ambivalence. Memories of particular cases and comparison with the United States tended to emerge in relation to the themes of the need for the death penalty and miscarriage of justice so have been subsumed under these in the discussion below.

The need for the death penalty

The need for capital punishment as a deterrent measure to help keep order in society was expressed by some interviewees, especially former police and prison officers. Malcolm, who worked as a police officer for thirty years, explained 'I saw the death penalty abolished', and at that time feared the murder rate would go up. This was borne out when '[t]he number of bodies quadrupled in the first few years after … abolition'.[19] Bill, another retired police officer, believed that capital punishment 'should be there for you know, like premeditated murder, murder of a policeman. Still, I mean, there's no deterrent and that's the top and bottom'.[20] Clive, a retired shipwright, proclaimed himself 'a believer, I must say, I'm a believer in the death penalty … because it would keep it down, keep the rate of murders and all down'.[21] Arnold, a retired detective, recounted his memories of capital cases, including those where policemen were killed, such as Bentley and Craig, and Podola, and also Gay Gibson's murder.[22] He had been involved with the case of the last man to be hanged in his coastal city, which had been a murder in the furtherance of theft. He remembered that the duty officer who had to witness the execution was 'normally a jovial, verbose man' but was very pale afterwards and did not talk about it. Nevertheless, Arnold regarded capital punishment as 'essential' as 'the fact there's no capital punishment anymore results in there being more murders'. People would refrain from such crimes if they feared execution.[23]

The death penalty's power as a deterrent was important to Dennis, a restaurant owner who had actively campaigned for the restoration of capital

---

19 Malcolm, Retired Police Officer, 1936, MMB900/19527.
20 Bill, Retired Police Officer, 1950, MMB900/11039.
21 Clive, Retired Shipwright, 1928, MMB900/02044.
22 On Gay Gibson, see Chapter Five. Guenther Podola was a German photographer who, in 1959, killed a police officer who had placed him under arrest. His case was contentious as he claimed to have no memory of the killing following a heavy beating from the police. During his initial court appearances, his face was clearly heavily bruised.
23 Arnold, Retired Detective Inspector, 1930, MMB900/15589.

punishment for child murder and killing a policeman. He felt 'there had got to be a deterrent' and the death penalty was necessary because life prison sentences did not mean life.[24] A man had been stabbed and killed in the street outside one of Dennis' restaurants, and the mother of the stabber maintained that her son would not have carried a knife if there had been the threat of capital punishment. Personal experience had also shaped the views of Elaine, who had been violently abused by her second husband and also her father. She thought if capital punishment were 'to come back it would save a lot of this [sic] things' and 'sincerely' believed in the restoration of hanging.[25]

The need for capital punishment was also expressed in relation to retributive sentiment. Ian, a retired journalist, described himself as 'a great believer' in both capital and corporal punishment and stated that he would support the reintroduction of the death penalty on retributive reasons alone. He had 'strong views on punishing the evil among us' and believed in the 'Old Testament adage of an eye for an eye and a tooth for a tooth'. Ian had met murderers when covering crime as part of his job and perceived 'the presence or feeling of evil in the presence of some people'. He recalled the rape and murder of a woman which 'made me feel physically sick to see it'.[26] Alan, a retired fisherman, also believed in capital punishment and the principle of 'an eye for an eye and a tooth for a tooth', and worried that current sentences were too lenient,[27] although he had no direct experience of crime himself. Irene, who was interviewed along with her husband, Mike, explained that as a policeman's daughter, she had been brought up to obey the law 'to the letter' but that society had become more dangerous since she was a child. Irene's sister had been murdered twelve years previously by a man who broke into her flat and stabbed her seven times. It 'grieve[d]' Irene that this young man was now free as she felt 'that people who take a life like that should pay for it with their own life'. She described herself as a Christian and pointed out that even the Bible says 'an eye for an and a tooth for a tooth'.[28]

Roy, a retired prison officer, did condemned cell duty when he was only 24 years old. He described an 'understanding', which existed between himself and the condemned prisoner, particularly as the prisoner had committed a crime of passion which 'was one that I could well have committed myself in the circumstances'. This man was reprieved. Roy expressed belief in capital punishment, 'possibly more so today because there are more heinous crimes being committed. I mean, there are some terrific crimes being committed nowadays that are just beyond belief really'.[29] Edna, a retired head teacher,

24 Dennis, Restaurant Owner, 1929, MMB900/16525.
25 Elaine, Retired Factory Worker, 1926, MMB900/06505.
26 Ian, Retired Journalist, 1933, MMB900/01091.
27 Alan, Retired Fisherman, 1920, MMB900/07005.
28 Irene, Wife of Mike, Retired Port of London Police Officer [an occupation for Irene is not given], 1924, MMB900/04077A.
29 Roy, Retired Prison Officer, 1925, MMB900/17032.

articulated concerns about people feeling unsafe in their own homes and criminals being released from prison too quickly. She approved of the death penalty and stated that '[t]he law must be more stringent'. She also drew comparison with the United States as a more punitive society, arguing '[w]e do sort of criticise America, but at least they're trying to do something about it'.[30] At the time of his interview, Andy was serving a prison sentence for aggravated burglary. He perceived crime as 'worse than it ever was, especially violent crime'. He favoured capital punishment 'for rapists, paedophiles and certain murderers' and referred to the recent murder of James Byrd Jr in Texas. Andy explained that Byrd Jr's murderer was 'gonna pay the price for it, he's gonna die by lethal injection, which he should do'.[31]

Belief in the necessity of capital punishment was connected to perceptions that society had become more dangerous and disorderly. Runaway modernity had compromised civilisation. Pro-death penalty views were bound up with narratives of decline, according to which, society had changed for the worse and rising violent crime could be directly attributed to the lack of an effective deterrent. In this discourse, the past figured as a better time to be contrasted with the less secure present. Respondents did not elaborate this contrast in detail, demonstrating the well-established nature of the decline narrative,[32] which operated as a cultural resource through which to express the need for capital punishment. Concerns about safety were not only articulated through a past/present divide, but as the quotes from Edna and Andy showed, could also be made in relation to comparison between Britain and America. Belief in harsh punishment as related to faith in the importance of abiding by codes of conduct was also evident,[33] and was strongly linked to the decline narrative, with respondents expressing bewilderment at the violation of these codes that excessive violence entailed.

Along with deterrence, retribution was an important sub-theme. Some respondents mobilised personal memories of past experiences to explain their belief in the need for retributive punishment. These included Ian's encounters with 'evil' as a crime reporter, and Dennis, Elaine and Irene, who in different

---

30 Edna, Retired Head Teacher, 1916, MMB900/04507.
31 Andy, Prisoner, 1975, MMB900/15093. James Byrd Jr., an African American, was murdered in Texas in June 1998 by three white men who tied him to the back of a pick-up truck and dragged him along the road, severing his head and arm. The murder was racially motivated and responses to it helped to pave the way for hate crime legislation in Texas and then federally. Two of the murderers were sentenced to death, one of whom has since been executed.
32 Criminologists have identified this narrative in relation to perceptions of disorderly youth, who become symbols of social decline and a bleak future: G. Pearson, *Hooligan: A History of Respectable Fears*, Basingstoke: Palgrave Macmillan, 1983; I. Loader, E. Girling and R. Sparks, 'Narratives of Decline: Youth, Dis/order and Community in an English Town', *British Journal of Criminology*, 1998, 38(3): 388–403 and King and Maruna, 'Is a Conservative'. In the MMB oral histories, the decline narrative was not specifically related to perceptions of youth, but to more generalised perceptions of danger, violence and insecurity.
33 A. King, 'Keeping a Safe Distance: Individualism and the Less Punitive Public', *British Journal of Criminology*, 2008, 48(2): 190–208, p. 204.

ways, were victims of violent crime. Consonant with previous research, experience of violent crime was not a pre-requisite for retributive views.[34] However, the compelling personal stories told by these interviewees demonstrate how cultural memory is mediated by individual experiences in order to interpret the world. Irene discussed the murder of her sister as exemplifying how society had become more dangerous since her childhood. King argues that individual psycho-social identities are significant to punitive views, as punitiveness derives from 'what is going on in people's own lives and how they make sense of it'.[35]

Interestingly, personal memories of direct involvement in the process of capital punishment introduced a note of ambivalence about the machinery of the death penalty to expression of the need for capital punishment theme. Arnold described the traumatic effects of witnessing execution on a police officer and Roy recounted the empathy that existed between himself and a condemned man. However, Arnold and Roy both believed that murder and violent crime had increased due to abolition.

Miscarriage of justice

Interviewees who expressed anti-death penalty sentiment nearly all mentioned the danger of miscarriage of justice, which they intertwined with refutations of deterrence and retribution-based justifications, and with other anti-capital punishment arguments such as the barbaric and/or immoral nature of the death penalty. Jim, an economic consultant, described the death penalty as 'abhorrent and immoral' and referred to seeing a picture in the previous day's newspaper that showed American inmates of death row who had been reprieved. He stated '[t]he chance of miscarriage of justice, it just seems to me is high and that's, sort of, intellectually unacceptable, but emotionally, I just feel it is totally unacceptable for civilised society to take life in that way'. Jim could not remember specific incidents of capital punishment in Britain but he remembered the death penalty as 'a very big doorstep issue that raised a lot of passion' when he canvassed for the Labour Party in the 1964 general election.[36] Rosamund had worked as a receptionist for Victor Gollancz in the 1950s and was also active in the National Campaign for the Abolition of the Death Penalty at that time. She described herself as an anarchist and argued 'it is quite wrong to have, for the state to have capital punishment, partly because they may put to death the wrong person, of course. But, erm, anyway, the state has no business taking lives like that'.[37] Rosamund was unusual in explicitly connecting her anti-death penalty views and activism to her wider political beliefs.

34 King and Maruna, 'Is a Conservative', p. 151.
35 King, 'Keeping', p. 192.
36 Jim, Economic Consultant, 1945, MMB900/01019.
37 Rosamund, Retired Teacher, 1929, MMB900/05058.

Reggie, a retired police superintendent, had 'never been a believer in the death penalty. I'm not an Old Testament person, I don't believe in an eye for an eye or a tooth for a tooth because there are occasions, very rarely, where the courts make mistakes'.[38] Reggie considered whether abolition might account for the rise in murders since the 1960s, but concluded that punishment was not an effective deterrent. He did think that sentences for killing someone were too short and 'would favour the American idea where life means life'. Edward, a judge, thought that caning was needed in school to discipline young people and that longer prison sentences reduced the likelihood of re-offending. However, he stated, 'I've never actually, despite everything I say, been an advocate of capital punishment. It's too final'. Wrongful imprisonment could be compensated but 'if he's been hanged, or she's been hanged, it's too late to put the mistake right'.[39]

Discussion of miscarriage of justice also entailed consideration of particular cases. Matt, who was serving a life sentence in prison, reflected '[i]f there had been capital punishment, I would have got done for it meself, wouldn't I?' He was present during a fight in which a man was killed and was found guilty of murder due to joint enterprise, a conviction he was attempting to appeal. Matt had sympathy for Derek Bentley as he did not 'see why people should be punished for something what they've not done'. Bentley's recent acquittal 'just shows you, justice, it stinks, it's all wrong'.[40] Andy, a prisoner whose pro-death penalty views were explored above, also mentioned Derek Bentley. He had watched *Let Him Have It* a couple of weeks previously and explained '[h]e didn't have the mind of his age, he had the mind of a child so how can they, you know, find him guilty and pass the death sentence on him when the geezer, the bloke who actually shot the copper, only served ten years out of his life sentence'. This illustrated for Andy that '[t]he law is all messed up'.[41]

Esme worked as a volunteer for the Prison Visitors' Association and Victim Support. In response to the interviewer asking her what she thought about the United States still having death row, Esme answered 'I don't believe in the death penalty, actually, because I think there are some people who were innocent and were hanged. I don't think Hanratty actually did do the, erm, A6 murder and of course he was hanged'.[42] Hanratty's case was the most frequently mentioned in the Millennium Memory Bank interviews. Rosamund remembered 'vividly' Hanratty's appeal being turned down by Rab Butler[43] and Angela, who advocated the reintroduction of capital punishment, recalled hearing the news report on the radio when Hanratty was hanged.[44] Ivan, a

---

38 Reggie, Retired Superintendent, 1933, MMB900/03580.
39 Edward, Judge, 1936, MMB900/12589.
40 Matt, Life Prisoner, 1970, MMB900/01595.
41 Andy, MMB900/15093.
42 Esme, Prison Visitors' Association and Victim Support Worker, 1924, MMB900/18096.
43 Rosamund, MMB900/05058.
44 Angela, Nurse, 1949, MMB900/02011.

coach tour operator, discussed his memories of the day Hanratty was executed. At the time, he was a schoolboy and on the morning of Hanratty's execution, looked at the clock on top of his school. He explained 'I remember my vision of capital punishment was, it's five to nine, when the bell goes for forming lines for your classes, that man is going to be dropped'. He was concerned about miscarriage of justice because 'people have been convicted with corrupt evidence, all sorts of things, lack of evidence'. Hanratty 'should never have gone to the gallows, not knowing what I've read since'.[45] Ben, a pupil at secondary school, described himself as having 'mixed feelings' about the death penalty. People who had killed deserved to die 'but there's always the chance of killing the wrong person. I think it was James Hanratty. He was killed and then he was cleared after he was killed, and that would be terrible if something happens nowadays'.[46]

Reservations about the danger of executing an innocent person were expressed by other interviewees who otherwise approved of the death penalty. Maxwell favoured strong punishments, such as following the Saudi Arabian practice of cutting off someone's hand if they had stolen something. He thought the death penalty 'should be enforced under strict situations' when guilt was '110 per cent sure'. He acknowledged that '[t]here's been quite a few miscarriages of justice' and that people had been 'fitted up'.[47] Dennis, who had campaigned for the restoration of capital punishment, mentioned execution as appropriate 'where it [guilt] was proved without doubt'.[48] Similarly, Elaine wanted the return of the death penalty but qualified this as '[w]hen they definitely know, I mean they probably made one mistake in hanging'.[49] Arnold, who had described capital punishment as 'essential', was prompted by the interviewer to consider innocence. He responded 'I do have that in mind' and conceded 'you can't put the clock back and that's a terrible thing'.[50]

In expressing pro-death penalty sentiment, some interviewees directly addressed the problem of miscarriages of justice. Clive, a 'believer' in the death penalty, contended '[n]ow, everybody says "you might hang an innocent man", right, but there is another way. Where there is 99 per cent doubt, OK, then keep them in [prison]. But if it is known – definite – that this man murdered this person'.[51] Edna rejected the innocence argument, stating it was 'all fine to say, for instance, that the death penalty was a terrible thing and it made some mistakes but you didn't get every Tom, Dick and Harry around the place wanting to kill people'.[52] Angela acknowledged that 'it's very sad if

45 Ivan, Coach Tour Operator, 1945, MMB900/05137.
46 Ben, School Pupil, 1985, MMB900/01066.
47 Maxwell, Heritage Park Guide, 1966, MMB900/13612.
48 Derek, MMB900/16525.
49 Elaine, MMB900/06505.
50 Arnold, MMB900/15589.
51 Clive, MMB900/02044.
52 Edna, MMB900/04507.

you get the wrong person and in the odd couple of instances that they have hung the wrong person, then that is beyond belief' but still felt that in certain cases 'it would be better to hang them than have them come out after 20 years, or 30 years'.[53]

Miscarriage of justice could therefore be rejected as an argument against the death penalty, but was the most important theme for articulation of opposition to it. Significantly, the irreversibility of capital punishment and the impossibility of correcting mistakes had influenced the views of respondents such as Reggie and Edward, who otherwise held fairly punitive attitudes. Maxwell, Dennis, Elaine and Arnold were all pro-death penalty but acknowledged the danger of miscarriage of justice as a problem, reflecting a degree of ambivalence, which is discussed further below.

The significance of miscarriages of justice does seem to reflect the high profile of this issue in the 1990s, with respondents mentioning cases overturned because of faults in the legal process, or the execution of the innocent. The importance of contemporary attention to historical cases in shaping cultural memory was illustrated by the references to Derek Bentley and James Hanratty, both of whom had received media attention in the 1990s, whereas no-one mentioned Timothy Evans by name. The film *Let Him Have It* was directly mentioned by Andy, and news reports and documentaries about the Bentley and Hanratty cases may well have been important vectors of cultural memories of miscarriage of justice. Personal memories of James Hanratty's execution or failure to win a reprieve were likely to be have been rekindled and reshaped by media attention to the campaign for his acquittal. In particular, Ivan's use of the trope of watching the clock was reminiscent of death penalty films in which clocks have figured as symbols of the condemned's impending doom.[54]

As a use of the past in the present, the miscarriage of justice theme had different resonances from the need for capital punishment theme. Rather than a stress on insecurity, vulnerability to violent crime or narratives of decline about the negative effects of social change, the articulation of past injustices implicitly highlighted the capacity for the state to be incompetent (pithily summed up by Matt as 'justice, it stinks') and did not invoke the past as a better or more desirable place. Jim's reference to the unacceptability of capital punishment in a 'civilised society' tacitly suggested the moral superiority of Britain in the 1990s to both the Britain of the mid-twentieth century and the contemporary United States. However, this kind of liberal interpretation, which implicitly evoked social progress, was not prevalent. Instead, negotiated memories of wrongful execution were largely expressed in relation to the

---

53 Angela, MMB900/02011.
54 Lesser describes the 'big clock' as a 'murder-story cliché', which features prominently in death penalty films such as *I Want to Live!*, W. Lesser, *Pictures at an Execution*, Cambridge, MA: Harvard University Press, 1993, pp. 237–38. British death penalty film, *Time Without Pity*, features clocks, large and small, as metaphors throughout.

uncertainty of justice and the ineradicability of error in the system. King's research into the psychological sources of punitive and forgiving stances towards offenders revealed that those with more forgiving views tended to view authority as highly fallible.[55] This perception of fallibility was, understandably, key to the miscarriage of justice theme in the oral history interviews, although this was not necessarily allied to a forgiving stance towards criminals.

The miscarriage of justice theme was articulated in relation to pro and anti-death penalty sentiment, demonstrating how inextricably entrenched it became within discussion of capital punishment in Britain. The significance of error in relation to the death penalty was further underlined by the high profile given to miscarriage of justice in the 1990s but, as Chapter Six explored, had already been established as a narrative on capital punishment in preceding decades.

Ambivalence

The danger of miscarriage of justice induced ambivalence about capital punishment for some interviewees as discussed above. Some respondents did not have clear views one way or the other on the death penalty but, like Ben, articulated 'mixed feelings'. Jonathan, a detective chief inspector, thought that capital punishment 'must be beyond, beyond, beyond reasonable doubt, and I'm not quite sure how you'd draw the line there', although he agreed that the death penalty was, in principle, appropriate 'at a certain point'.[56] Malcolm saw capital punishment as a deterrent and thought that murder had increased as a result of abolition. However, he 'was not saying the death penalty should be here now … , I've no strong feelings on that'.[57] George, a retired prison officer, remembered '[a] friend of mine who did take a prisoner into the execution chamber to be executed came in with a white streak over his hair'. George found it 'difficult to say whether I agree with capital punishment or not'. He noted that America still had 'atrocious murders' despite the death penalty and 'couldn't say whether it would be a success, whether it would help murders or not'.[58]

Elsie discussed her father's experience of being on a jury in a capital case, recalling 'Daddy was in a terrible state. You knew jolly well that the boy had done it [murdered both parents], but you were saying that that man could be hanged, and that was a terrible thing to say, that you had said he should be hanged'. The case had 'a profound effect on my father. Because my father said "I don't think jurors ought to make that sort of decision"'. However, Elsie was troubled by what she interpreted as the cultural changes wrought by the 1960s, and despite her father's trauma stated '[y]et there are days now

55 King, 'Keeping', p. 204.
56 Jonathan, Detective Chief Inspector, 1958, MMB900/15631.
57 Malcolm, MMB900/19527.
58 George, Retired Prison Officer, 1921, MMB900/21016.

when you think, yes, I'm sorry there should have been, that should have continued [capital punishment]'.[59] The toll that the death penalty could take on those involved in the case was also discussed by Jeff, a retired police officer. He explained 'I always feel that although a lot of people cry out for the death penalty to be introduced and I don't think it'll ever work because even in those days when we had the death penalty, the jury would bend over backwards to try and bring in a charge of manslaughter'. Jeff thought 'it would solve a lot of problems if they were [hanged] today' and that the death penalty was deserved by those who had taken a life.[60] Similarly, Godfrey, a retired solicitor, believed that capital and corporal punishment were deterrents but did not think reintroduction was possible as he did not 'think you'd ever get the judges to sit on a capital case'.[61] The emotional and contentious nature of capital punishment was recognised as problematic by Jeff and Godfrey even though they approved of it in principle.

The issue of particularly serious crimes was considered by some interviewees. Josephine, a retired librarian, thought that hanging 'depends on the degree of murder'. She mentioned 'really, really horrible' murders as worthy of the death penalty and referred to Myra Hindley as an example but drew a distinction with cases where a 'woman conks her abusive husband over the head'. Josephine described capital punishment as 'a difficult one' and did not want to go back to 'hanging a child for stealing a loaf of bread, more or less'.[62] Gordon, a retired solicitor, discussed how his views on capital punishment had changed, stating '[w]ell, I used to, in my young days, to be in favour of the death penalty but for many years I have not been. I would never bring it back and, erm, I'm afraid I'm anti-death penalty these days'. His views had changed due to his recognition that 'I don't think I'd have had a wink of sleep' if his work as a solicitor 'could affect the verdict when a man's life was at stake'. There was also the problem that 'nowadays we've had several cases, which, erm, highlight the fact that there's no going back after an execution if it's found to be wrong'. However, Gordon had 'a lot of sympathy for people who try to argue that in terrorist cases, it should be brought back. I can understand their arguments'.[63] Jacob, a local government officer, had also modified his views due to miscarriages of justice. He explained 'I did believe it, that there should be a death penalty, but in the last couple of years, there's been so many appeals on murder charges and people are getting off, it makes you think sometimes, "is the legal system right?"'. As far as terrorism was concerned, though, 'there shouldn't be no qualms, I think they should be shot or whatever, or injected or whatever they do like, because that's premeditated murder'.[64]

59 Elsie, Retired Teacher, 1939, MMB900/02002.
60 Jeff, Retired Police Officer, 1922, MMB900/12531.
61 Godfrey, Retired Solicitor, 1913, MMB900/18057.
62 Josephine, Retired Librarian, 1920, MMB900/12518.
63 Gordon, Retired Solicitor, 1930, MMB900/16562.
64 Jacob, Local Government Officer, 1959, MMB900/13619.

The expression of ambivalence from some respondents highlighted the complexity of their views – it is clear from some interviewees' statements that they were neither straightforwardly for or against the reintroduction of the death penalty. This kind of response illustrates how data from unsophisticated surveys could be quite misleading, as such methods cannot capture the feelings of those who both simultaneously approve and disapprove of capital punishment. As with some of the personal memories negotiated in relation to the two previous themes, George and Elsie articulated the traumatic effects of execution on those who bore the responsibility for sending the condemned to their death. Elsie struggled to reconcile the memory of her father's distress as a capital juror with her anxieties about social change since the 1960s, and her associated feeling that the death penalty would help to restore social order and safety. Jeff's memory of the reluctance of juries to convict for capital murder was constructed as an instrumental reason not to reintroduce the death penalty, despite his belief in retribution and suggestion that capital punishment would improve society. Similarly, Godfrey cited the unwillingness of judges to sit on capital cases. Arguably, Jeff and Godfrey's ambivalence existed in this gap between what they articulated as possible and what should be done. Like respondents who perceived a need for capital punishment, Josephine felt that 'horrible murders' deserved the death penalty, but her evocation of a past where children could be hanged for stealing bread did not portray a 'golden age', but a time when punishment was cruel and disproportionate.

Gordon and Jacob were the only interviewees to explicitly mention terrorism and, interestingly, both of them cited it as a compelling reason to reintroduce capital punishment, even though they referred to miscarriages of justice as influencing their unease about the death penalty's use and despite Jacob's anxiety about the functioning of the legal system. One of the limitations of secondary data is that these views cannot be probed further and only speculation is possible. It could be that Gordon and Jacob did not readily associate cases such as the Guildford Four and Birmingham Six with the death penalty, or did not accept them as miscarriages of justice. Like Josephine, they found capital punishment persuasive for especially heinous murders, with Jacob mentioning the 'premeditated' nature of terrorist murders as aggravating.

Conclusion

As qualitative data, the MMB interviews demonstrate the fluidity of post-abolition views on the death penalty, where the danger of miscarriage of justice or the seriousness of the murder influenced whether some interviewees approved of capital punishment or not. As Jackson *et al.* argue, the original context of the data collection needs to be considered in the analysis of secondary data. Interviewees who worried about the leniency of prison sentences to an extent echoed the 'tough on crime' rhetoric that had been embraced by both major political parties in the late 1990s. However, those who saw the death penalty as necessary for reasons of retribution or deterrence drew on longstanding arguments in favour of capital punishment. Expression of punitive views also did not necessarily align with approval for capital punishment, with some respondents favouring long prison sentences but objecting to the death penalty. Discussion of miscarriage of justice also shows the diverse currents within cultures of punishment, which in the 1990s included punitive talk of the need for harsh punishment and scepticism about the ability of the legal system to dispense justice. The two themes of the need for capital punishment and danger of miscarriage of justice showed orientation towards the consideration of different, but not mutually exclusive, threats – disorder and violence in society, or the incompetence of the state.

As oral histories, the interviews demonstrate the uses of the past to understand the present and the negotiation of memory. As such, they reveal the contested and multiple nature of cultural memories of capital punishment. The era of the death penalty could figure as representative of a more orderly, less violent time preceding social change and 'decline', or a time in which irrevocable injustices were allowed to happen.[65] Certain respondents also negotiated memories of personal experiences, or of experiences of relatives or colleagues, in relation to their views on capital punishment. These memories either served as evidence of society's increased danger, or highlighted the traumatic aspects of administering capital punishment – something emphasised even by those who supported the death penalty in principle. The contested terrain of the reconfiguration of memories of capital punishment in Britain shows the deep ambivalence of this issue, an important theme to emerge from the MMB oral histories.

Archival collections

British Library Sound Archive, Millennium Memory Bank (MMB)

Bibliography

Anderson, A., 'Loafing in the Garden of Knowledge: History TV and Popular Memory', *Film and History*, 2000, 30(1): 14–23.
Frisch, M., *A Shared Authority*, Albany, NY: SUNY Press, 1990.
Gallwey, A., *Lone Motherhood in England, 1945–1990: Economy, Agency and Identity*, Unpublished PhD Thesis, University of Warwick, 2011.
Gaubatz, K. T., *Crime in the Public Mind*, Ann Arbor: University of Michigan Press, 1995.
Girling, E., Loader, I. and Sparks, R., *Crime and Social Change in Middle England*, London: Routledge, 2000.

65 As explained above, respondents were asked to talk about living memory and changes within their lifetime. Consequently, evocation of the collective past was of the relatively recent past of the twentieth century – with the reference to children being hanged for stealing a loaf of bread being the exception.

Jackson, P., Smith, G. and Olive, S., 'Families Remembering Food: Reusing Secondary Data', Working Paper, University of Sheffield, undated: www.sheffield.ac.uk/polo poly_fs/1.1450761/file/FRF-resuse-paper-WP-pdf.

King, A., 'Keeping a Safe Distance: Individualism and the Less Punitive Public', *British Journal of Criminology*, 2008, 48(2): 190–208.

King, A. and Maruna, S., 'Is a Conservative Just a Liberal Who has Been Mugged? Exploring the Origins of Punitive Views', *Punishment and Society*, 2009, 11(2): 147–69.

——'Moral Indignation in the East of England', S. Karstedt, I. Loader and H. Strang (eds), *Emotions, Crime and Justice*, Oxford: Hart Publishing, 2011, 123–43.

Lesser, W., *Pictures at an Execution*, Cambridge, MA: Harvard University Press, 1993.

Loader, I., Girling, E. and Sparks, R., 'Narratives of Decline: Youth, Dis/order and Community in an English Town', *British Journal of Criminology*, 1998, 38(3): 388–403.

Loader, I. and Mulcahy, A., *Policing and the Condition of England: Memory, Politics and Culture*, Oxford: Oxford University Press, 2003.

Pearson, G., *Hooligan: A History of Respectable Fears*, Basingstoke: Palgrave Macmillan, 1983.

Perks, R., 'A Century Speaks: A Public History Partnership', *Oral History*, 2001, 29(2): 95–105.

Sasson, T., *Crime Talk: How Citizens Construct a Social Problem*, New York: Aldine de Gruyter, 1997.

Smith, M., Sparks, R. and Girling, E., 'Educating Sensibilities: The Image of "The Lesson" in Children's Talk about Punishment', *Punishment and Society*, 2000, 2(4): 395–415.

Sturken, M., *Tangled Memories*, London: University of California Press, 1997.

Thomson, A., 'Four Paradigm Transformations in Oral History', *The Oral History Review*, 2007, 34(1): 49–70.

Tyler, T. R. and Boeckmann, R. J., 'Three Strikes and You're Out, but Why?', *Law and Society Review*, 1997, 31(2): 237–66.

Index

21341490R00112

Printed in Great Britain
by Amazon